Visions of Victory

Visions of Victory explores the views of eight leaders of the major bel-ligerents in World War II – Hitler, Mussolini, Tojo, Chiang Kai-shek, Stalin, Churchill, de Gaulle, and Roosevelt – and compares their visions of the future assuming their side emerged victorious. While the leaders pri-marily focused their attention on strategies for fighting and winning the war, these strategies were often shaped by their aspirations and hopes for the future. Weinberg assesses how subsequent events were impacted by their decisions and examines how their visions for the future changed and evolved throughout the war. What emerges is a startling picture of post-war worlds: Besides the extermination of the Jews, Hitler intended for all the Slavs to die off and for the Germans to inhabit all of eastern Europe. Both Mussolini and Hitler intended to have extensive colonies in Africa. Churchill hoped to see the reemergence of the British and French Empires. De Gaulle wanted to annex the northwest corner of Italy (but Truman forced him to back down). Stalin wanted control of eastern Europe, and he got it. Roosevelt's vision of the future was the closest to being fulfilled, including, importantly, the establishment of the United Nations. Aston-ishing in its synthesis and scope, Weinberg's comparison of the individual portraits of the wartime leaders is a highly original and compelling study of history that might have been.

Gerhard L. Weinberg is Professor Emeritus of History at the University of North Carolina, Chapel Hill. He is the author of numerous books and articles on the origins and course of World War II, including *A World at Arms: A Global History of World War II* (Cambridge, 1994), which won the George Louis Beer Prize of the American Historical Association, and *Germany, Hitler, and World War II* (Cambridge, 1995).

Visions of Victory

THE HOPES OF EIGHT
WORLD WAR II LEADERS

Gerhard L. Weinberg
University of North Carolina, Chapel Hill

CAMBRIDGE
UNIVERSITY PRESS

CAMBRIDGE UNIVERSITY PRESS
Cambridge, New York, Melbourne, Madrid, Cape Town, Singapore, São Paulo

Cambridge University Press
40 West 20th Street, New York, NY 10011-4211, USA

www.cambridge.org
Information on this title: www.cambridge.org/9780521852548

© Gerhard L. Weinberg 2005

This book is in copyright. Subject to statutory exception
and to the provisions of relevant collective licensing agreements,
no reproduction of any part may take place without
the written permission of Cambridge University Press.

First published 2005

Printed in the United States of America

A catalog record for this publication is available from the British Library.

Library of Congress Cataloging in Publication Data
Weinberg, Gerhard L.
Visions of victory : The Hopes of Eight World War II Leaders / Gerhard L. Weinberg.
p. cm.
Includes bibliographical references and index.
ISBN 0-521-85254-4 (hardback)
1. World War, 1939–1945 – Biography. 2. Heads of state – Biography. I. Title.
D736.W46 2005
940.53′092′2–dc22 2005000785

ISBN-13 978-0-521-85254-8 hardback
ISBN-10 0-521-85254-4 hardback

Cambridge University Press has no responsibility for
the persistence or accuracy of URLs for external or
third-party Internet Web sites referred to in this book
and does not guarantee that any content on such
Web sites is, or will remain, accurate or appropriate.

To my students

CONTENTS

vii

LIST OF MAPS

PREFACE

When working on my general history of World War II, I was intrigued by what appeared to me at the time to be a highly unusual concept of Charles de Gaulle, the leader of the Free French movement. He evidently wanted the southern portion of the Italian colony of Libya annexed after victory to what was then French Equatorial Africa. The area involved is desert, with one oasis. At the time, France already controlled most of the Sahara Desert; why acquire more desert? Into what sort of vision of the postwar world held by de Gaulle did such an annexation fit? It was this question that led me to the idea of looking at the postwar visions of major leaders of World War II.

In my work on this project, I have again been indebted to the William R. Kenan Jr. Charitable Trust. A period as scholar in residence at the United States Holocaust Memorial Museum provided time and support for my work, though nothing in this book represents the views of the museum or its council. The librarians at the University of North Carolina at Chapel Hill have been as patient and helpful as always. Any errors and shortcomings are, of course, my own.

To assist the reader who would like to pursue the issues touched on in the text further, I have tried to provide sources in English wherever possible. If it looks at first as if numerous citations are to a collection with a German title, the big series *Dokumente zur Deutschlandpolitik*, it is important to note that the documents from British and American archives reproduced in this collection invariably appear in the original English and with proper archival references. The broader context of the war can be followed in my *A World at Arms: A Global History of World War II*, where relevant published and unpublished sources are provided in considerable detail and my many debts to institutions and individuals are acknowledged. In the text, the spellings and names of places are generally those used at the time. Thus, the colonies of European powers appear under their old names, Chinese names have not been altered to the new system, and Japanese names are in the Japanese form, with the family name first.

If the focus in this work is on a small number of individuals at the top of their respective states, there are two reasons for this. The first is what I would call the intrinsic fascination of the leaders of the major powers involved in the greatest war in history. There are many biographies and other studies of them and their activities, but none that compares their views of the future assuming their side of the war emerged victorious. The second reason is that, especially in wartime, the urgent demands of the conflict almost automatically make the individual at the top more important and, in terms of the society that the individual leads, more powerful. This was most certainly the case during World War II.

Whatever rivalries existed in National Socialist Germany, there can be no doubt that the major decisions on policy were made by Adolf Hitler himself. Benito Mussolini was obliged to defer minimally to those elements that had enabled him to assume power, but not only did he resent them, he generally kept them out of the decision-making process – until they succeeded in removing him from office. Tojo Hideki, as Chapter 3 demonstrates, was not in the dictatorial position that Hitler and Mussolini held, but he played an important role in the complicated way decisions were arrived at in Tokyo all the same. After the great purges, there was certainly no one in the Soviet Union who could imagine an internal challenge to the absolute dominance of Josef Stalin. It should be remembered that when assuming the office of prime minister, Winston Churchill also insisted on creating and holding the office of minister of defence. He did this so that he could work either directly with the military chiefs of staff or do so through an intermediary, General Hastings Ismay, whom he had chosen himself. Charles de Gaulle in a real sense personified as well as led the Free French movement. Franklin D. Roosevelt carefully emphasized his constitutional role as commander-in-chief, and no one in the political or military hierarchy of the United States had any doubts about that. When he agreed with proposals submitted to him, he would note in the margin, after the initials of the proposer, "OK FDR." But if he disagreed, the typed indication of his disapproval would be followed by his full signature with "Commander-in-Chief" typed underneath.

The leaders of World War II belligerents were in practice limited by the human and material resources at their disposal as well as by the geographic factors that often made some choices either impossible or especially inviting. What I have found striking is the extent to which each of the leaders examined here tended to assume that limitations of human and material resources could be coped with by careful planning, the assistance of associated powers, and, in the final analysis, by sheer determination and will-power. The

occasionally voiced view that the Allies won the war by sheer numbers of men, planes, ships, and tanks would have come as astonishing news to the British pilots in the Battle of Britain, the Red Army
soldiers fighting in the streets of Stalingrad, and the sailors on the
three American aircraft carriers coping with the six Japanese carriers in June of 1942. The English Channel was equally wide and
stormy for the Germans at the height of their victories in 1940 as it
was for the Allies as they planned an invasion of northwest Europe
in 1943 and 1944. Certainly both resources and geography had to be
taken into account; what is so interesting is that in the urgencies of a
desperate war all leaders concentrated on aims first and strove to har-
ness resources and strategic decisions to them. It was the hundreds
of millions of ordinary people across the globe who fought, suffered,
labored, and died in the war, and they were the ones who had to
live, and work out the best adjustments that circumstances allowed,
in the postwar world that was so largely not of their own making.
It was also by no means precisely the postwar world that the leaders
studied here wanted or expected, but the aspirations that they held
during the great conflict are surely worthy of some attention.

The world created by the war is still very much the world in which
we live. Decisions and the outcomes of battles in places that few
can identify today have shaped our world. In many ways the successes and the failures of the years of fighting have created the issues
that confront the governments of our own time. It is true that one
can now travel under the English Channel on a train, but the heritage of choices made by World War II leaders continues to affect
the relations of Britain with France and other states on the continent. The position of the United States in the world and the mul-
titude of newly independent countries in the United Nations – itself a wartime creation – are both examples of developments that

cannot be understood unless their origins in World War II are taken into consideration. This book is designed to assist in that process of understanding.

Over a period of forty-five years of teaching, my students, both undergraduate and graduate, have inspired, challenged, and cheered me. It is to them that this book is dedicated.

Efland, North Carolina, July 2004

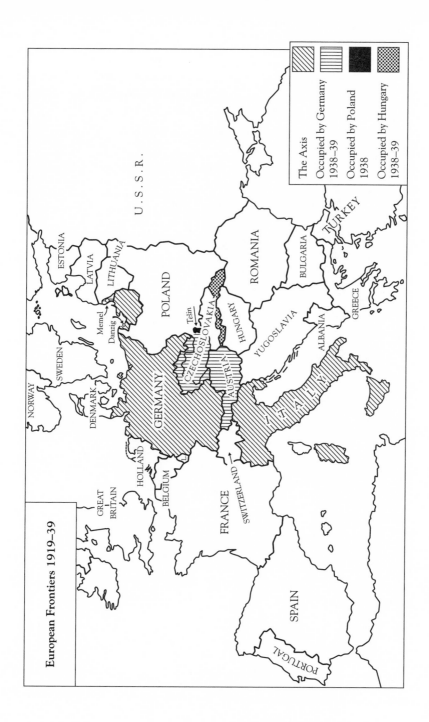

European Frontiers 1919–39

The Axis

Occupied by Germany 1938–39

Occupied by Poland 1938

Occupied by Hungary 1938–39

U.S.S.R.

NORWAY

SWEDEN

ESTONIA

LATVIA

LITHUANIA

Memel

Danzig

POLAND

Těšín

TURKEY

ROMANIA

BULGARIA

GREECE

CZECHOSLOVAKIA

HUNGARY

YUGOSLAVIA

ALBANIA

AUSTRIA

ITALY

GERMANY

DENMARK

GREAT BRITAIN

HOLLAND

BELGIUM

FRANCE

SWITZERLAND

SPAIN

PORTUGAL

xvii

Northern Europe June 1941

Arctic Ocean

North Cape
Altafjord
Tromso
Bardufoss
Harstad
Banak
Kaafjord
Petsamo
Murmansk
KOLA
PENINSULA
LOFOTEN
ISLANDS
Narvik

Arctic Circle

Bodo
Glomfjord
Gällivare
Kemi
KARELIA

Norwegian
Sea
Mosjoen
Lulea
Suomussalmi
Kuhmo

Atlantic
Ocean
Namsos

Alesund
Trondheim
Maloy
Andalsnes

SHETLAND
ISLANDS
BRITISH
Bergen
Taelvag
Hamar
Haugesund
Lake
Tinnsjo
Rjukan
Oslo
Turku
Helsinki
Terioki
Stavanger
Vermork
Hangö
Gulf of Finland
Porvoo
Porkkala
Vipuri
Lake
Ladoga
Narva
Kronstadt
Leningrad
Arendal
Kristiansand
Stockholm
Tallinn
Haapsalu
Pärnü
Skagerrak
Gothenburg
Backebo
Riga
North Sea
Vederso
Aarhus
Libava
DENMARK
Odense
Malmo
Baltic Sea
Memel
SOVIET
UNION
HELIGOLAND
BORNHOLM
Kiel
Copenhagen
Peenemunde
Swinemunde
Gdynia
Königsberg
Vegesack
Lübeck
Rostock
Kolberg
Danzig
Stutthof
Rastenburg
Hamburg
Stettin
Bremen

Berlin

GREATER GERMANY

HOLLAND

BELGIUM

SWEDEN

NORWAY

FINLAND

Gulf of Bothnia

Vogelsang

xviii

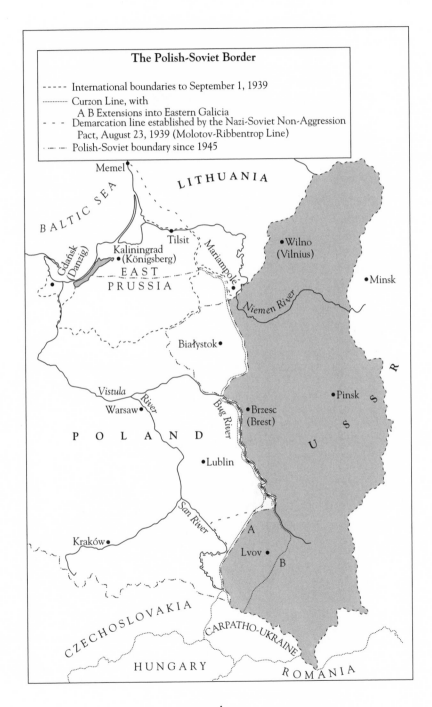

The Polish-Soviet Border

----- International boundaries to September 1, 1939

.... Curzon Line, with
A B Extensions into Eastern Galicia

- - - Demarcation line established by the Nazi-Soviet Non-Aggression
Pact, August 23, 1939 (Molotov-Ribbentrop Line)

-.--.- Polish-Soviet boundary since 1945

Memel

LITHUANIA

BALTIC SEA

Gdańsk (Danzig)

Tilsit

Kaliningrad (Königsberg)

EAST PRUSSIA

Mariampole

•Wilno (Vilnius)

Niemen River

•Minsk

Białystok•

Vistula River

Bug River

Warsaw•

P O L A N D

•Brzesc (Brest)

•Pinsk

U S S R

•Lublin

San River

A

Kraków•

Lvov •

B

CZECHOSLOVAKIA

CARPATHO-UKRAINE

HUNGARY

ROMANIA

The Polish-German Border

Polish-German Boundary 1921–39 ----- since 1945 ———

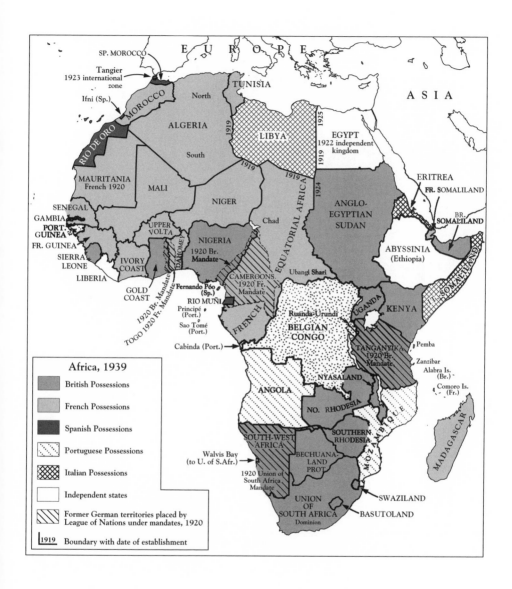

EUROPE

ASIA

SP. MOROCCO

Tangier
1923 international
zone

Ifni (Sp.)

MOROCCO

North

ALGERIA

South

TUNISIA

1919

LIBYA

1919

1925

EGYPT
1922 independent
kingdom

1919

1924

ERITREA

FR. SOMALILAND

BR.
SOMALILAND

RIO DE ORO

MAURITANIA
French 1920

MALI

NIGER

Chad

ANGLO-
EGYPTIAN
SUDAN

1919

SENEGAL

GAMBIA

PORT.
GUINEA

FR. GUINEA

SIERRA
LEONE

LIBERIA

UPPER
VOLTA

NIGERIA
1920 Br.
Mandate

ABYSSINIA
(Ethiopia)

GOLD
COAST

1920 Br. Mandate

TOGO 1920 Fr. Mandate

DAHOMEY

IVORY
COAST

Fernando Póo
(Sp.)

RIO MUNI

Principé
(Port.)

Sao Tomé
(Port.)

Cabinda (Port.)

CAMEROONS.
1920 Fr.
Mandate

Ubangi Shari

FRENCH

EQUATORIAL AFRICA

Ruanda-Urundi

BELGIAN
CONGO

UGANDA

IT. SOMALILAND

KENYA

Pemba

Zanzibar

Alabra Is.
(Br.)

Comoro Is.
(Fr.)

Africa, 1939

British Possessions

French Possessions

Spanish Possessions

Portuguese Possessions

Italian Possessions

Independent states

Former German territories placed by
League of Nations under mandates, 1920

1919   Boundary with date of establishment

TANGANYIKA
1920 Br.
Mandate

NYASALAND

ANGOLA

NO. RHODESIA

SOUTHERN
RHODESIA

MOZAMBIQUE

MADAGASCAR

SOUTH-WEST
AFRICA

Walvis Bay
(to U. of S.Afr.)

1920 Union of
South Africa
Mandate

BECHUANA-
LAND
PROT.

UNION
OF
SOUTH AFRICA
Dominion

SWAZILAND

BASUTOLAND

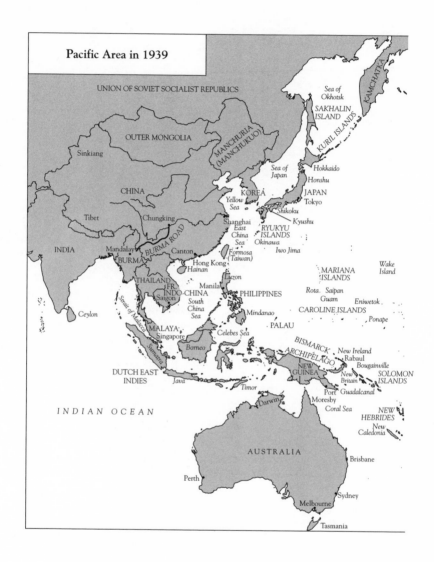

Pacific Area in 1939

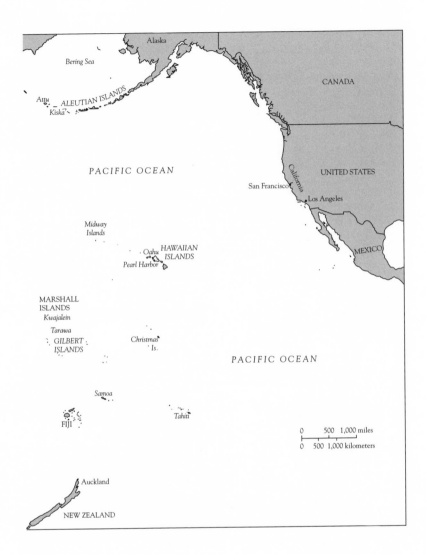

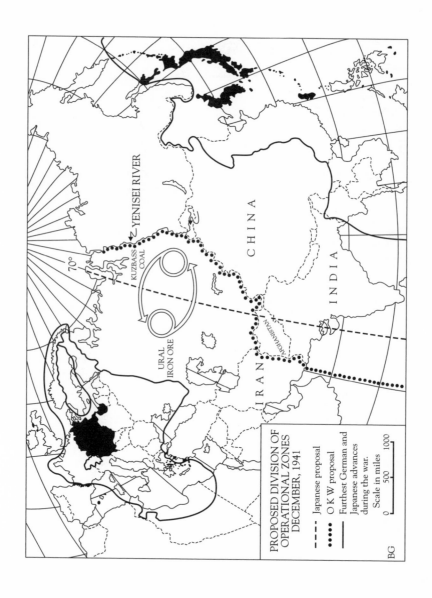

PROPOSED DIVISION OF
OPERATIONAL ZONES
DECEMBER, 1941

---·---·--- Japanese proposal

•••••• O K W proposal

———— Furthest German and
Japanese advances
during the war.

Scale in miles

0   500   1000

BG

Z YENISEI RIVER

KUZBASS
COAL

URAL
IRON ORE

70°

CHINA

INDIA

IRAN

AFGHANISTAN

INTRODUCTION

URING WORLD WAR II THE LEADERS OF THE MAJOR BELLI-
gerents concentrated their attention and their energies on
the immediate requirements of the fighting; but not only did they
from time to time give some thought to the postwar world that might
emerge at the end of the war – assuming that their side won – but
also the very decisions they made were frequently affected by the
hopes and aspirations they entertained about that future. The war
was, after all, not fought because countries had large armed forces
and did not know what to do with them. The belligerents fought for
aims, however vaguely defined; and even those who found themselves attacked, and hence involved in hostilities against their own
prior preference, either already had or developed concepts of what
the postwar world should be like when the fighting ended.

The course of events, the changing fortunes of battle, the entrance or departure of powers from the conflict, and revisions in the
understanding of events would from time to time produce changes in
perceptions of a desirable future. These changes could in turn influence policies and military deployments and allocations and in other
ways affect the course of hostilities. While the public in each country might have a variety of views and aspirations, fears and hopes,

I

about the future, the focus of this study is on the leaders of eight major belligerents. Because of the short periods of time that they led their countries during the war, Neville Chamberlain, Clement Attlee, Harry Truman, Koiso Kuniaki, and Suzuki Kantaro will not be discussed.[1] The subjects of scrutiny are, in order, Adolf Hitler, Benito Mussolini, and Tojo Hideki on the Axis side, Chiang Kai-shek, Joseph Stalin, Winston Churchill, Charles de Gaulle, and Franklin Roosevelt on the Allied side. The leaders of the countries that took the initiative in starting the war are placed first, in the sequence in which they came to be involved in open hostilities, followed by the Allied leaders in the sequence in which they came to be involved.

In each case an effort based on the often fragmentary evidence is made to show what the hopes and ambitions of each of these major actors were, and also whether and why and in which direction their views appear to have changed during the war. In many cases there will necessarily be a speculative element in the presentation; and not only might alternative readings of the currently available evidence be possible, but also new evidence may yet come to light. It is, however, worthwhile to look beyond the course of hostilities and to examine the aspirations of those in charge of the main belligerents. This procedure will assist us in understanding the choices and decisions those leaders made at the time and also provides some basis for assessing the extent to which the subsequent course of events was affected by their decisions. It will hopefully also help to show how developments during as well as after the war came to confound their hopes or conform to their expectations.

In examining the thinking and planning of these leaders, the reader who knows how the war developed and especially how it ended must always be extremely careful not to project that knowledge backwards. At the time, the men who led their nations in the greatest war ever fought had their hopes as well as military plans that might lead to the realization of those hopes; but however clear their understanding of the current situation in the conflict, they had no way of knowing for certain how it would all come out. It is fair to say that each had a substantial degree of confidence in an outcome that would be favorable to the country that he was leading. Hitler was not prepared to admit that Germany was about to be defeated until the late spring of 1945. Mussolini started to have serious doubts by the end of 1942 and therefore began to urge his German associate to make a separate peace with the Soviet Union. Tojo may well have had doubts about the outcome of the war at some point before his dismissal over the Japanese defeat in the Marianas in July 1944. Whatever disastrous defeats Britain suffered, Churchill was always confident that victory would come, however many years it might take. The prior experience of England in the wars against Philip II of Spain, Louis XIV and Napoleon of France, and also in World War I affected a man who was very conscious of history – and had written much history himself. De Gaulle was similarly confident that sooner or later victory for the Allies would include a France freed from German control and restored in full glory to the status of a major power in the world.

Stalin, during the fall of 1941, again in 1942 and well into 1943, was probably the one leader on the Allied side who at times had doubts and fears about the possibility of defeat or at least such exhaustion as to weaken his country in the trials that he was certain lay ahead. The example of Lenin's willingness to make enormous concessions to Germany in order to retain control of the bulk of the country in early 1918 was always there for him. It was concern about the possibility of loss of control in the first part of the war on the

Eastern Front – together with the subsequent realization, after the German recovery following the great Soviet victory at Stalingrad, that the road to Berlin would be a terribly costly one – that inclined Stalin alone to give serious thought to a compromise peace with Germany, a possibility that Hitler invariably rejected.[2]

Chiang Kai-shek, after the rejection of any mediated peace by the Japanese government in early 1938, was determined to fight the Japanese invaders until they tired of an endless conflict. After December 1941 he was sure that American participation in the war against Japan in effect guaranteed victory. Roosevelt was always certain that the Allies could and would crush the Axis powers and was no more dissuaded from this view by the early major American defeats than was Churchill. Whatever the confidence or lack of it, whatever the timing of changed perspectives, all the leaders on both sides knew that until the last shot was fired, the clash of arms, the solidity of the home front, and the elements of uncertainty and contingency would dominate events.

1. Adolf Hitler

Adolf Hitler, Hermann Göring, and General Field Marshall Keitel looking at map (ca. 1942). Library of Congress, Prints and Photographs Division, LC-USZ62-116157.

B ORN INTO THE FAMILY OF AN AUSTRIAN CUSTOMS OFFICIAL in 1889, Adolf Hitler had moved to Munich as a young man and served in a Bavarian unit of the German army on the Western Front in World War I. After the war he was briefly assigned to give indoctrination lectures to soldiers and then to observe a small new political party in Munich, which he soon joined and came to dominate. A failed coup attempt in 1923 brought him a short time in jail but also his first national publicity. After his release, he devoted himself to building up the National Socialist German Workers Party. A temporary alliance with the extremist German Nationalist Party gave him the opportunity to bring his message to large numbers of Germans, and by the beginning of the 1930s his party was the largest in the country. A small group of individuals around the president of Germany, Paul von Hindenburg, persuaded the latter to appoint Hitler chancellor of Germany on January 30, 1933. Over the subsequent year and a half, Hitler succeeded in consolidating his hold on the country by ending all civil liberties, dissolving all other political parties, and establishing an effective police and terror apparatus.

In any review of Hitler's hopes and aims in World War II, two interrelated aspects of his thinking before he became chancellor of

7

Germany must be noted. Already in the 1920s he was clear in his own mind that Germany deserved to conquer the globe and would be able to do so if only he were given the opportunity to lead it in the manner he thought appropriate – and his closest followers fully understood this concept.[1] In November 1930 he explained to the faculty and students of Erlangen University in a subsequently published speech that no people had more of a right to fight for and attain control of the globe (*Weltherrschaft*) than the Germans.[2]

Hitler was under no illusion that a goal that others might consider preposterous could be attained without a great deal of fighting. He recognized that this privately held and publicly proclaimed ambition would necessarily require a series of wars. This makes it more understandable why he explicitly asserted in the book he dictated in the summer of 1928 that each war Germany fought would merely provide the starting point for the next one in the series.[3] Dictated after his party's very poor showing in the May 1928 election, this text, which was designed to reinforce the very views on foreign policy that he thought had cost his party votes, offers support for the increasingly accepted view that Hitler was a man driven by ideology rather than simply an opportunist seeking power.

It had been within the framework of a series of wars that he had decided in early May 1938 to attack Czechoslovakia that fall. The purpose of conquering Czechoslovakia was to strengthen Germany's strategic position in central Europe and also provide, through the utilization of the portion of the country's population that was of German cultural background, the opportunity to raise additional divisions for the German army to employ in the next war. Such potential reinforcement was especially important to Hitler because the second war in the series was the one he believed likely to be the most difficult, namely, the war against the Western powers, Great Britain and France.⁴ At the last moment Hitler changed his mind, called off that war, and settled at the Munich Conference for what others thought of as a German triumph but Hitler came to consider the worst mistake of his career. The "lesson" he derived from Munich was that no one was ever going to cheat him of war again, and in 1939 he so conducted German diplomacy and military preparations that there would be no possibility of a negotiated settlement.⁵ Since the Polish government, unlike those of Hungary and Lithuania, had not been willing to subordinate itself to Germany as the latter moved to initiate its war against France and Great Britain, Poland would be crushed first, with the two Western powers either attacked thereafter or in the same conflict if they supported Poland.

The war started by Germany on September 1, 1939, was therefore seen as the next in a series; it was to pave the way for a war against the Soviet Union, thereafter a war against the United States, and another to follow, as explained below. For a number of reasons growing out of the actual course of hostilities, the wars against the Soviet Union and the United States were initiated by Germany before the preceding one in the expected series had been finished, and therefore Hitler's aims in this wider conflict are what must be examined.⁶ But before that can be done, something has to be said about the war that was expected to be next in the series.

Because Britain had not surrendered after the fall of France to the German invasion of that country in May and June of 1940, Hitler was most anxious for Japan to enter the war. That country could provide a great surface navy, and although Hitler had planned such a navy and the Germans had begun construction on it, they had not yet had the time to complete it. When the Japanese explained to their German ally that they could not attack the British base at Singapore without going to war with the United

States to protect the flank of their advance south, Hitler personally promised Japanese Foreign Minister Matsuoka Yosuke that in that case Germany would immediately join in war against the United States. He worried all during the negotiations between Japan and the United States in 1941 that an agreement might be reached between them, and he did what he could to encourage the Japanese to strike. Furthermore, to judge by recently published evidence, he had driven the German army forward toward Moscow in December 1941 in part for fear that the authorities in Tokyo might get cold feet at the last moment and not plunge into the wider war about which they had just asked Berlin and Rome for reassurance.[7]

The enthusiasm for Japan to enter the war, strike at the British base at Singapore, and assure Germany of the participation of a major navy on the side of the Axis did not, however, imply any great German fondness for that power. Relations between Berlin and Tokyo during their joint war against the Western powers were distant, and not only in miles. All the evidence points to the assumption that Hitler, just as he had been willing to make extensive concessions to the Soviet Union in 1939 to obtain its assistance until Germany was ready to move East, was willing to sign over to the Japanese whatever they wanted in order to get them into the war on his side until they in turn could be conquered in a subsequent war.[8] Since Germany was defeated by the Allies rather than victorious, that subsequent war did not take place; and it is to the aims of the one that Germany began on September 1, 1939, that attention must be devoted.

It seems appropriate to examine first the territorial dimensions of the empire Hitler intended to take over for Germany as a result of the conflict he had been so insistent on starting before dealing with the developments he expected to bring about within that empire. Inside Europe, the countries of Scandinavia – Denmark, Norway, Sweden, and Finland – were to be annexed to Germany. In the West, Luxembourg had already been incorporated into Germany in 1940. The small pieces of land Germany had lost to Belgium and the tiny jointly ruled area of Moresnet had also been annexed that year; the rest of Belgium was expected to follow. Alsace and Lorraine were placed under the direct administration of the adjacent portions of prewar Germany, and much of northern France and all of Burgundy were to be annexed later. The evidence suggests that some sort of dependent French puppet state, possibly with Brittany detached as a special region aligned with Germany, would make up the remainder, although a portion adjacent to Italy might be allocated to the latter.[9] Most of Switzerland would be annexed to Germany; the southeastern quarter was to be Italy's share.

The whole United Kingdom, including all of Ireland, was to be under German control. No decision had been reached as to whether this would be a puppet state of some sort, posssibly under the Duke of Windsor, or incorporated directly as a *Gau*, a German province. The preparation and printing of a lengthy arrest list, a detailed administrative plan that included provisions for the deportation of all males between seventeen and forty-five, the designation of the police chief who would subsequently be nominated for Moscow, and the assumption that all Jews living in Great Britain would be killed point in the direction of a form of control that very few on the islands would have found acceptable.[10]

Spain and Portugal were expected to become subordinate satellite states, with Spain turning over bases on and off the coast of northwest Africa to German sovereignty. Portugal was expected to surrender much of its African colonial empire as well as bases on the Azores in the Atlantic to the Third Reich. The precise details of the future division of the French colonial empire in northwest Africa between Spain and Italy constituted a subject on which Hitler preferred not to commit himself during the war. In any case, Spain was to receive Gibraltar, which in Hitler's eyes was always seen as a stepping stone on the way to northwest Africa rather than as a base commanding the western entrance to the Mediterranean.[11]

In southeast Europe, there would be governments subordinate to Germany in Slovakia, Hungary, Romania, and Bulgaria. A piece of northern Yugoslavia was annexed to Germany during the war; other portions would be under German control, as would parts of Greece, with the bulk of the latter country, including the strategically important island of Crete, allotted to Italy. The future of Turkey had not been decided, but Hitler would probably have been willing for it to go to Italy, along with the Middle East. Austria had been annexed in 1938, and the main portions of the former Czechoslovakia were destined to be incorporated into Germany and populated exclusively by Germans as well.

Once Italy left the war in 1943, the aggrandizement that Hitler had earlier been willing to allow the Italy of Benito Mussolini was canceled. The Italian zones of occupation in France, Yugoslavia, and Greece were taken over by Germany, and the puppet state of Croatia, formely under partial Italian control, came completely under German control. Furthermore, Italy was to lose not only Albania but also very large portions of prewar Italian territory as well. Hitler now intended to annex to Germany the southern Tyrol area that he had once been willing to see Italianized, along with very extensive additional parts of northeast Italy, including the port city of Trieste on the Adriatic.[12] In view of this enthusiasm for taking into the Third Reich purely Italian parts of Italy proper, it can be assumed that the

Italian empire once scheduled for North Africa and the Middle East would now be added to Germany's spoils of war instead.

In eastern Europe, a victorious Germany would extend to the Ural Mountains, thus including all of prewar Poland, the Baltic States, and European Russia, including the Caucasus, whose oil was expected to fuel Germany's navy and air force in war with the United States. Looking east beyond the Urals into Asia, Hitler was, for the time being, willing to be content with a border that extended some two to three hundred kilometers into Central Asia, as he explained in late July 1941.[13] This relative modesty compared with the suggestion from the High Command of the German Armed Forces (OKW) that Germany take all of central Siberia to the Yenisei River may help explain Hitler's willingness to accept the Japanese proposal for a division at the seventieth degree longitude.* This meant that for the time being Japan would seize more of central and eastern Siberia while Germany would control less of Siberia but take Afghanistan and the part of British India that is now Pakistan instead.[14] As for Germany's former colonial possessions in the central and south-west Pacific, which had been turned over to Japan, Australia, and New Zealand as mandates after World War I, these were – at least temporarily – to be sold to Japan on the basis of highly complex negotiations and exchanges of notes that do not, from the available evidence, appear to have been reviewed with Hitler.[15] What Hitler actually thought about these former German colonies is not discernible from the record; his thinking about colonies – as contrasted with land for German agricultural settlement – was concentrated entirely on Africa.

* See map, p. xxiv.

Hitler's view of the future of Africa saw that continent divided essentially into three parts; since he had not studied Latin, this was not an echo of Caesar's Gaul. The northern segment of the continent was to be Italy's. This would include Egypt, the Anglo-Egyptian Sudan, Kenya, French and British Somaliland, Tunisia, Algeria, and at least some portions of French Morocco, to use the names then current for the territories to be added to the prewar Italian colonies of Libya, Eritrea, and Italian Somaliland and the recently conquered Ethiopia. Some of French Morocco and Mauretania might be added to Spain's colonial empire. In any case, the German troops sent to fight in North Africa were to help maintain Mussolini's empire and status and to implement Germany's policy of killing all Jews, not establish a German colonial presence in this portion of the continent. Only naval and air bases on and off the coast of northwest Africa were to be under Germany's complete control, as already mentioned.

Germany's own colonial empire was expected to be a broad swath of land in central Africa from the South Atlantic to the Indian Ocean. It was expected to include the former German colonies in that part of Africa, that is, Togo, Cameroon, and German East Africa, as well as the French and British colonial possessions from Senegal to Uganda and Northern Rhodesia. This would entail the inclusion in Germany's empire of the British colonies of Gambia, the Gold Coast, Sierra Leone, and Nigeria; the French colonies of Dahomey, French Guinea, the Ivory Coast, and French Equatorial Africa; the Belgian Congo; and at least the northern parts of the Portuguese colonies Angola and Mozambique. It was expected that the land south of this huge German colonial empire would be controlled by a pro-Nazi Afrikaaner government that would take over in the Union of South Africa as one result of Germany's victory over

Britain and the British Dominions. That regime might be asked to return former German Southwest Africa, today's Namibia, in exchange for the British protectorates of Bechuanaland, Basutoland, and Swaziland, plus possibly southern portions of the Portuguese colonies.[16]

The thinking of Hitler about future German control of the Western Hemisphere was, from all evidence, far vaguer than his plans for Europe and parts of Asia and Africa. Always assuming that the United States would not give up its independence without a fight, he had asserted as early as the summer of 1928 that preparing for war with that country would be one of the main responsibilities of a National Socialist government of Germany.[17] While there would presumably have to be some agreement on a division of the area with Japan, as there had been on the division of Asia, Hitler remained vague on details. It is by no means clear how he saw the role of the large German settlements in Brazil, Argentina, and elsewhere in Latin America. There is no evidence to show whether he was aware of the interest of segments of the Nazi Party in Patagonia, the southernmost portion of Argentina.[18] At times he referred to the possibility of encouraging the descendants of German settlers in the Western Hemisphere to move back to European lands under German control,[19] but the whole issue of the disposition of the Americas once Germany obtained world domination remained cloudy in Hitler's thinking and comments.

Hitler assumed that during the course of then current hostilities Australia and New Zealand would come under Japanese control. Whether that was to be their final disposition will have to remain an open question. His only lengthy recorded discussion of New Zealand reveals a degree of ignorance that exceeds anything foolish he said and believed about the Soviet Union and the United States. He seriously argued that the people there lived in trees and had not learned to walk upright.[20] Had they ever come under German control, their fate would presumably not have been very nice.

If these were the dimensions of the vast empire Hitler expected to conquer in the war then under way as a first major installment of Germany's march to world conquest, how did he envision what was to happen inside that domain? How were its peoples to be structured and controlled; what sort of life – or death – could they expect? Perhaps the best way to try to picture the German-controlled areas of the post–World War II era as the German leader imagined it during the war would be to divide Hitler's plans into three separate but closely interrelated aspects. First, there are the intentions that were to affect all of Germany's empire regardless of the individual status of its parts. Second, it will be important to look at his plans for the lands that were already or were in the near future expected to be inhabited by Germans and what he considered Germanic peoples (whether the latter recognized their own Germanic character or not). Third, it will be necessary to examine plans for those conquered lands that were not settled or expected to be settled by Germans.

There was no doubt in Hitler's mind that the German empire would be ruled from its capital, "Germania," as Berlin was to be renamed. The changes intended, and in part already being implemented, for that city will be reviewed below, but that all people would look to Germania as the seat of absolute power – as they had once looked to Rome – was beyond question. Certainly two categories and perhaps a third category of persons were to be exempted from this perspective because they would be killed wherever they were located. The German government had in 1939 initiated a program for the systematic killing of all handicapped people as the

German government from time to time defined that category. Although begun inside the country, this process had been applied in German-occupied Poland right away and, while the subject has not received the scholarly attention it deserves, was clearly designed to be of universal application. Hitler's personal authorization for this, the first bureaucratically organized mass murder program, was signed by him in late October 1939; he had backdated it to September 1, 1939 – a clear sign of his sense of the connection between the killing and the war.[21] It was in this terrible step into uncharted territory that the Germans experimented with the social and mechanical procedures for defining, identifying, and murdering large numbers of people, disposing of enormous numbers of corpses, and recruiting individuals who would kill others from morning to lunchtime and then all afternoon, six days a week, as their steady occupation.

Although inside Germany the killing of the handicapped was decentralized after August 1941, the process continued until the German surrender of 1945, and those involved in it attempted to maintain it afterwards until physically halted by the occupation authorities. By that time, among the tens of thousands murdered were numerous German World War I veterans, and a start had been made on German World War II veterans as well. Germany's defeat saved not only innumerable old people, handicapped individuals, and persons in mental institutions inside and outside the prewar Third Reich but also tens of thousands of Germany's own seriously wounded veterans from death at the hands of their own government.

A second group targeted for total extermination was the Jewish population not only of Germany and all of Europe but also of all other parts of the globe as well, what Hitler, with his Eurocentric perspective, referred to as Jews living "among non-European peoples."[22] Whether this had always been his intention is beyond our knowledge, though reference to total extermination as a desired fate for the Jews appears in his public speeches as early as April 1920.[23] When urged by German medical professionals and so-called racial scientists to initiate the killing of the handicapped in the 1930s, Hitler had explained that this could be done only when the country was at war; as has just been shown, it was in this context that he authorized it. After deciding to go to war for certain in 1939, he mentioned the forthcoming destruction of Germany's Jews to the Czechoslovak minister for foreign affairs on January 21, 1939, and soon after, on January 30, he predicted in a speech to the German parliament that in another war – on which he had already decided – all Jews in Europe would be killed.[24] In numerous public speeches in subsequent years, Hitler would refer to the prediction he had made in this speech, always misdating it to September 1, 1939, just as he had misdated his directive for the killing of the handicapped.[25] These shifts forward and backward to the same date – the one on which he started the war – surely provide some insight into the way he saw those killing programs, that is, as part and parcel of a conflict fought not so that he could see the Eiffel Tower but to bring about a total demographic and racial reordering of the globe.

In this field, as in that of the killing the handicapped, the Germans were entering new territory, and it should therefore occasion no surprise that the actual implementation of the policy came in steps, some of them tentative, to see what the reaction would be. Systematic killing of Jews in newly occupied Yugoslav and Soviet territory began in the spring and summer of 1941. As there appeared to be no substantial opposition from the German military, but considerable assistance and support instead, by the end of July Hitler clearly believed it possible to expand the killing to all areas under German control or influence, as he explained in late July 1941 to the visiting war minister of Croatia.[26] The details of the way in which Hitler's aspiration was implemented do not belong in this context and are adequately described and analyzed elsewhere.[27] The critical point is that application of this policy, like the killing of the handicapped, was initiated on a large scale during hostilities.

Hitler's earlier support of the emigration of Jews from Germany to Palestine and elsewhere must be understood as a product of his genuine belief in the legend that Germany had lost World War I, not because of defeat at the front, but as the result of a stab in the back by Jews and others. Driving as many Jews as possible out of the country – after stealing most of their assets – before he started the first of his wars, therefore, was motivated by his concern to ensure a solid home front in that war, a solidity that would guarantee victory this time. As for the Jews in Palestine, they were to be killed along with all other Jews then living in the Middle East, as he assured the Grand Mufti of Jerusalem in November 1941.[28] Hitler did not feel confident that he could rely on the Italians to carry out such a program when they received the area, an assessment that was as correct as the expectation he had voiced earlier in his conversation with the Croatian minister of war, that the Hungarian government would be the last in German-controlled Europe to surrender its Jews for killing. The murder of the very large number of Jews then living in the areas of North Africa and the Middle East was a task of such importance to Hitler that he intended his own forces to carry it out. Naturally he did not explain to the Grand Mufti, who wanted a German declaration favoring Arab independence, that the area would instead be incorporated into Italy's colonial empire when the Axis powers had won the war.

The question of whether the total elimination by systematic killing of the Sinti and Roma, the gypsies, was also intended by Hitler is still not entirely clear. The available evidence and the scholarship devoted to the subject show very extensive persecution, large-scale killing, and some indications of additional killing intended for later. At the same time, there are signs that some Roma who had not intermarried with others and also the descendants of "pure" Roma were expected to survive, if under special restrictions.[29] This author inclines to the interpretation that there was to be no room for Roma in the thousand-year Reich, but the evidence, especially on Hitler's role, views, and expectations, is not nearly as definite as it is for the other two categories, the handicapped and the Jews.

If these were the groups that Hitler expected to remove from the face of the earth, what fate was in store for those whom he considered Germans or sufficiently Germanic to qualify for membership in the superior race that would inhabit the territories Germany already held or planned to annex? First, an issue has to be dealt with that concerns the population itself. The killing of all considered handicapped, whatever the changing definition of this category over time, has already been mentioned. In addition, male and female Germans who Germany's doctors and so-called racial experts believed might beget defective babies would be subjected to surgical sterilization. This had been provided for in the first piece of legislation in the field of family law that the new Nazi government had included in the mass of laws enacted by the cabinet on July 14, 1933, a date chosen for its symbolic significance.[30] By the end of the Nazi regime, some four hundred thousand Germans had been forcibly subjected to this procedure; it was assumed that a victorious Germany would continue this practice. An additional precaution, alongside extensive education in what was called "racial hygiene," was a series of legal provisions requiring permission to marry, permission that could be withheld for a number of reasons that the Nazi leadership imagined as having racial significance.[31] Although there appears to be no evidence on the subject, such procedures, both sterilization of certain categories and marriage permission for others, would no doubt have been applied to all those whom the Nazis were prepared to include in their definition of "Aryans" and hence to include among those favored by the regime.

If the measures that have been mentioned and that were already being applied to the German population before the war were designed to eliminate the imagined danger of racial degeneration – and hence might be called the negative side of racial policy – what about the positive side of racial policy? On this side of the ledger there was a whole series of special measures. Beginning in 1933, a variety of laws and other procedures were instituted to encourage the "right" people to marry and have lots of children. Simultaneously, the legal and social status of illegitimate children was to be improved. Women were pushed toward staying at home and away from higher education, from the professions, and, to the extent possible, from any gainful employment outside the home (other than on farms). During World War II, the regime was obliged to make temporary adjustments to several of these policies, but there was the clear intent to reverse these concessions to the needs of the moment. Furthermore, women, as Hitler personally emphasized, were under no circumstances to be paid equally for equal work.[32]

Additional steps were taken during the war to increase the number of Germans for the planned expansion of German settlement. The families of soldiers were provided with substantial support payments. To increase the number of Germans as well as decrease and weaken the peoples in occupied eastern Europe, the regime instituted a procedure called "hay action" (*Heuaktion*). This was a massive kidnapping operation in which thousands of young children who looked "Germanic" to the Nazis were stolen from their parents and entrusted as so-called orphans to German families for raising.[33] Special procedures were introduced to offset the losses in men that warfare entailed. For example, Germany established a form of marriage to a dead man (*Totenehe*). If a woman could demonstrate by letters, testimony, or other evidence – such as a pregnancy – that a soldier who had in the meantime lost his life at the front had intended to marry her, she would be retroactively legally married to him. She would then be eligible for a widow's pension, any baby would be legitimate, and her prospects for a later marriage and the bearing of additional children would be greatly enhanced.[34] More dramatic procedures were planned for the postwar era but were deferred because of the possible morale implications on the home front if enacted in wartime. Just as systematic mass killing had had to be postponed until it could be covered by hostilities, so a drastic revision of the whole concept of marriage had to await the end of the war because victory would further empower the regime and increase popular support for its policies.

By January 1944 Hitler realized that the losses of the German armed forces during the war would be so large that millions of women would become widows and, like the young unmarried, would be unable to find a husband after Germany's expected victory. At that time Hitler estimated that the number would be between three and four million; in fact the number substantially exceeded five million.[35] Having previously strongly endorsed the 1939 order of Heinrich Himmler calling on the men of the SS to have children inside and outside marriage, Hitler now laid out the reasons for the surviving men to have multiple marriages. The provision of various forms of state support for the women in these marriages would assure them that they could have children with firm legal status and without fear for their own and their children's financial future. Those children would be needed, if for no other reason, for the future wars in the series Germany would have to fight for world dominion. It must be noted that, just as the reason for his interest in the Germans inside Czechoslovakia was the additional number of army divisions their incorporation into Germany would make possible, the main reason for his concern with the multiple marriage concept was the number of army divisions that Germany would lose in the future without such a measure.[36] Since, as will be reviewed subsequently, there were to be no churches in the Germany of the future, religious objections to such a dramatic alteration in the concept of marriage would have no institutional support at a time when, as Hitler insisted, the Nazi Party, and especially its women's organization, preached the new approach to childbearing.

The style of life he planned for Germans in the future was also expected to lead to the raising of large families. Since very many, if not all, German males were expected to serve in the postwar army, their situation after service would, in effect, apply to a substantial proportion of couples. As Hitler explained in detail on July 27, 1941, the term of service for an army of one and a half to two million would be twelve years, with much attention during the last two years spent on preparing the man to be a farmer. Each man upon discharge would be given a farm for free since the land would have been stolen from those "inferior" Slavic people living on it previously. The fate of the displaced Slavic residents is reviewed below. The discharged German soldier would be obliged to marry a woman willing to be a farm girl and to raise a large family, whose members in turn would be provided with additional stolen land. Hitler was always strongly opposed to the system of dividing farms among children. That system, which had long obtained in much of Germany, would be abolished inside the country as well as for these settler families, with all given land in the East whose inhabitants had been killed or expelled. Hitler suggested further that in the territory of the Baltic States, Dutch, Norwegian, and possibly Swedish settlers would be included in this expansion of Germanic settlement.[37]

As for those who were to be displaced, three options were under review by Hitler and his associates. There were the two obvious options of either killing them or letting them starve to death, both much discussed and in part already practiced during the war. The other possibility, in this author's opinion, was to implement a policy related to the extensive horrendous experimentation initiated in the concentration camps in 1942 in an effort to discover some means of mass sterilization. Unlike the individual surgical sterilizations that had been carried out on a large scale in Germany since 1933, these were to be applied wholesale to masses of people without their immediately knowing what had been done to them.[38] In a world that would be without the handicapped, without Jews, and entirely or almost entirely without Roma, who was to be mass sterilized? Is it not most likely that this process, if ever developed, was designed for Slavic people whose work on farms and in factories, mines, and construction was still needed – but who would have no progeny?

While a larger percentage of Germans than in the past were to live on farms and in new villages in eastern Europe, what about those who continued to live in cities? They, too, would see major changes. One of Hitler's main interests in life had always been architecture. His focus, however, was not on a particular style or only on projects for specific buildings but rather on the role of architecture in the fashioning of a total urban environment that would be conducive to the political aims of his regime. Long before he became chancellor of Germany, he had begun to sketch designs for buildings of colossal size to be built in the world capital that Berlin was to become. Designed to overawe all those living in the city and those who would visit it, these buildings would give Berlin an entirely new form. As the most comprehensive study of the subject shows, once in power Hitler not only moved forward with these projects, utilizing a totally compliant Albert Speer to implement his plans, but decided to have a large number of German cities altered to fit his concept of broad avenues for mass demonstration marches, large central Party headquarters, and other common features.[39]

Two special features characterized all the plans for Germany's cities of the postwar era. In the first place, because Christianity was to disappear, no space was provided for churches in the plans for the German cities, towns, and rural settlements of the future. Second, the public structures that were to dominate the cities of the future Germany were to be constructed of stone so that even after the end of the thousand-year Reich their ruins would impress subsequent generations the way the ruins left behind by the Roman Empire still impressed observers more than a thousand years after its fall. Contracts for the enormous quantities of stone needed for the huge building program were still being worked on in Scandinavia in 1943. Both before and after that date, the concentration camp system was directly structured and located so that the inmates could help provide the stone and brick required for the buildings.[40] The people living in these cities would know from their surroundings that they were small, indistinguishable elements in a huge empire that from time to time would expect them to assemble either to participate directly in the ritual parades or to observe them cheering from the sidewalks.

A few cities were each expected to have a special feature. Berlin would have the world's largest structures and widest streets. Hamburg was to have the world's largest bridge, one deliberately constructed in such a fashion that its total surface would exceed that of the Golden Gate Bridge in San Francisco, then the world's longest suspension bridge.[41] Linz, the city in what had been Austria with which Hitler most identified personally, was to receive, in addition to other major structures, a museum that was to put all others on earth in the shade.[42] Partly as a product of systematic looting all over Europe, Linz would obtain a huge art collection – including Hitler's own – a great art library, a coin collection, and a collection of weapons. This project was actually initiated in 1938, and in February 1945 Hitler had the models for the future of the whole city of Linz brought to Berlin for him to study as the Red Army closed in on the German capital. The city of Königsberg (now Kaliningrad) in East Prussia was to have an art museum for the eastern portion of the German empire, but Hitler was considerably more explicit about his plans for the Norwegian city of Trondheim.

The North Sea port of Trondheim was to become one of Germany's most important cities and naval bases. This city was to have a German population of 300,000 and was to have the art museum for the northern part of Germany's empire, a museum that would hold only works by German masters.[43] As Germany's major naval base, designed to be the home port of the superbattleships and aircraft carriers of the postwar German navy, the city would be completely reconstructed by Albert Speer with the enthusiastic cooperation of the leadership of the German navy.[44] At the time,

Trondheim was, of course, separated from Germany by the exits from the Baltic to the North Sea. This minor detail would be overcome by one portion of Hitler's plans for the transportation system of the future: a four-lane highway running from Klagenfurt in the south by bridges across the Little and Great Belts all the way to Trondheim. All other areas of German-controlled Europe would be similarly joined by highways, while the Danube and the Main and the Danube and the Oder would be joined by canals.[45]

The one German city that was to be downgraded in the future was Vienna. Unlike such cities as Moscow and Leningrad, it was not to be razed to the ground, but its importance, especially as a cultural center, was to be drastically reduced. Hitler did not want the old capital of the Habsburg Empire that he so hated to be in any position to challenge Germania for predominance in any segment of life. The very structures in Vienna that had so impressed him in his youth when he lived there now contributed to his concern about the possibility of a challenge to the primacy of Germania and inspired a strongly negative attitude toward the city.[46]

The cities of the enlarged postwar Germany would be connected not only by four-lane highways and the existing railway and airplane routes. In addition, Hitler was planning a network of super-railways running on tracks about double the width of the west and central European standard track (and hence substantially wider than the Russian railway track). Colossal engines would haul large and luxurious coaches for the members of the master race, while something like barracks on wheels would haul slave laborers from eastern Europe to whatever destinations seemed desirable. Hitler worked on the details of this project with Fritz Todt, his favorite construction engineer, and kept it secret from the German railway administration as well as Albert Speer.[47] In his enthusiasm for the wide-track railway, Hitler even anticipated extending this system of tracks to India and Vladivostok, the Soviet port on the Pacific![48] This final destination was not explained to the Japanese, to whom the Far East provinces of the Soviet Union were assigned in the territorial division previously mentioned.

What kind of education and what sort of life could the favored members of the master race expect in the cities and on the farms to which they had been sent? On the subject of education, Hitler's views were clear in outline if lacking in detail. There was to be a very strong emphasis on physical education, on the one hand, and an end to anything resembling a liberal arts education, on the other. How the latter was to be implemented in view of Hitler's very great interest in and emphasis on wide popular participation in and attendance at cultural activities like concerts and theater performances was left open.[49] The major emphasis in the school system was to be on the physical rather than the mental aspect of development of the young, thus preparing the young males for their role as warriors and the young females for their role as bearers of numerous children. It was presumably within the education system that Hitler expected to further his goal of convincing everyone of the advantages of a vegetarian diet and nonuse of tobacco.[50] Until after the war, he reserved his lectures on these subjects, endless and repetitive though they were, to his evening companions at headquarters.

An aspect of the life of Germans in the future on which he was consistently emphatic was the disappearance of religion, a subject already touched on in connection with his concepts of city planning. In order to avoid any danger of lowering morale during the war, he repeatedly deprecated overt steps in this direction while hostilities were in progress, and at times he felt obliged to restrain his more exuberant followers in this regard. But once the war had been won, all would change. Since he was certain that National Socialism and Christianity were incompatible, he was never seriously interested in the experiments of those who called themselves "Germanic Christians." Constituting a major faction within the German Protestant Church, these believers tried to remove the Jewish core from Christianity, make Jesus into a non-Jew, and create a form of Christianity that was compatible with the racial concepts of the new Germany.[51] Whatever temporary support this widely popular tendency within the German Protestant Church received from the Nazi government in 1933–34, there was no doubt in Hitler's mind as to the future. In July 1941 he explained to his immediate associates that there was no possible coexistence of National Socialism and the Christian churches; in May of the following year he explained this in some detail to the leaders of the Nazi Party and to its regional chiefs.[52] As he confided to Joseph Goebbels, when Christianity was terminated in postwar Germany, many of the bishops would be executed.[53]

As for the physically rather than mentally educated German citizens, they not only were to enjoy their superior status as compared with any surviving members of "inferior races" but also were to have great opportunities for personal and social advances (though these would always be restricted to males). Hitler was a strong opponent of hereditary status and class divisions and privileges. A vehement critic of both the old royal and princely houses as well as of nobility in general, he wanted a society in which any man of any background could aspire to any position or rank. His disdain for the old class divisions in Germany made him something of a social revolutionary in his own estimation and practice, though few historians have paid much attention to this aspect of National Socialism.[54] And, of course, all German families could expect to have cars – no longer a sign of class status – and could use them to roar across the thousands of kilometers of the thousand-year Reich's superhighways.

Hitler's views about the future of the German economy were dominated by his invariable insistence that politics dictated economics, not the other way around. Where and when private initiative and ownership operated in accordance with the political directives from the top, they could continue and, within limits set by the government, be rewarded. But whenever the political demands established by the leader were not met by the private sector, then there would be government-owned factories and other such controlled operations. The establishment in 1936 of the Four Year Plan, with its massive mining and industrial complexes, can be seen as something of a model for any field where private industry might be recalcitrant in the future. On the one hand, when in 1933 IG Farben had been willing, even enthusiastically willing, to pursue a vast expansion of synthetic fuel production as long as it was guaranteed a cost-plus price, the government had been happy to oblige. On the other hand, when the leaders of Germany's steel industry had declined to become involved in the processing of low-grade iron ore, which they disdainfully called "potting soil" (*Blumenerde*), they next read in the newspapers about the establishment of a government-owned organization that would do that work and was to begin with capital the steel industry itself was to provide. There was, in other words, not a doctrine of either a free market or government ownership; the regime would give direction and set goals that could be reached by any means, either private or public.[55]

It was Hitler's intent that the administrative apparatus of the Germany of the future would, under a genius like himself, undergo an important change – a change that would, ironically, be implemented by the actual victors of World War II. Hitler wanted the state of Prussia to be broken up into smaller units. As for taxes, these would be collected centrally and then allocated to the provincial governments. Since these would be controlled by the Nazi Party, there could be regional variations within the system, for the party would maintain a common ideological orientation.[56] Hitler was always skeptical about the ideological purity of judges and administrators and insisted that they be appointed or dismissed as he thought appropriate. He had arranged for the last session of the Reichstag, the German parliament, to enact in April 1942 a law that stripped all Germans of procedural protections of any type. Anyone could now be punished in any way the leader thought appropriate and without the affected person having any rights on the basis of prior service, position, or established procedure. The unanimous enthusiasm with which this stripping of all Germans of any and all rights had been greeted by the Reichstag reflects the careful way in which its members had been selected before Nazi Germany's last "election" in April 1938. A joke current in Germany at that time – that someone had stolen the results of the next election – provided a grim but accurate foretaste of what the future would bring to German voters.

Before we turn to the two other categories of territory controlled by Germany – those believed suitable for German settlement and those destined for permanent colonial status – it is important to recall that the "Germans" whose future land and lives have been reviewed would include numerous persons from states outside the borders of the Germany of 1939. As they grasped the concept that they were indeed Germans, or at least members of a branch of the so-called Aryan family of tribes, Norwegians and other peoples of Scandinavia, as well as the Dutch, at least the Flemish segment of Belgium's population, and the inhabitants of the already annexed Luxembourg, were expected to become full-fledged citizens of the Reich. Furthermore, in addition to the large program of kidnapping children believed to be Germanic-looking mentioned earlier, there were complicated procedures, some already implemented, some only in the planning stage, to separate out individuals and families thought to be suitable for Germanization who were living in the occupied territories of central and eastern Europe. The area where such a procedure was first developed and experimented with was Poland, the first country overrun by the German army, partially in 1939, with the rest occupied in 1941. It was in Poland that the Germans not only first exported their policy of killing the handicapped but also experimented with a variety of schemes for transforming conquered territory into settlement land for Germans.

Already in October 1939, Hitler had appointed Heinrich Himmler to the newly created position of Reich Commissioner for the Strengthening of Germandom, an office that was to play a central role in the settlement and resettlement of Germans, the displacement and murder of non-Germans, and the development of long-range plans for the transformation of conquered lands into areas of German living space.[57] Although Hitler and Himmler frequently conferred in the subsequent years of the war, the extent to which Hitler personally directed or approved all the measures that Himmler implemented in his new capacity cannot be stated with certainty; what is clear is that Poland provided the place for all manner of horrendous experiments in the establishment of the New Order, as the Nazis chose to call it. Germanization would mean massive expulsions, killings, resettlements, deportations, and other procedures. Hitler had every reason to feel confident that Himmler understood what was intended in general and would move in the desired direction as quickly and as ruthlessly as possible. If these measures involved temporary reversals, for example, the repeated shuffling of the same people back and, forth, that was simply a part of great new experiments with few if any precedents. What worked could be applied subsequently further east; what did not work could be changed in the next area to be affected. What mattered in Hitler's eyes were the direction and the sense of pressure; the details could safely be left to Himmler, who would, as his official record of daily activities shows, check with Hitler whenever a major appointment or new project needed approval.[58] What Hitler had specified at the beginning of the occupation of Poland was that the clergy and the intelligentsia were to be killed, that the standard of living of the remaining Poles was to be kept as low as possible while they were still alive, and that many would be made into slave laborers for the Germans.[59]

If German policies in Poland and the first parts of pre-1941 Soviet territory seized by the Germans provide a useful glimpse into how Hitler envisioned the transformation of eastern Europe into an area of German settlement, what were his plans for those lands that he did not believe suitable for such settlement but intended to hold as colonial possessions instead? From the beginning of his interest in colonies, Hitler thought about the central segment of the African continent. He had entrusted German planning for that colonial empire to an old associate, Franz Ritter von Epp, a retired army general who had been an ardent supporter of the Nazi Party already in the 1920s, had been rewarded with an appointment as Hitler's representative in Bavaria, and was to be the new minister for the colonies.[60] In these colonies there would be German administrators and police, but Hitler did not envision massive German settlement, as he intended for eastern Europe. There was a serious argument between him and his military advisors on the subject of recruiting Africans to serve in a military role, as they had done in World War I, especially in the German force that had held out in German East Africa until the end of that war. Against the preference of his highest military advisors, Hitler opposed such recruitment and instead intended each German division to spend one year in colonial service on a rotating basis.[61] The colonies were expected to provide Germany with raw materials that were otherwise difficult, expensive, or impossible to obtain; their populations would be required to work for the benefit of their German masters. Under von Epp's direction, and with the enthusiastic support of many German ministries and agencies, especially the German navy, there was very extensive planning for the great colonial empire Germany assumed it would control. Other than vast quantities of paper, only the proof coins for use in the colonies remain as silent testimony to great schemes that the peoples of a wide swath of Africa, unlike those of eastern Europe, were spared.[62]

A word needs to be said about those territories in western Europe that Germany either had conquered during the war or expected to occupy in the course of winning but that were neither lands destined for German settlement in the near future nor included in the anticipated African colonial empire. As mentioned, the Norwegians, Danes, and Dutch were assumed to be of kindred "Aryan" background and would be treated like Germans once they had come to understand their true racial nature. A similar future was accorded to the German-speaking Luxembourgers and Swiss as well as the Flemish population of Belgium. The French-speaking populations of Belgium and Switzerland as well as the bulk of the population of France itself could expect a harsh rule. The long-term fate of these people was not, however, clear.[63] The dreams possessed by such leaders of Vichy France as Henri Pétain and Pierre Laval of a secure if subordinate place in a German New Order were most likely to remain mere dreams in view of Hitler's hatred for and distrust of the French.[64] The policy of collaboration was always a one-way street: the French could collaborate but there was no way that in German eyes they could remove the stain of being French.[65] As already mentioned, the Germans had made extensive detailed preparations for the administration of the occupied United Kingdom, but other than extreme harshness, these provide few clues as to the longer term future. Only two aspects are clear: all Jews on the two islands would be killed, and the enthusiastic admirers of Hitler's Germany in the IRA would see Ireland united into one territory under Nazi rule.[66]

It had been Hitler's initial expectation that the process of attaining world control as a result of a series of victorious wars would be completed by 1950.[67] Although he would not accept the reality that Germany was about to be totally defeated until late April 1945, he did begin to recognize by the fall of 1943 that total German victory was unlikely in the near future. In a lengthy discussion with Goebbels on October 26, 1943 – after the defeat of Germany's summer offensive on the Eastern Front and the landing of the Western Allies on the Italian mainland – Hitler took the position that Germany might best make a deal with Stalin on the 1939 model, returning to its 1941 border in the East and then concentrating on crushing Great Britain. A renewed war against the Soviet Union to seize land in the East would have to come later, and it might have to be led by a successor, as he himself might by then be too old.[68] Two aspects of the discussion should be noted: Hitler held to his preference for a temporary peace in the East to facilitate the defeat of Britain in the face of the lengthy arguments of Goebbels for the opposite course, and any reference to the United States was completely absent from the record Goebbels made of this conversation.

The first aspect confirms the reality of Hitler's obsessive hate for England – contrary to the often repeated fables on this topic.[69] The absence of any reference in this record to the fact that Germany was at war with the United States demonstrates once again the extent to which preposterous assumptions about that country remained a fixture of the thinking of the highest authorities in Germany during the war.[70]

It was in part this underestimation of the United States that led Hitler to throw his last major reserves into an offensive against American forces in December 1944 – what the Germans called the Ardennes Offensive and others have come to call the Battle of the Bulge. Partly in anticipation of that operation, partly as a result of the attempted coup against him and his government by domestic opponents of the Nazi regime on July 20, 1944, Hitler focused his attention on domestic German affairs following Germany's assumed winning of the war. As he explained to Goebbels at the beginning of December, both the aristocracy and the traditional officer corps would vanish. New elections were to be held for the Reichstag, it being assumed that the law allowing only the Nazi Party to nominate candidates would continue to be in effect. This Reichstag would establish a new constitution that would provide for a dictatorially ruled republic but contain only a minimum of other provisions. The Nazi Party would be the main pillar of the regime. Stringent measures would be taken against the churches. On the other hand, Hitler reiterated his interest in the furthering of what he considered the appropriate cultural life of the German people. The enormous bribes already distributed to the highest military and political leadership of Germany were to be further increased, especially with the allocation of landed estates (though he failed to specify where at this stage of the war that land was to be located).[71]

By March 11, 1945, the development of the military situation led Hitler at least to mention the United States; perhaps the crossing of the Rhine by American troops at Remagen a few days earlier had reminded him of that allegedly inferior country's role in the war. He now hoped that a local defensive victory on the Eastern Front, preferably accompanied by massive Red Army casualties, would facilitate a separate peace agreement with Stalin. Hitler hoped that such an agreement would yet allow for a partition of Poland with the Soviet Union and leave Hungary and Croatia under German control. (At this time, Croatia was still under German occupation.) Germany would then defeat the Western powers of Britain and the United States. The administration of a death blow (*Todesstoss*) to England would give the war its real meaning.[72] It was Hitler's thinking along these lines that contributed to his choice of Admiral Karl Dönitz as his successor – here was an enthusiastic Nazi among the highest military leaders, one whose whole career had been devoted to the crushing of Great Britain.[73]

The trajectory of Hitler's view of the future was as terrible as it was consistent. He began with an aspiration for world domination by the racially superior Germans and ended, in his last testament, with an admonition to the German people to adhere to his racial concepts. And he wanted them to do so under the leadership of a successor whose vision reached across the oceans to the wider world that might yet, some day, fall under German domination.

When in his last days Hitler pondered what had gone wrong, he thought that his major mistake was not the terrible war that he had been so insistent on unleashing but rather his drawing back from war in 1938; for it was then, he was certain in retrospect, that Germany's prospects had been at their best.[74] He thought of himself thwarted in his hopes, not by Churchill or Stalin or Roosevelt, but by Neville

Chamberlain. In his speech to Germany's military leaders on August 22, 1939, he had explained that his only concern was that at the last moment some "pig-dog" (*Schweinehund*) might propose a compromise that would make it difficult for him to start a war this time, leading him to duplicate the failure of the year before. No one will ever know how a war started by Germany in 1938 would have developed; Hitler did get war in 1939, and it ended in Germany's utter defeat. Although Admiral Karl Dönitz believed after his arrest, trial, and imprisonment that he was in fact still the country's legal head of state, no other German is known to have shared this view.[75]

2. Benito Mussolini

Benito Musolini. Library of Congress, Prints and Photographs Division, LC-USZ62-88713.

B ENITO MUSSOLINI WAS BORN IN 1883 TO A FAMILY LIVING in fairly poor circumstances in northern Italy. An ardent socialist in his youth, Mussolini broke with that movement to advocate Italy's entrance into World War I on the side of the Allies and against Austria-Hungary. He himself served in the Italian army fighting the Austrians. After the war he played a role in the formation and organization of the Fascist Party. Leading it in the confused politics of the country, he was catapulted into power in 1922 by a combination of threats from the outside and maneuvers and compromises on the inside. During the immediately following years, he consolidated his power and established a single-party dictatorship. Not surprisingly he thought of himself as both the first fascist leader to attain power and the senior partner in any alignment with such latecomers as Adolf Hitler. It is from this perspective that his reluctance at first and his resentment later of having to depend on Hitler's forces to rescue his country from military disasters and then himself from captivity can readily be understood.

In view of recent divisions among scholars about the foreign policy plans and war aims of Benito Mussolini, it appears best to set forth at the beginning of this chapter the author's reading of the evidence that has been adduced for the two conflicting interpretations. As between the most recent argument of Richard J. B. Bosworth, that Mussolini had only limited aims that he originally believed might be attained in an alignment with Britain and France,[1] and the position of MacGregor Knox and Robert Mallett, that the Italian dictator always contemplated a massive program of expansion that he recognized could only be accomplished at the side of Germany and against Italy's World War I allies,[2] this author is convinced of the correctness of the latter interpretation.

The evidence regarding Mussolini's policy and his private comments, especially those made to his son-in-law and foreign minister from 1937 to 1943, Galeazzo Ciano, show a leader who did recognize the possible danger for Italy of an excessively strong Germany but who expected to profit from Germany's attempts at expansion at the expense of and in war with the Western powers.[3] Italian unification had been attained in the nineteenth century in a series of wars primarily against the Austrian Empire, but at the end of World War I, the Habsburg empire had disappeared from the scene. Many Italians, including Mussolini, believed that they had not acquired as much territory from the ruins of the Habsburg and Ottoman empires as they considered Italy was entitled to by treaty and because of her sacrifices in the war. It had been assumed that further territory that was included in the new South Slav state of Yugoslavia as well as additional portions of the Ottoman Empire would accrue to Italy. Italy, it was felt, had been cheated by her own allies. The colonial concessions in Africa turned over to Italy by France and Britain to compensate her for disappointments in Europe in no way diminished the resentment and disappointment.

An alignment with the World War I enemy Germany entailed a risk that the Italian alliance with Prussia against Austria in 1866 had not involved. The risk was that a revived and more powerful Germany on Italy's northern border might reclaim southern Tyrol. This territory, with its very substantial German-speaking population, had been turned over to Italy in the peace with Austria by the extension of the Italian border northward to the Brenner Pass rather than to something resembling the cultural and linguistic divide. Furthermore, a Germany victorious over the Western powers might demand the cession of Trieste, also acquired from Austria, as a German port on the Adriatic in spite of that city's mainly Italian population.

The fact remained, however, that Italian expansion in the Mediterranean and southeast Europe could most likely be attained only in alliance with Germany and against Great Britain and France – but in a war that might leave Germany so powerful as to threaten Italy's hold on Tyrol and Trieste. Here was a conundrum to which no Italian leader who wanted Italian expansion beyond what had been attained in Italy's 1912 war with the Ottoman Empire and in World War I could find an answer. Mussolini certainly hoped to square this circle but would fail dismally.

Two contradictory patterns of planning and implementing plans, emerged early in Mussolini's pursuit of his imperial ambitions. On the one hand, as early as 1925 he expected to seize Abyssinia (as Ethiopia was then called) and by the mid-1930s was moving both toward that aim and making plans for attacks on the Anglo-Egyptian Sudan, Kenya, and British Somaliland.[4] In 1938 his aims for expansion extended to Corsica, Tunisia, Albania, French Somaliland, and the southeastern portion of Switzerland.[5] While the Italian navy was hoping to seize the Seychelles from Britain as a base in the Indian Ocean well beyond that in Italian Somaliland, Mussolini explained to the Fascist Grand Council on February 4, 1939, his hopes of taking over Turkey, Malta, Cyprus, Greece, and Yugoslavia.[6] Well before the Germans began World War II, the Italian dictator envisioned an empire that included most of the Mediterranean coastal regions, southeast Europe, and northeast Africa. The war of conquest against Abyssinia in 1935–36, the massive Italian intervention in the Spanish Civil War in 1936–39, and the occupation of Albania in 1939 must all be seen as steps toward this general goal.

Yet the actual preparations of Italy's armed forces for the war alongside Germany against the Western powers that was implicit in Mussolini's ambitions were more in the propagandistic realm than in the reality of Italy's armaments program. Deluded to some extent by his own boasting and his insistence on being shown to the Italian public as all-knowing, on the one hand, and limited by the reality of Italy's small industrial and raw materials base as well as the effects of its antiquated social structure on the army, on the other hand, Mussolini did an unbelievably poor job of preparing the country for war against major enemies. Much of the country's artillery in World War II, along with the rifles carried by its soldiers, was of World War I vintage.[7] Furthermore, the budgetary and military strains imposed by the war against Abyssinia and the fighting in Spain dramatically limited the extent of the intended improvements and expansion in the Italian armed forces, especially the navy.[8] Since Mussolini had insisted on holding the service ministries himself, he could hardly acknowledge the discrepancies between grandiose war plans and hopelessly inadequate preparations for war without admitting his own massive failure as Italy's invariable wise, correct, and far-seeing leader.

It was in part at least in the context of some awareness of the enormous discrepancy between his territorial ambitions and the military means at hand for realizing them that Mussolini had urged Hitler to refrain from war in 1938. For the same reason he had also insisted in May 1939 that the military alliance with National Socialist Germany signed at that time was to be implemented by war against the Western powers in three years – a time by which the Italian leader imagined his armed forces would be ready for such a conflict.[9] He had been enormously impressed by what he saw when he visited Germany in 1937, and in view of an earlier German commitment to move those of German descent out of the Italian portion of Tyrol, he had acquiesced in the German annexation of Austria. Why he, in 1939, trusted the assurances of a government that had made itself notorious for breaking them is difficult to understand. Count Ciano, who had originally favored the alliance with Germany, would turn permanently against Berlin when in August 1939 he learned on a visit to Germany that the German government had decided to go to war that year rather than wait the three years he believed had been promised to Italy just four months earlier.

The German initiation of World War II in 1939 placed Mussolini in a quandary largely of his own making. On the one hand, he knew that the country was neither ready for war nor in the least enthusiastic for it. On the other hand, he had relentlessly preached in public the merits of fighting, and he also very much wanted to avoid any accusation that Italy was as unreliable an ally for Germany this time as it had proved to be for the Central Powers in World War I. For several months he wavered between remaining out of the war that he really desperately wanted to enter and joining Germany at a time that would assure Italy its share of the booty, a point about which he felt very strongly and that he repeatedly stressed to the doubting Ciano.[10]

Certain that Germany would defeat the Western powers, he had decided in his own mind by March 23, 1940, that Italy would enter the war on Germany's side.[11] As he explained to the still skeptical Ciano, Italy would acquire a Mediterranean empire and access to both the Atlantic and Indian Oceans. He assumed that Hitler would be prepared to split the spoils of war, an assessment that was surely correct at that time but presupposed an Italian military effort that events would show was not forthcoming.[12] As German forces appeared to be moving toward victory in the spring and early summer of 1940, Mussolini decided that the time for Italy to enter the conflict had indeed come. In view of the news of German military successes, he could now count on far broader support for such a step from Italy's elite and public than had been true earlier (and than Italians preferred to believe in retrospect).[13] His assumption appears to have been that the war was practically over, that Italy would have to make only a brief show of fighting, and that this minimal active participation would assure it a seat at the peace table, with the prospect of all sorts of additions to its empire. While all of these assumptions quickly proved to be completely erroneous, it is important for any understanding of Mussolini's policy to examine what it was that these additions were expected to be as well as what he expected to do in the future inside that enlarged empire as well as in Italy itself.

In late June and early July 1940, in the first weeks of Italian participation in the war and at a time when Mussolini believed that the fighting was essentially over and a peace settlement was about to be developed, his view of Italy's expanded empire was as extensive as it was explicit. In addition to Italian expansion in the Balkans at the expense of Yugoslavia and Greece, he expected to secure the acquisition of Nice and Corsica from metropolitan France as well as Tunisia, parts of Algeria, Djibouti (French Somaliland), and a southward extension of Libya at the expense of French Equatorial Africa. Malta, Cyprus, Egypt, British Somaliland, Aden, and the island of Socotra would be taken from the British Empire, while Iraq and Iran as well as the balance of the Arabian coast (which in Mussolini's thinking probably included Palestine, Lebanon, and Syria) would also come under Italian control.[14]

As indicated in the first chapter, all of this, with the possible exception of the southward extension of Libya, fitted in with Hitler's views (since that portion of the French colonial empire was to become a part of Germany's swath across central Africa). It was for tactical reasons that Hitler found it useful to restrain Mussolini's demands on France during the armistice negotiations with that country in June 1940. Hitler at that time hoped thereby to keep the French navy and colonial empire from continuing the war on the side of Britain. Hitler similarly vetoed Mussolini's plans for an attack on Yugoslavia and Greece in early August 1940 since he wanted the Balkans quiet while he prepared for his next war, that against the Soviet Union. The broad outlines of Mussolini's territorial ambitions, however, could easily be fitted together with Hitler's previously described ones as long as the military development of the war took the course the two Axis leaders at that time confidently anticipated.

What was to happen inside the greatly expanded empire and in Italy itself when the new settlement was in effect? Unlike the situation with Hitler, who held conquered territory for years, initiated large-scale killing and resettlement programs in them, and left extensive recorded discussions of his intentions and hopes for the future of these lands, the evidence regarding Mussolini's plans for his empire is relatively slight. It can safely be assumed that two aspects of his prior actions in the colonial sphere were to be continued as well as applied to whatever territory was added.

Substantial Italian settlement had occurred in Libya and more moderate settlement in the northeast African territories. There is extensive evidence that Mussolini expected very large numbers of Italians to settle in Abyssinia, hundreds of thousands of the local population in the conquered territory to become soldiers in the Italian army, and the area as a whole to provide bases for Italy's air force and navy.[15] Some Italians had already settled in Tunisia; presumably Mussolini expected that the stream of emigrants from Italy who had in the past headed for the Western Hemisphere, other European countries, and the colonies of other European powers would in the future be redirected to the greater empire that the war was expected to bring under Italian control. In some ways his colonial expansionist ambitions can be seen as a continuation of the general European colonial policies of the late nineteenth century. There was, however, in Mussolini's vision of the future undoubtedly a larger element of deliberately redirecting emigration from Italy to Africa than had been characteristic of the policies of other European powers in the race to divide the African continent in the years 1870–1900. In those years, there had certainly been some European settlement in Algeria, southern Africa, and Kenya, but at the same time far larger numbers of people leaving Europe had gone to live in North and South America rather than in any portion of the African continent.

A second feature of prior Italian policy that would also presumably be implemented in any newly acquired territory – as well as in the old one – was absolute ruthlessness in the suppression of dissent and revolt. Thousands had been killed in the putting down of the Senussi rebellion in Libya, and even larger numbers of civilians had been killed by poison gas and random slaughter during the Italian conquest of Abyssinia. Italy's record in this regard was both clear and very well known at the time; it throws an interesting light on those in the Arab world who could hardly wait for Italy and possibly Germany to replace Britain and France as colonial masters in the Middle East. To mention only one example, Mussolini was as willing as Hitler to meet with the Grand Mufti of Jerusalem, but he was just as unwilling as the German dictator to issue a public declaration in favor of Arab independence.[16]

A distinction must, however, be made between Hitler's concept of completely replacing the local Slavic populations of eastern Europe with Germanic settlers and Mussolini's embracing of the most violent measures for repressing any signs of resistance. The indigenous population of the expanded Italian empire could look forward to a hard life. They would live subordinate to Italian officials, would have to serve in Italian military forces, and would be subjected to harsh controls; but those who survived conquest and repression could expect to continue to live in the Italian empire, unlike the Slavic peoples of eastern Europe. Their labor would be exploited, and there would be other exactions, but they would not be headed for extinction. On the other hand, unlike the inhabitants of Germany's African colonial empire, they would see substantial numbers of people from Italy living among them, though of course in more elegant homes and at a higher standard of living.

In Italy itself there would be major changes. As the price of attaining power in the first place, Mussolini had been obligated to accommodate the crown, the Vatican, and the conservative elite of the country and to temper his preference for radical change other than the very drastic one of terminating the country's relatively open political system.[17] War, Mussolini believed, would harden the people, and victory would enable the regime to make changes that had been impossibly risky earlier. Imperialism abroad was to facilitate revolutionary change at home.[18] The monarchy was to disappear at the earliest possible moment, a move certain to meet with Hitler's enthusiastic approval.[19] The influence of the Vatican was to be removed from Italian life, and many of the Christian holidays – including Christmas, which Mussolini denounced as celebrating the birth of a Jew – were to be eliminated.[20] Grandiose buildings would illustrate the power of the regime and demonstrate that the new Roman empire, in its works, was as mighty as, if not mightier than, the old. Some construction projects had already been started, and by no means coincidentally they involved the levelling of several churches. In a literal way with huge statues as well as figuratively by his role, Mussolini himself would tower over a capital that harked back two thousand years across the allegedly decadent and backward ages in between.[21]

One might see an echo of his earlier years as a strong anticlerical in Mussolini's building program. His attitudes as an advocate of radical socialism seem to have been revived in his project to eliminate class differentiation in Italy's railroad carriages.[22] His endless diatribes against Italy's middle and upper classes reflect his continued belief in a society in which all were equally at the service of the state, devoted to it, prepared to give their lives for it, and, of course, subject to his will. With the disappearance of the country's traditional, rather rigid social differentiations, the only distinction that would remain in the Italy of the future was that between the ruler and the ruled.

At least some of the changes Mussolini had hoped to implement inside Italy itself might be considered a foretaste of his attempted alterations during his short-lived activities as a German puppet in northern Italy after his rescue from imprisonment by the Germans in

1943. However, the wider hopes with which the Italian leader had entered the war in June 1940 were quickly dashed because of the poor performance of Italy's armed forces. The few days of fighting on the border with France quickly showed how poorly the regime had prepared Italy for a serious conflict. As early as July 5, 1940, Ciano described Mussolini as worried that the French might find a way to slip into the German camp and thereby leave Italy defrauded of the territorial booty he wanted and expected.[23] Thereafter he was concerned that a peace between Germany and England might deprive him of the opportunity to conquer those portions of the British Empire he hoped to secure for Italy, and it should be added that he remained worried about this possibility for several years. He would quickly discover that there was to be neither peace nor conquest.

Italian forces were not prepared to seize the key island of Malta in the summer of 1940 when its defenses were at their weakest. The temporary Italian conquest of British Somaliland in northeast Africa and a minimal advance into Egypt from Libya were merely preludes to disastrous Italian defeats in both campaigns. Already in the winter of 1940–41, British forces defeated Italian armies in Eritrea, Ethiopia, and Italian Somaliland as well as retaking British Somaliland. Almost simultaneously, they crushed the Italian force that had entered Egypt, captured much of the Italian army in Libya, and threatened to seize that whole Italian colony. Part of Libya was saved for Italian control in 1941 only because of the diversion of British units to Greece and the arrival of a German force under Erwin Rommel, which was sent because Hitler feared that the loss of the rest of Italy's colonial empire would lead to the fall of Mussolini.

As if these disasters – of which the first signs were visible by the fall of 1940 – were not enough, Mussolini decided to attack Greece in October 1940. Having been told by the Germans in

August that he was not to invade Yugoslavia because Hitler wanted the Balkans kept quiet, the Italian dictator was livid when he learned in September that the Germans were in the process of occupying Romania without notifying Italy well ahead of time of this Balkan venture. Since the Germans had also failed to explain to him that the occupation of Romania was a preliminary step in their preparations for the invasion of the Soviet Union scheduled for the following year, Mussolini decided that the way to maintain Italy's status in the alliance was to invade Greece. Instead of the swift victory this operation was to produce, it led to a most embarrassing defeat and, as in the case of the Italian failure in North Africa, to a need for the Germans to bail out their ally.

Two further calamitous errors of Mussolini would serve to compound the weakening of his position. As a means of emphasizing the role of Italy in the war and to ensure a place at the side of Germany when it won – as he still expected – Mussolini insisted in the summer of 1941 on sending an expeditionary force to the Eastern Front to fight the Soviet Union alongside the Germans.[24] This step, which was incomprehensible to the Italian population, to say nothing of the soldiers sent to fight on battlefields they had not the slightest interest in, would dramatically undermine Mussolini's position at home, especially after most of a whole Italian army was destroyed in the later stages of the Soviet offensive at Stalingrad in early 1943. By that time, Mussolini, who underestimated the United States even more than Hitler and could hardly wait to take on another enemy, had enthusiastically declared war on that country in December 1941.[25]

Under these circumstances, Mussolini could only mourn the loss of the whole Italian colonial empire. The gracious permission of the Germans for Italy to annex a part and occupy additional portions of the former Yugoslavia and also to occupy parts of France and most of Greece hardly seemed adequate compensation for that loss. Mussolini dearly wanted to regain the former Italian colonies and was, therefore, especially intent on making sure that the war against England continued until final victory rather than being terminated by compromise peace.[26] As pointed out in the first chapter, this was one issue about which he need not have worried. Instead he might have paid more attention to the efforts of those in or close to government circles who preferred to remove him from office, as they successfully did in July 1943.[27] Far from expanding Italy's empire, he had lost it all; his soldiers ended up in Allied captivity or, if not murdered by the Germans, enslaved by them.[28] Like Hitler, he ended in death together with his mistress.

There is a very important additional aspect of Mussolini's view of the postwar world that must be examined. Unlike Hitler, who looked toward a future in which Germany ruled the world and there would be no other independent states on any continent, Mussolini was, in spite of his fascist ideological concepts for the structure of Italian society,[29] in an important way a far more traditional leader. Certain countries, especially Britain and France, would be greatly weakened, and some, like Switzerland, Yugoslavia, and Greece, would disappear as independent states completely. There would, however, be other states in a world greatly changed but not transformed as Hitler expected. If any of the Scandinavian states survived hostilities, that would not bother Mussolini in any way. Similarly, he was prepared to see such countries as Portugal continue to exist, to say nothing of the nations of the Western Hemisphere. Italy under his rule had maintained good relations with both China and Japan; beyond the Middle East, he had no ambitions in Asia other than to maintain a naval presence in the Indian Ocean.

Recognizing that Mussolini envisioned the world changed in detail but not transformed basically, one may more easily understand his urging Hitler, beginning in the winter of 1942–43, to make peace with the Soviet Union and to concentrate all the military effort of the Axis powers on the war against Britain and the United States. This was a position that the Japanese had been urging on Berlin since the fall of 1941 and that the French collaborator Pierre Laval and the Hungarian Arrow Cross leader Ferenc Szálasi would adopt soon after.[30] Like the similar advice of others, that of Mussolini had no impact on Berlin. The Italian dictator, like the other leaders of Germany's allies and satellites, never understood the worldwide ambitions of Germany, imagining that this war was similar to earlier ones, in which specific territories, bases, and spheres of influence were at stake rather than the fate of the people of the whole globe.

It should, however, be noted that in the future world that Mussolini envisioned, the continued existence of many independent states would certainly not be in any way compromised by some new international organization. He had happily withdrawn Italy from the League of Nations; looked upon such structures with the same derision as Japan and Germany, which had also left Geneva; and had no interest in any revived or alternative international body. In his view, the allocation of territory and influence was to be shifted in favor of the so-called young and vigorous nations at the expense of what he considered the decadent democracies. Once the appropriate adjustments had been made, the map of the world would look very much the way it had in the nineteenth century, with only the coloring on the map changed to reflect the growth of some and the decline of other colonial empires and individual states. He believed that this was what had happened after World War I, taking no account of such innovations in the direction of decolonization as the separate representation of the British Dominions at the Paris Peace Conference and the establishment of the Mandate system. If Italy had not received as much of the spoils of the last war as he believed it entitled to, it would attain them – and preferably considerably more – this time around. But when it was all over, the basic state system of the late nineteenth century would still be there, though substantially modified in favor of Italy and its allies. And inside that enlarged Italian empire, he would rule supreme over a classless society of abject subjects and repressed colonial peoples.

3. Tojo Hideki

Prime Minister of Japan Tojo Hideki speaks at the podium of the Diet during World War II, Tokyo, Japan. © CORBIS.

UNLIKE HITLER AND MUSSOLINI, WHO BOTH SERVED IN THE army in World War I but were not professional soldiers, Tojo Hideki was born in 1884 into the poor family of a career soldier and became one himself. He graduated from the military academy during the Russo-Japanese War of 1904–05 and began his service as an officer on garrison duty in Manchuria thereafter. His father's rise to the rank of general inspired him to a kind of dedicated service in the army that helped to bring him promotion even in peacetime. Assignments by the Ministry of War, where he was quickly regarded as a man with a future, brought Tojo to Germany as military attaché after World War I. On his return to Japan, Tojo continued to rise in rank and became associated with those military leaders who shot their way into positions of authority in Tokyo. By 1937 he had risen to the rank of lieutenant general and became chief of staff of the Kwantung Army, the Japanese force stationed in Manchuria, which had been seized from China in 1931. Though not himself directly involved in initiating the fighting with Nationalist China in that year, Tojo took part in one of the early campaigns. In 1938 he returned to Tokyo to serve briefly as vice-minister of war under General Itagaki Seishiro. After a stint as inspector general of the Air Force, he was appointed minister of war in July 1940, a position he would retain until 1944.

From October 1941 to July 1944, Tojo Hideki was prime minister of Japan. He not only continued to hold the office of minister of war but periodically added further positions to these two. At times he held the offices of minister of the interior, minister of commerce and industry, minister of munitions, and, after mid-February 1944, chief of staff of the army![1] When he found the Foreign Ministry not as enthusiastic about policies he favored as he thought it should be, he had a large portion of its jurisdiction removed to a new Greater East Asia Ministry and forced the resignation of the foreign minister, who, not surprisingly, had objected to this amputation of much of his ministry's jurisdiction.[2]

Under these circumstances, one might have expected a substantial scholarly literature dealing with Tojo's role in the conduct of the Pacific War and his views about the future of the vast empire that Japan conquered in the early months of that conflict. Unfortunately, the reality is otherwise. The publications dealing with Tojo concentrate on his role in the Japanese decision to attack the United States, Great Britain, and the Netherlands in 1941, his removal from power in July 1944, and his attempted suicide and trial as a war criminal after the Japanese surrender. On his role in the direction of the Japanese war effort, its aims, and his views about the future, there is essentially no scholarly work in any language and only indirect evidence of any kind.

Perhaps the most important and certainly the best-known source on the higher direction of Japan's role in the Pacific War is the diary of Admiral Ugaki Matome for the years 1941–45. Ugaki was chief of staff of the Combined Fleet under Admiral Yamamoto Isoroku, subsequently served on the Naval Staff, commanded a major fleet, and had a key role in the final defense of Japan. In his diary Tojo appears only once, and then for sending a congratulatory telegram on one of the many Japanese defeats that Tojo publicly acclaimed as victories.[3] Similarly, the diary of Marquis Kido Koichi, the Lord Keeper of the Privy Seal from 1940 to 1945, refers to Tojo's views only in the most minimal way.[4] In these circumstances, the account that follows is necessarily based on general policies followed during Tojo's tenure as prime minister insofar as they can reasonably be attributed to him, a critical document from his Ministry of War, and such steps taken by him in public as can be seen as reflecting his aspirations for Japan and its empire.

Any understanding of Tojo's views on the postwar world must be related to three critical characteristics of his general position. First, he assumed a leadership role in a country that had already left the League of Nations in 1933 – the first major power to do so – and under no conditions was about to rejoin anything similar. It had been the League's vote to approve the Lytton Commission's report denouncing Japan's aggression in Manchuria that had been the ostensible reason for Japan's exit; and it was in the Japanese army that carried out the seizure of Manchuria that Tojo had first become prominent. Like Hitler and Mussolini, therefore, Tojo at no time envisioned a new international organization of some kind, as did all the leaders of the Allies, whatever their differences in regard to the specifics.

Second, by the time Tojo became prime minister, Japan held territories taken from China, Russia, and Germany in prior wars; had seized Manchuria from China and established a puppet regime there; had further been at war with China since 1937; and had occupied militarily all of what was then French Indo-China. In the talks before the Japanese attack on the Western powers, Tojo had been among those most insistent that absolutely none of this be given up; he was certainly not about to withdraw from any of it after December 1941.

Third, unlike Hitler and Mussolini, Tojo, who might have wanted to be an absolute dictator and did try to move in that direction, never actually became one. He operated within a framework that had been established by the Japanese constitution, even though in practice it had been modified by the military's usurping authority through assassination and intimidation in the decade preceding Tojo's appointment as prime minister. Japan in World War II was an authoritarian, not a totalitarian, state. Its courts ordered fifty-seven executions during the war – as compared with the thousands in Germany – and in 1942 there were elections to the Diet. While the army subsidized an approved list of candidates in this election, it was still possible for many others to run and for some of those not approved to win seats in the Diet. There were pressures, restrictions, censorship, and police persecutions, but the system was still characterized by roles for old political and economic elites, an occasionally stubborn bureaucracy, and a more than nominal adherence to prior forms and procedures.[5]

The first question to consider about the postwar world envisioned by Tojo as he led his country into a wider war must necessarily be its geographic dimensions. Of course the conquests secured in Japan's earlier wars with China, Russia, and Germany would be retained, along with the recently seized large and important portions of China as well as occupied French Indo-China. The planned division of Asia with Germany has already been mentioned. It would mean Japanese control of the eastern part of the Soviet Union, including most of Siberia, in addition to all of South and Southeast Asia east of the seventieth parallel. Since it was the Japanese government that formally proposed this very specific division of Asia to Berlin,

Tojo must have approved it, though there is no known record of his personal role in the internal discussion of this question in Tokyo, as there is for Hitler's role in Berlin.

The best available document illuminating the broader thinking in Tojo's Ministry of War on the size and nature of Japan's future holdings is a "Land Disposal Plan in the Greater East Asia Co-Prosperity Sphere" prepared in December 1941 in the Research Section of the Ministry of War.[6] Since all authors who have written about Tojo agree that he controlled his ministry very tightly, it is unlikely that those working on such projects departed widely from the thoughts of their minister as he had expressed them or as they had good reason to believe would be congenial to him. Although there cannot be certainty on this point, the empire outlined in this plan may be taken as a reasonably accurate reflection of their master's voice at a time when Japan was plunging forward in the Pacific and Southeast Asia but was not yet at war with the Soviet Union.

This document assumed that the puppet government Japan had established in Manchuria would continue and that the collaborationist government the Japanese had induced the Chinese collaborator Wang Ching-wei to set up in the parts of China conquered by the Japanese army since 1937 would continue to operate there. The islands north of the equator that had been taken from Germany after World War I and had been allocated to Japan as C-Class Mandates by the League of Nations; the Marianas, Carolines, Marshall Islands, and some others had been the subject of earlier negotiations with the Germans and therefore do not figure in the new project.[7] Under a projected "Government General of Formosa" would come Hong Kong, the Philippines, the Paracel Islands, and Macao (to be purchased from Portugal) as well as the island of Hainan (to be purchased from the puppet government of China).

A "South Seas Government Office" would take over Guam, Nauru, Ocean Island, the Gilbert Islands, and Wake. An office called either "Melanesian Region Government-General" or "South Pacific Government-General" was to administer the British and Australian (eastern) parts of New Guinea, the Admiralties, New Britain, New Ireland, and the smaller islands near them, the Solomon Islands, the Santa Cruz Archipelago, the Ellice Islands, the Fiji Islands, the New Hebrides, New Caledonia, Loyalty Island, and Chesterfield Island. It should be noted that this last grouping included not only formerly German and British territories but also islands then under French control or joint French–British administration. An "Eastern Pacific Government-General" would be in charge of Hawaii, Howland Island, Baker Island, the Phoenix Islands, the Rain Islands, the Marquesas and Tuamotu Islands, the Society Islands, the Cook and Austral Islands, all of the Samoan Islands, and Tonga. If there were any coral reefs that the Japanese planners overlooked, these must have been missing from their maps.

What was called the "Australian Government-General" was expected to govern the whole of Australia along with Tasmania. A tentatively entitled "New Zealand Government-General" was to govern both the North and the South Islands of New Zealand along with Macquarie Island and the southwestern portion of the Pacific Ocean. A "Ceylon Government-General" would control, in addition to Ceylon itself, the southern third of India defined by a detailed line running approximately west to east from the Portuguese colony of Goa. The "Alaska Government-General" was expected to comprise all of Alaska, Canada's Yukon Province together with the western portion of the Northwest Territory, the provinces of Alberta and British Columbia, as well as the state of Washington. A "Government-General of Central America" was to include Guatemala, San Salvador, Honduras, British Honduras, Nicaragua, Costa Rica, Panama, Colombia, the Maracaibo [western] portion of Venezuela, Ecuador, Cuba, Haiti, Dominica, Jamaica, and the Bahamas. The future of Trinidad, British and Dutch Guiana, and the British and French possessions in the Leeward Islands was left open for negotiations with the Germans after the war. Furthermore, if Mexico, Peru, and/or Chile entered the war against Japan, substantial parts of those states were also to be ceded to Japan.

If all these territories were to come under direct Japanese administration, a set of so-called independent states was to be established on the model of Manchoukuo, as the puppet state established by the Japanese in Manchuria was called. There was to be an "East Indies Kingdom" that would include all the Dutch possessions in the East Indies, those portions of Borneo that were not under Dutch control, that is, British Borneo, Labuan, Sarawak, and Brunei, and, in addition, the Cocos and Christmas Islands, the Andaman and Nicobar Islands in the Indian Ocean, and the Portuguese portions of Timor, which were to be purchased. A "Kingdom of Burma" would have the Indian province of Assam and a substantial portion of Bengal transferred from India to British Burma as the core of this new construction. Malaya and Thailand were to be separate kingdoms, while French Indo-China was to be divided into two kingdoms: the "Kingdom of Cambodia," comprising Cambodia and French Cochin China, and the "Kingdom of Annam," comprising Annam, Laos, and Tongking.

During the six months following the preparation of this ambitious project, Japanese forces did either overrun or threaten a substantial part of the projected empire. Allied forces, however, effectively halted the Japanese advance by the summer of 1942. Japanese forces failed even to get close to Tasmania – to say nothing of Cuba

or Jamaica, whose inhabitants would surely have been astonished
to learn that they were to be included in Greater East Asia. Within
the area that the Japanese did conquer temporarily, they actually
made two territorial changes, and in these Tojo played a direct role.
The four northern Malay states that had been ceded by Thailand
to British control in 1909 were returned to Thailand in the spring
of 1943.[8] Ironically, as will become apparent in the discussion of
Winston Churchill's vision of the postwar world, this same border
was to be moved, but in the opposite direction. Tojo, in addition,
had a part of Burma added to Thailand over the opposition of some
in the Tokyo government.[9] It was, however, clear to all in Tokyo,
including most definitely Tojo himself, that the Japanese military
would actually run the nominally independent constructions that
were being set up in Burma and were subsequently proclaimed for
the Philippines and other Japanese-controlled areas at a time when
the tide of war was turning increasingly against Japan. This subject was discussed at considerable length at a Liaison Conference
meeting in Tokyo on March 10, 1943, in which Tojo played an active role.[10] Even the high-flown rhetoric of Tojo and others at the
"Assembly of Greater East Asian Nations" of November 1943 could
not disguise either the reality of Japanese control in the newly established or proposed puppet states or the steady decline of Japan's
military fortunes.[11]

The shifting balance in the Pacific war in 1942, though not publicly admitted by Tojo, did lead to policy changes by his government,
in addition to the establishment of nominally independent states in
portions of the conquered territories and support for Japan's efforts
to develop an atomic bomb.[12] Even before expanding the war with
China into a wider conflict in December 1941, the Japanese government had been urging Germany to make a compromise peace with

the Soviet Union. With no comprehension of Germany's true war aims, the Tojo government ever more insistently tried to persuade Hitler that a newly worked out arrangement with Stalin and concentration on fighting Britain and the United States was the wisest course to take.[13] While these efforts produced no results for the Axis powers, but instead strengthened the position of the Soviet Union by increasing the fears of precisely such a deal by the Washington and London authorities who read the decoded texts of Japanese telegrams, the Japanese did what they could on their own to maintain good relations with the Soviets. There would be no interference with the stream of American aid to the Soviet Union, of which fully half moved across the Pacific. Fishery rights were abandoned, and other concessions were made. In the endless discussions about an air link between Germany and Japan, the Japanese always insisted that there be no flights over Soviet territory for fear of offending Moscow.[14] There would even be hopes that the Soviet Union might be tempted by massive territorial concessions to reverse alliances and join Japan against the Western powers, but these futile hopes were entertained in Tokyo after Tojo had been pushed out of office. A more significant adjustment in Japan's position than the attempt to maintain good relations with the Soviet Union was made by the government when Tojo was still in charge: a so-called New Policy toward China.

The Japanese government was never able to define a clear policy toward China and then adhere to it for at least a few months. Shadowy approaches toward a possible peace with the Nationalist government of Chiang Kai-shek alternated with solemn public announcements that the Nationalist government had to be crushed and would never be negotiated with. The puppet government of Wang Ching-wei was alternatively strengthened, at least nominally, and undermined.[15] Perhaps the New Policy of 1943 can be seen as fitting in with any of these contradictory policies, though that may attribute too much rationality and planning to a situation marked by permanent confusion. The Japanese government announced the surrender of its extraterritorial rights in China, returned nominal control of the International Settlement in Shanghai, and made a series of concessions in Chinese cities to the Chinese puppet government.[16] Emphasized by personal visits of Tojo to Shanghai and Nanking, these measures could be interpreted either as a means of strengthening the status of Wang Ching-wei or as a hint of a possible accommodation to Chiang Kai-shek. In practice they had neither effect, because Wang was still far too obviously a subordinate client of a Japan hated by the overwhelming majority of Chinese, and Chiang could see that Japan was going to be defeated in any case.

In the following year, with the consent of Tojo, who by this time was also chief of staff of the army, the Japanese launched major offensives into China and India. The latter, if successful, would have cut the air supply route to China by the seizure of the bases from which the American "Hump" airlift to China over the Himalaya Mountains was flown and would also have cut the railway that brought supplies to those bases and the whole Allied effort in northern Burma. This operation ended at Kohima and Imphal in the biggest defeat the Japanese army had suffered up to then in the war. The Japanese offensive in China, on the other hand, was successful in capturing most of the air bases from which the Americans had begun to bomb the Japanese home islands. More important in the long run, this "Ichigo" offensive, as it was called, destroyed much of the remaining military power of Chiang Kai-shek and thereby paved the way for the Communist takeover of China. This military victory of

Japan could not, however, offset the essentially simultaneous defeat suffered by the Japanese army and navy in the Marianas as the Americans took Saipan and defeated the Japanese naval units sent to ward off that invasion. It was this defeat on Japan's doorstep that enabled Tojo's opponents within the ruling circles in Tokyo to force him out of office.

Aside from territorial adjustments and rearrangements, how did Tojo visualize the internal future of Japan and its empire? In Japan itself, the evidence regarding Tojo's expectations is reasonably clear. He had left the formal institutions unchanged, and nothing suggests that in case of a Japanese victory he would have altered them in any substantial way. Unlike Mussolini, who could hardly wait for the day when he could put an end to the Italian monarchy, Tojo certainly expected the imperial system of Japan to be maintained. A careful study of his relationship with Emperor Hirohito shows Tojo to have been a man deeply and sincerely devoted to the imperial institution.[17] The fact that he knew that some of the courtiers surrounding the emperor were either doubtful about him or actively hostile to his role as prime minister at no time led him to consider, let alone initiate, changes to this institution. As the war turned increasingly against Japan, he certainly put more pressure on the police and the judiciary to contain and repress domestic dissent, but there was nothing analogous to Hitler's April 1942 attainment of full power to disregard the rights, status, and procedural protections of any and all German citizens that was so enthusiastically endorsed by the German parliament.[18]

The Diet, the Japanese parliament, continued to meet during the war, and there is no evidence that Tojo expected this to change. There was, however, one significant initiative by him in regard to the nature and composition of the Diet, an initiative with potential

major long-term implications for the government structure of a victorious Japan. As already mentioned, in the 1942 elections to the
Diet, the army had established an approved list of candidates and
provided those on the list with campaign funds.[19] After the election,
which saw most but by no means all on the government's candidates
winning their contests, Tojo moved in a new direction. Tojo's predecessor as prime minister, Konoye Fumimaro, had organized the
Imperial Rule Assistance Association (IRAA) in October 1940 as
a means of providing a broad political basis – separate from and basically in opposition to and as a replacement for Japan's political
parties – for the policies he wanted to follow.[20] In practice, neither
Konoye nor Tojo had been willing or able to make this organization
into the formidable political national basis for a uniform centralized
government that Konoye had originally intended.

Following the April 1942 Diet election, Tojo established the
"Imperial Rule Assistance Political Association," which, at least in
his thinking was over time to become the only political party in the
country and of course the Diet.[21] In practice, rather little came of
this effort to copy the Soviet, Italian, and German models of a single
party that would produce a parliament that, like those in Moscow,
Rome, and Berlin, could be expected to perform at all times like a
well-rehearsed choir. The point that ought, however, not to be lost
sight of is that in case of a Japanese victory Tojo would have had im-
mensely greater prestige. Under those circumstances, the likelihood
of such a development would have been high indeed, and it would
certainly have marked a significant departure from prior Japanese
experience. In this regard, as in the case of Mussolini's Italy, triumph
in war could prepare the way for major domestic political change.

There is no evidence to suggest that Tojo thought of any substantial alterations in the domestic social or economic structure of Japan.

The major role of the great industrial and banking conglomerates, the *zaibatsu*, was not something he was prepared to challenge. If anything was likely to change as a result of the continued shift from agriculture to industry in Japan, their role was more likely to increase rather than to be reduced. Japan would import raw materials and export manufactured goods, but in larger quantities than before. Well into his term as prime minister, Tojo presumably began to comprehend something that he did not understand earlier, namely, that after conquest by Japan, the tin mines, oil wells, and rubber plantations of Southeast Asia could not be moved to the Japanese home islands but would remain exactly where they had been before. It was simply that their products would now have to be moved in Japanese rather than foreign-owned ships, ironically the field in which Japan was deficient when it went to war and was becoming increasingly so as the Allies took a steadily larger toll of Japanese shipping. Unlike Hitler and Mussolini, Tojo had no plans for extraordinary buildings to be erected in Tokyo or elsewhere in the home islands. There is no evidence to suggest that he ever thought about the reordering of urban Japan beyond the obvious task of reconstruction wherever there had been damage during the war.

The one major area where there might have been the prospect of significant economic change in postwar Japan was in the field of synthetic products. The evidence, in the opinion of this author, is not clear as to the extent to which Tojo was himself aware of and/or involved in the endless negotiations with the German government and German firms about patents and blueprints for new technologies, including not only information on new weapons systems but also the techniques for producing synthetic oil and rubber from coal.[22] The other side of this, of course, is that a Japanese victory in the war with the Western powers would have obviated the need for the new weapons – which could not possibly be produced in time for the conflict then under way – as well as the need for the new and very expensive industrial procedures, because oil and rubber would then be available in areas under Japanese control.

Since the Japanese army had always thought of the Soviet Union as the most important and most dangerous enemy of Japan, a victory by Japan in association with a German victory in Europe would, as already detailed, have meant a partition of the Soviet Union at the seventieth parallel, a partition that Tojo's government had proposed to Berlin. There is no evidence on the subject of Tojo's plans or hopes about Japan's relations with the Soviet neighbor in the north if Japan won but Germany either made the compromise peace on the Eastern Front that Tokyo was always urging or actually lost altogether. Certainly the troop units that were being withdrawn from Manchuria by Japan as the war in the Pacific became ever more deadly – units to be employed against the Allies in the Pacific and Southeast Asia – would, after a Japanese victory, have been returned to their prior stations. But beyond that, it remains impossible at this time to ascertain what, if anything, Tojo may have had in mind for Japan's relationship with its powerful neighbor if that state survived the war.

The future situation in the territories Japan already had or expected to conquer must be examined cautiously because Tojo's views on this issue are by no means very clear.[23] It is safe to assume that there would have been some settlement by Japanese in these areas, as there already was in Manchuria. Whatever the accompanying hardships for any local people displaced by such settlers, there was at no time any sign of an inclination to follow procedures of the type the Germans planned and were beginning to implement, namely, to *replace* with German settlers practically the entire local population

after their extermination or massive removal elsewhere. In this regard, it could be said that the anticipation in Tokyo was rather like
that in Rome. As for the political administration of the conquered
areas, Tojo's own close ties to the army in which he had made his career points to a decisive continuing role for military officers of high
rank as governors or as so-called advisors to the nominally independent states that had been or were to be created. The treaties with
Wang Ching-wei and the arrangement for Burma all point to the
prior experience with the puppet state of Manchoukuo established
in Manchuria as the model that would be followed. The exigen-
cies of war led the Japanese to recruit units of Indian, Burmese, and
Dutch East Indies men into military units, but these were clearly to
remain under complete Japanese control.[24] Some of the Japanese
officers who were involved in these recruitment projects may well
have been sincere in their desire to develop some form of comradely
association between Japan and the new entities, but any moves in
that direction were quickly halted by Tokyo military authorities,
who looked down on the peoples of the conquered lands not only
on military but also on essentially racist grounds.[25]

This last point, the attitude of the Japanese to the people of the
conquered territories, is central to any understanding of what happened and Tojo's own role in it. The occurrence of a descent of the
Japanese military from what was generally considered a model of fair
treatment of prisoners of war in the Russo-Japanese War of 1904–
05 and in World War I to a policy involving the most horrible mistreatment of prisoners as well as civilians was already dramatically
evident in China from 1937 on. There is no evidence that Tojo in
any way dissented from this moral collapse; if anything, it continued to an ever worse extent under his leadership. Such events as the
Bataan Death March, the murder of 50,000 Chinese in Singapore,

the tying of British prisoners of war to stakes to be used for bayonet practice, the killing of American airmen who had parachuted and been captured by the Japanese, the tens of thousands of prisoners and conscripted local laborers worked to death on the Thailand-Burma railway, and an endless array of other atrocities all either took place or began when Tojo was both prime minister and minister of war.[26] Since he was minister of war at the time, the kidnapping of women to be sex slaves of Japanese forces all over the different areas into which they moved during hostilities, the so-called comfort women, clearly had Tojo's authorization.[27] There were and unfortunately will be incidents of a terrible kind in all wars, but in the case of Japan during World War II, what happened was a reflection of policy established at the highest levels, not a matter of local incidents. There is no evidence that anyone was ever brought before a court martial or even severely reprimanded as the most brutal policies were implemented. And in a military organization, policies are established at the top.

What has all this to do with the future of Japan's expanded empire as Tojo saw it? There is no indication that the attitude of Tojo, or that of the leadership of the Japanese military, toward the peoples of the territories they conquered would in any way have differed after the war from their attitude during the war. Not only would any efforts at resistance have been crushed with the utmost ruthlessness, but also the general view of all others as racially and culturally inferior to the Japanese would have ensured an extraordinarily repressive regime. The especially harsh mistreatment of white prisoners of war and civilian internees did not bode well for those whites living in Australia, New Zealand, and the parts of the Western Hemisphere scheduled for Japanese conquest. Japan's record as a colonial power – as in Korea – was arguably the worst of those who engaged in colonialism at the end of the nineteenth century. In the twentieth, all signs point to a record that would have been even more terrible and only exceeded in its cruelty by that of a victorious Germany. For Japan, defeat meant the loss of the imperialist acquisitions of the preceding fifty years. For Tojo, it meant trial, conviction, and then hanging.

4. Chiang Kai-shek

Chiang Kai-shek inspecting high-ranking officers of Officers Training Corps at Lushan, Kinkiang, Jiangxi Sheng. Library of Congress, Prints and Photographs Division, LC-USZ62-112372.

B ORN INTO A MERCHANT FAMILY IN 1887, CHIANG KAI-SHEK early developed an interest in military affairs. He entered training for a military career in both China and Japan. From the beginning of the Nationalist movement led by Sun Yat-sen, he played a part in its military organization. He married a sister of Sun's wife and in the confusions that both preceded and followed Sun's early death became a key leader of the Kuomintang, the party Sun had founded. In the 1920s Chiang at times allied himself with the Soviets and at times fought the Chinese Communist Party that was emerging out of the student radical movement at that time. By the end of the decade, substantial but by no means complete progress had been made in pulling together major portions of China into one country under Kuomintang influence if not control.

Unlike Hitler, Mussolini, and Tojo, Chiang would very much have preferred to stay out of war with Japan or any other country. It was his hope that after the internal upheavals in China following the 1911 revolution that had ended the imperial system and brought a republic to China, there might be many years of internal consolidation. But not only were civil war and local warlords rending the society in which he was asserting his supremacy, there was also the heritage of what were called the "unequal treaties" imposed on China in the preceding century. These treaties allowed foreigners access to their own courts in China on the basis of extraterritoriality and imposed other restrictions on Chinese sovereignty in regard to customs and certain other areas. Furthermore, the European powers, Japan, and the United States had imposed a large indemnity after the Boxer Uprising at the turn of the century, maintained urban areas within China under their control, and had the right to station troops at designated places. In addition to these international servitudes, there was the current danger of Japanese aggression.

In regard to the unequal treaties, Chiang, like essentially all Chinese, resented them and hoped for their abolition. Perhaps more important for Chiang's view of China's future in the long run was his firm belief that the end of these treaties was one of the critical prerequisites for China to develop its economic potential. The economic development that would follow could be a mixture of private and public ownership; Chiang was not a doctrinaire advocate of either a free market economy or of government ownership of the means of production.[1] It was the unequal treaties that had held the country back, in his eyes. The key factor responsible for the sad state of the country was not internal decay or prior misrule by the Manchu (Ch'ing) dynasty but the aggression of outsiders and their imposition of the unequal treaties.[2]

It would ironically be the threat from Japan that in the short run produced the end of the unequal treaties but in the long run enabled the Communists to take over the country. As the Japanese seized first Manchuria in 1931 and then expanded their control into additional parts of northeast China, Chiang at first held back, hoping for further domestic consolidation to strengthen the country and also for assistance from other foreign powers that could see their own interests in East Asia threatened by Japan. But when no other country proved willing to defend its own interests against Japan by military means, he decided in 1937 to resist further Japanese advances by military force. By moving the fighting from northeast to central China, Chiang obliged the Japanese to make a major commitment of their armies to a campaign in much of China. It was the resistance of the Chinese to these wider attacks by Japan that effectively elevated China – and Chiang with it – to a major role on the world stage.[3]

Since both the Nationalist government of China and the new leadership that had established itself on the ruins of party government in Japan had good relations with Germany, and the latter did not want to have to chose between the two, there was a serious mediation effort by Germany to end the conflict between her two friends in the winter of 1937–38. The Japanese government of Prince Konoye Fumimaro, however, destroyed all hopes of a peaceful settlement in January 1938.[4] Although there would be occasional indirect contacts thereafter, there would be no realistic opportunity for a peaceful settlement between China and Japan in the years that followed. Whatever the contacts and feelers, nothing substantial in the way of a possible accommodation ever came into view.

In the early stages of the fighting, Chiang had very much hoped that the Soviet Union would join in the war against Japan. For some time Stalin encouraged this expectation and provided considerable supplies to the Chinese. However, especially after the fall of Wuhan to the Japanese in October 1938, the Soviet leader not only refrained from entering hostilities and reduced the flow of supplies but also turned increasingly to Germany – a country that in the same year gave up its position in China and tried for an alliance with

Japan.[5] It was in these circumstances that Chiang decided that an alignment with the United States was the best possible policy for China, and he would pursue this policy, and even hope for a formal alliance with the United States, both during the war and as a part of his view of the postwar world. The fact that such a formal bilateral alliance was never agreed to by the American government should not be allowed to obscure the significance of this policy line for Chiang. Whatever the frictions and disappointments, and there were plenty of them, he pursued this line all through the remaining years of his rule. Many specific aspects of Chiang's postwar plans can only be understood if this constant feature of Chinese foreign policy is kept in mind.[6]

When, as Chiang had long expected, Japan went to war against the United States, Great Britain, and the Netherlands in December 1941, he anticipated more assistance from those powers in the immediate future and expected that before too long they would surely defeat the Japanese by means of their vastly superior power. In the short run, there was enormous disappointment as the Japanese swept across Southeast Asia and the southwest Pacific, toppling all forces in their way. By the conquest of Burma, the Japanese advance cut the one remaining overland supply route from the Western world to China at a time when the Soviet Union was fighting for its own life against the German invasion and hence not in a position to send substantial supplies over its land route into China. As if these disasters suffered by the Allies were not sufficiently discouraging, the East Asian theater of war was generally at the bottom of the priority list for reinforcements and supplies. Winston Churchill refused to take the problems of China seriously, and President Roosevelt not only had to cope with dangers in other theaters but also faced some reluctance to aid China within his own administration.[7] The massive disasters suffered by British forces in North Africa in the summer of 1942 led to the shifting of American reinforcements for the China-Burma-India theater to the Middle East instead, only one dramatic example of many in 1942–43.

In spite of grave disappointments, Chiang remained at war. Certainly the inability of the Japanese to decide how to extricate themselves from seemingly endless fighting in China made this course easier for Chiang.[8] A slowly growing trickle of aid from the United States, which came to include an aerial supply route over the Himalayas called "The Hump," also helped. The puppet government established by the Japanese in much of the Chinese lands they had occupied never attained substantial popular support; and Chiang's occasional indirect dealings with this regime, led by Wang Ching-wei, was for Chiang essentially a means of obtaining intelligence.[9] Chiang kept the intensity of fighting against Japan at a low level, expecting the Allies, and especially the Americans, to defeat the Japanese. He looked forward to a postwar situation in which his forces, strengthened by American aid, would be able to crush the Communist Party of China, with which he was at times allied and at times in combat.

One of the most significant ways in which the steadfast position of the Kuomintang government was rewarded during the war was the termination of the unequal treaties and with that the abolition of extraterritorial rights for foreigners, formally conceded by the British and the Americans by treaty in January 1943.[10] In the negotiations for this major step, Chiang at one point raised the question of the new territories that had been added by lease to the British colony of Hong Kong, but he dropped the issue for fear – certainly justified – that the British government might use it as a reason for not agreeing to the end of extraterritorial rights.[11] The leased new territories, of course, were only one part of the whole problem of Hong Kong, and that issue has to be seen in the framework of Chiang's views of future territorial questions in general.

Chiang always assumed and insisted in inter-Allied negotiations that all the territories taken by Japan be returned to China. This meant not only the very extensive lands occupied by Japanese forces in the fighting since the summer of 1937 but also, most specifically, all of Manchuria. Furthermore, the territory lost to Japan as a result of the Sino-Japanese War of 1894–95 was to be returned as well. This meant Taiwan (Formosa) and the Pescadores Islands.[11] On the subject of the Ryukyu Islands, the group that includes Okinawa, Chiang was less certain. Since these had not been under regular Chinese control and the population had long been administered by Japan, he was not inclined to insist on their being turned over to China.[12]

The return of Manchuria to China would automatically raise highly important and controversial issues about the role of the Soviet Union. Who would control the Chinese Eastern Railway, which cuts across Manchuria from a connection to the Trans-Siberian Railway in the northwest to the Soviet port of Vladivostok in the southeast? Who would control the South Manchurian Railway, which is connected to the Eastern Railway at Harbin, the Manchurian capital, and runs between there and the ports of Dairen and Port Arthur? And who would control the latter?[13] Certainly Chiang wanted all of this under Chinese control once again, but in view of the real possibility that Stalin would insist on a major role for the Soviet Union, he preferred to have the United States utilize the ports and simultaneously have base rights on Taiwan.[14] In this fashion, he hoped to engage the United States in holding back Soviet power in East Asia.[15]

Chiang's postwar plans for Korea were also modified to some extent by his very great concern about Soviet expansionist ambitions. From an early date, he wanted Korea to regain its independence. It might look to China for leadership but would be independent once Japan had been defeated.[16] As Chiang discovered that the United States government in general and President Roosevelt in particular did not think that Korea was ready for immediate independence but would need to be under some temporary form of trusteeship until it could become independent, Chiang wanted the United States to join China as trustees, thereby hopefully excluding the Soviet Union from a role in the peninsula.[17] While Roosevelt was not willing to exclude the Soviet Union from any and all roles in Manchuria and Korea, the evidence is clear that this would have been Chiang's preference. In addition, Chiang not surprisingly wanted to make sure that Outer Mongolia was returned to full Chinese sovereignty and no longer under Soviet influence and control, another issue on which he would be unable to have his way.[18]

When one considers Chiang's views about the future of territories that had not recently been a part of China, one needs to distinguish between those areas beyond Mongolia that had been ceded to Russia by unequal treaties in the nineteenth century, on the one hand, and the colonial possessions of France, the Dutch, the Portuguese, and the British in South and Southeast Asia, on the other. There is no evidence that Chiang, unlike his Communist successors, ever publicly raised the question of lands ceded to Russia in the nineteenth century by the Treaties of Aigun and Nerchinsk.[19] It is not possible at this point in time to explain Chiang's reticence on this issue. Perhaps he was certain that the Soviet Union would never consider the return of those portions of its East Asian territories – surely a correct assessment – and that raising the issue (as Mao Tse-tung subsequently did) could only poison relations with the mighty neighbor to the north for no conceivable useful purpose. Chiang's opinions and aspirations regarding the colonial question were, however, clear and consistent. They can best be understood in the framework of his general view of imperialism.

It was his belief that whatever expansion China had engaged in during prior centuries was in no way similar to the imperialism of the European powers before and during the nineteenth century. He was opposed to all such actions by anyone, and that most definitely included Japan, though he was prepared to have good relations with that country once it abandoned its expansionist course.[20] Not only was China to reclaim her full independence, but the reassertion on the international scene of full independence for China appeared to Chiang as a major step toward an analogous return of independence to all those peoples who had come under imperialist control.[21] Among other immediately important implications, this meant that, unlike Sun Yat-sen, the founder of the Chinese Republic, and Mao Tse-tung, the leader of the Chinese Communists, Chiang rejected the idea of Chinese control over Thailand, Indo-China, and Korea.[22] Further, his perception of the future end of imperialism may make it easier to understand his January 1942 request to President Roosevelt, that Roosevelt urge the British and Dutch to agree to apply the Atlantic Charter, with its promise of self-government, to their colonial possessions.[23] French Indo-China was also to become independent. Since in regard to this territory President Roosevelt once again argued for an intermediate stage of trusteeship, Chiang thought – and Roosevelt agreed – that China might act as the trustee. In this case, unlike that of Korea, there would be no need in Chiang's eyes for a joint trusteeship with the United States, as he assumed that Indo-China would probably not be an object of Soviet ambitions.[24] At all times Chiang hoped that India would gain its independence. When Wendell Willkie, who had been the presidential candidate of the Republican Party in the 1940 election and was touring the world with President Roosevelt's agreement, visited Chiang in October 1942, he suggested that the United States might guarantee that independence.[25]

As for the future of Japan, Chiang, as already stated, expected that its prior expansion would be reversed. He wanted those facilities that the Japanese had built up or developed in territory that he considered properly to belong to China to be turned over to Chinese ownership. Beyond that, the enormous damage that the Japanese had wrought in the years of war and through their acts of deliberate destruction was to be offset, at least to some extent, by the transfer of industrial equipment from Japan to China. War criminals were to be punished and the country was to be disarmed. On the question of Chinese participation in an occupation of Japan, as well as the future of the imperial system of government in postwar Japan, Chiang was evidently prepared to change his concept of the future somewhat during the war, as will be seen in the discussion of the Cairo Conference between him and Roosevelt in 1943.[26] There was, however, in Chiang's view of the postwar world no concept of a permanent Chinese enmity toward Japan. If that country became peaceful once again, he saw no reason why the two states could not be friends.[27] Although there is no explicit evidence on the point, it may well be that he viewed future good relations with a disarmed and peaceful Japan as a means of gaining an economic partner and creating an added counterweight to the role of the Soviet Union in East Asia.

Many, even if not all, of the questions about postwar Asia that Chiang was especially interested in were subjects of discussion at the Cairo Conference at the end of November 1943. Roosevelt and Churchill were meeting with Chiang before the former two went on to Teheran to meet with Stalin (at a time when the Soviet Union still held to its Neutrality Treaty with Japan). Unlike the leaders of the Axis powers, who at no time met to conduct even the most minimal discussion of their plans for the postwar world, the leaders of the Allies did have at least some discussions of this type, even if the pressing questions of military operations took up most of the time at their conferences. Charles de Gaulle was always excluded. Churchill and Roosevelt and Churchill and Stalin met several times, with the third leader not present; the three met twice while the war with Germany was still going on, and once (with changes in individuals) after Germany was defeated but Japan was still fighting. In all of these meetings, there was at least some discussion of issues concerning the postwar world.

While Churchill, in line with his general disdain for the Chinese and their leader, was not greatly interested in any meeting with Chiang, Roosevelt very much was, and the two would have a lengthy conversation during the Cairo Conference. Since Roosevelt did not want a formal record made of that talk, the available sources on their exchange are quite fragmentary and largely of Chinese origin, but they do allow a reasonably accurate reconstruction of the agreements and disagreements between the two leaders as well as the extent to which each of them subsequently modified his approach to the major issues.[28]

In 1942 Chiang had established a "Research Committee on Postwar International Peace Organization," whose proposals he took along to Cairo, but as shown later these proposals would not be important for Chiang's procedure on this matter.[29] Some of the hopes of the Chinese leader on other matters were to be ignored or thwarted at Cairo. The expectation of an equivalent of the Atlantic Charter for the whole world – meaning especially the colonies of the European powers – was disappointed. On the other hand, he found both Roosevelt and Churchill in agreement with his insistence on the complete defeat of Japan, an issue of supreme importance for the Chinese leader and one on which he had entertained some doubts when the early great victories of the Japanese led him to fear that the United States and Great Britain might be amenable to some sort of compromise with Japan. Similarly, there was agreement to his demand that Manchuria and Taiwan be returned to China – a point implicitly included in the final public statement from Cairo, which asserted that Japan would have to surrender all territories it had seized. On the subject of Korean independence, there was something of a compromise. Chiang wanted it to follow immediately upon the end of hostilities, but Roosevelt believed that the country was not ready for independence and would need to be under some form of trusteeship until independence looked feasible.

On the future status of the former French, Dutch, and British colonies in Southeast Asia, Chiang had the agreement in principle of President Roosevelt but could not obtain any assurances because not a single one of the colonial powers was willing to move in that direction at that time. Certainly Roosevelt shared Chiang's hopes for postwar cooperation between their two countries. In response to the American president's suggestion that China take the lead in a postwar occupation of Japan, Chiang demurred and agreed only to a small part in such an occupation while stressing that his country would need substantial additional aid to make even this role possible. On the issue of the future of Japan's imperial institution, the discussion implicitly left that matter open.[30]

It should be noted that leaving the question of the institution of the emperor open while hoping for a democratic government in postwar Japan meant, in practice, that the institution was likely to be retained because of the generally understood sentiments of the Japanese people on this point. In the face of some contrary opinion within his own party, Chiang held to this view subsequently and supported the decision of the U.S. government under Roosevelt's successor Harry Truman to keep the emperor as an instrument, first to ensure the surrender of all Japanese armed forces and then to control an administrative apparatus in Japan as the Americans occupied and restructured the country.[31]

Certainly Chiang did not come away from the Cairo Conference with all that he had hoped for. Nevertheless, in addition to the concrete promises that most interested him – no compromise peace with Japan and the return of all Chinese lands that had been seized by the Japanese – there was surely a symbolic aspect of the meeting that was important for him and for his government. A Chinese leader had met with the key leaders of the United States and the United Kingdom under circumstances that would be well publicized and that showed a China becoming recognized as one of the world's great powers. And, by definition, that placed a special and new status on the leader who had been invited as China's representative to the meeting. The final official communiqué issued at the end of the meeting came from the three leaders jointly. Churchill and Roosevelt might frequently ignore Chiang in their subsequent meetings and decisions, but at least on this occasion the way things were presented to an attentive world audience placed Chiang alongside the other two. Coming a few months after the formal abandonment of extraterritorial rights by Britain and the

United States, the symbolic significance of the Cairo meeting should not be underestimated.

After the Cairo Conference, Chiang continued to work toward independence for Korea after Japan's defeat; close relationships with Korean elements looking in that direction would be a part of that policy. While he still hoped to exclude the Soviet Union from a role in the Korean peninsula, he appears to have thought of China's postwar relationship to the newly independent Korea to be restricted to assisting in its defense.[32] Postwar developments, of course, would alter all this, but during the war Chiang's views on the subject remained essentially unchanged.

The year and a half after the Cairo Conference was also a time when the critical steps were taken toward the establishment of the new international organization to replace the League of Nations. While Chiang was very much interested in full Chinese participation in this project, he quite deliberately held back from advancing specific proposals. Although some plans were prepared inside the Kuomintang government for the preliminary meeting at Dumbarton Oaks, these were not put forward by the Chinese delegation during the sessions, evidently under specific instructions from Chiang.[33] A similar policy was followed, again under Chiang's instructions, at the San Francisco Conference for the formal establishment of the United Nations Organization in 1945. Chiang's reticence in pushing for specific detailed proposals at these meetings was very much the product of his concern that if the Chinese pushed for things that the United States and Great Britain might oppose, this might endanger implementation of the promises that China had obtained at the Cairo Conference.[34] Since there was never any doubt in the mind of the Chinese leader that all prior expansionist acquisitions of

Japan had to be given up, he was entirely willing to have his delegation at San Francisco support the transfer of Japan's former mandates in the Pacific to the United States as Strategic Trust Territories.[35]

Ironically, Chiang's position and his hopes for the postwar world were being undermined at home in the very years of the war in which the international position of China was in the process of being elevated to the status of a major world player, shown by the guarantee of a permanent seat on the Security Council of the new United Nations Organization as well as the termination of the unequal treaties of the preceding centuries. The corruption in leading circles and the authoritarian character of Chiang's rule meant that the regime did not build up the domestic support it needed for success in the difficult postwar situation. In addition to the internal disorganization of the Kuomintang government, there was the great Chinese military defeat of 1944. Both in order to secure a railway connection between north and south China under complete Japanese control and to seize air bases from which American planes were beginning to raid the Japanese home islands, the Japanese launched the Ichigo offensive. Ordered in December 1943 and initiated in April 1944, this offensive effectively destroyed the military forces of Chiang Kai-shek during the following months.[36] The attempts to rebuild Chinese military capacity were not successful in spite of substantial and for a time increasing American assistance. As if this were not bad enough, the development of a civil war with the Chinese Communists in its early stages meant that a planned Nationalist offensive toward Canton in southern China – with the possibility of Chinese troops liberating Hong Kong from Japanese control – had to be abandoned in order to enable troops to be moved north to fight the Communists.[37] That fight, of course, ended in the triumph of the Communists on the mainland of China and the removal of the Chinese Nationalist leadership to Taiwan. From there Chiang would continue for years to instruct the Chinese delegation in the United Nations, but others controlled most of China and its policies.

Something should be said about Chiang's vision for the future of China even if he failed to be in a position to implement the policies he advocated. It was, after all, these ideas that to some extent influenced his policies during the years before, during, and after World War II.[38] Rightly or wrongly, Chiang thought of himself as the inheritor and executor of Sun Yat-sen, the founder of the Chinese Republic. In one way or another, Chiang either in reality or just cynically tried to make his views fit in with the Three Principles – Nationalism, Democracy, and the People's Livelihood – that Sun had proclaimed as his central doctrine. As Chiang saw the concept of Nationalism, it meant first and foremost the abolition of the unequal treaties. This is clear from all of his writings and from the speech he made to the people of China on January 12, 1943, the day after the signing of the formal treaties with the United States and Britain ending extraterritoriality and related impositions on China.[39]

The end of the unequal treaties would, in his eyes, not automatically bring to an end their impact on the people of China. Those treaties, he believed, had created a sense of inferiority among China's population. In a psychological reconstruction, they would have to rebuild their self-respect over a period of years. Furthermore, it was his opinion that a rebuilt sense of social cohesion would have to develop in the country. As for the principle of Democracy, Chiang never viewed it in the way that people in western Europe and the United States interpreted it. He believed in a centralized state with a leading single political party (the Kuomintang), a strong and ruthless police force, and only minimal tolerance for divergent political tendencies and public discussion.[40] The goals referred to under the rubric of the People's Livelihood would be reached by a long-term program of industrial development that he envisioned requiring some thirty to fifty years. And in this industrialization process, what might best be called state capitalism was to play a central role. Certainly industrialization and modernization in general would have changed the appearance of China's urban landscape, as had been the case in Europe in the preceding century, but there is no evidence to suggest that Chiang entertained visions of grandiose buildings similar to those so dear to Hitler, Mussolini, and Stalin.

It is very difficult to imagine what his estimation of the evolution of Taiwan in the last decades of the twentieth century would have been or what he might have said about the post-Mao developments in Communist China. History and historians, especially in Europe and the United States, have not been kind to Chiang Kai-shek. There has been an astonishing reluctance to compare the police repression and the corruption of the Communist regime that followed with those of the Kuomintang government that Chiang led. Two aspects of the latter's role in Chinese history do, however, deserve more attention than they have generally received. One of these is the extent to which he and his movement were able to make substantial strides toward consolidating a country shattered by a decrepit Manchu regime's heritage, foreign intervention, and civil commotion – and to do so and modernize the country sufficiently to hold up in years of grueling war against a strong and tightly organized invading power. The other is the extent to which, inside and outside China, Chiang became a personal symbol of a country defiant against the odds.

5. Josef Stalin

Russian Premier Stalin talks to his Foreign Minister Molotov at the Palace, Yalta, Crimea, Russia (ca. February 1945). Franklin D. Roosevelt Library, photo no. NLR-PHOCO-A-48223659.

B ORN OF POOR PARENTS IN GEORGIA IN THE NORTHWESTERN
Caucasus in 1878, the man who took the name of Josef Stalin
received what schooling he had in a seminary. Expelled from the
seminary, he joined the Social Democratic Workers' Party and became a professional revolutionary. Repeatedly exiled to Siberia, he
became an associate of Lenin and a member of the government after
the Bolshevik revolution of 1917. After Lenin's early death, Stalin
used his position in the Communist Party to move toward power.
Turning against others in the party's leadership, he steadily consolidated his position so that by the end of the 1920s he was effectively
in control of the party and the state apparatus. A series of purges
removed any and all who in his imagination might even dream of
challenging his supreme authority.

Stalin had, therefore, been in complete control of the government of the Soviet Union for a decade before the Germans initiated
World War II. Under his driving leadership, the Soviet state had
made massive strides in an industrialization process that was exceed-
ingly wasteful of resources and human lives and was very much oriented toward strengthening the country's capacity for military activity, but this was not for immediate military operations. As Japanese

aggression in Manchuria in 1931 – following upon its occupation of much East Asian Russian territory temporarily a decade earlier – suggested the possibility of further Japanese advances, Stalin had been quite willing to appease the authorities in Tokyo by yielding some of the rights in Manchuria that Russia had obtained in prior years. On the other hand, at border incidents in 1937 and 1939 Stalin was quite determined to allow no encroachment on what he considered the territory of the Soviet Union or its Mongolian satellite. In heavy fighting, the Red Army asserted a decisive local superiority over Japanese forces.[1]

In a similar fashion, Stalin operated very carefully in regard to the revisionist powers in Europe. The Soviet Union maintained good relations with Mussolini's Italy and did not allow the fighting support of the two states for opposite sides in the Spanish Civil War to interfere with those relations. There were repeated efforts to maintain good relations with Hitler's Germany, but until 1939 these were met by rebuffs from Berlin.[2] On the assumption that it would be best for the capitalist powers to fight each other, lest they join together to attack the Soviet Union, Stalin encouraged the Western powers to fight Germany and Germany to fight the Western powers. They would weaken each other in the process, and the Soviet Union would assist whichever was the weaker in order to prolong the fighting. He expected that this would be Germany.[3]

Stalin's view that Germany was the weaker of the two potential warring camps can only have been reinforced by Germany's drawing back from war at the last moment in 1938. By that time the Japanese had already involved themselves on their own initiative in a war with China, thus greatly reducing any danger to the Soviet Union in East Asia. The Germans clearly needed encouragement to begin a war against the Western powers, and Stalin was prepared to provide that. In the face of the urgings of President Franklin Roosevelt that Stalin ally himself with the Western powers lest a Germany victorious in western Europe turn thereafter against both the Soviet Union and the United States, Stalin preferred to ally himself with Hitler.[4] We will never know whether Germany would have taken the plunge into war in 1939 without Soviet encouragement; the reality remains that Germany unleashed a second world war with the knowledge that the Soviet Union would neither stand aside as a neutral nor side with Germany's enemies. It would instead join in the war on Poland and assist Germany in minimizing the impact of any Allied blockade of the kind that had been so damaging in the prior great conflict.

An especially clear sign of Stalin's preference can be seen in the way his forces, clearly under instructions from the top, handled the same issues of liaison in 1939 and 1945. At all levels the Red Army cooperated as fully as conceivable with the German army in Poland when the two forces met in the country they had both invaded. German soldiers who had been captured by the Poles were promptly and courteously returned to Germany when liberated by the Red Army. In both respects, the situation in 1945 was the exact opposite: Moscow made cooperation with the Western Allies as difficult as possible at the point the armies were about to meet in the field, and liberated British and American prisoners were put through an additional ordeal before their return to the Soviet Union's allies.[5]

The agreement with Hitler's Germany appeared to bring to Stalin's Soviet Union some significant territorial gains. Eastern Poland was annexed to the Belorussian and Ukrainian Soviet Socialist Republics. The Germans had originally proposed that Estonia be Soviet, Lithuania German, and Latvia divided at the Dvina River between the two countries. Stalin, however, asked for all of Latvia, a request to which the Germans hastily agreed. Once Poland had been crushed militarily by German and Soviet forces, Stalin suggested that the central part of that country between the Vistula and Bug Rivers, which had originally been assigned to the Soviet sphere, be exchanged for Lithuania. In the German-Soviet negotiations at the end of September 1939, the Germans agreed to this exchange, although a small portion of Lithuania around the town of Mariampole was to become German when the country's independence was ended, a subject that will be examined further.[6] In the course of their negotiations with the Soviets before starting the war, the Germans had also agreed to turn over Finland to their new friend as well as rather vaguely defined territories in the Balkans. They had been prepared to make even greater concessions, but Stalin had not asked for more. Instead, he had instructed all communist parties in the world to oppose the war as a conflict between capitalist states. As Stalin explained his views in the Kremlin on September 7, 1939, "It would be fine if at the hands of Germany the position of the richer capitalist countries (especially England) were shaken."[7]

Just before invading Poland, Stalin had extended diplomatic recognition to the puppet state of Slovakia, which the Germans had created out of the eastern half of Czechoslovakia at the same time as they had authorized Hungary to seize the Carpatho-Ukraine, the easternmost portion of that country. The Soviet government was the only one outside the Axis that thus formally accepted the end of the Czechoslovak state, a point that has to be kept in mind in connection with later developments in Stalin's policy toward that country.

In the immediate aftermath of the fighting in Poland, the Soviet Union forced the three Baltic States to accept the stationing of

Soviet military forces at bases in them. The effort to oblige Finland to make territorial and other concessions failed in the face of Finnish objections. Stalin thereupon ordered an attack on that country and, evidently expecting a swift victory, had a Communist client regime established for Finland. It is not clear at this point in time whether this step was a preliminary to the total annexation of Finland on lines similar to those Stalin adopted toward the three Baltic States in the following year. In any case, the war did not develop as expected. The Finns fought hard and at first successfully, as a poorly led Red Army stumbled badly. Worried about possible implications, Stalin had massive forces assembled to crush Finnish resistance in February 1940. Then, rather than push on to occupy the whole country, Stalin made peace with Finland in March and dropped the Communist government he had intended to install in the Finish capital of Helsinki.

Several aspects of the Soviet–Finnish peace shed light on Stalin's views of the future. On the one hand, Finland was allowed to retain its independence, with a Soviet garrison only at a leased territory, Hangö, near the capital of Helsinki, but not at various places in the country, as had been imposed on the Baltic States. The border between the Soviet Union and Finland was pushed back to turn over to the Soviets substantial territory north of Leningrad and in the central portion of the border. On the other hand, in the far north, where the Red Army had occupied the Finnish Arctic port of Petsamo and the nearby nickel mines, almost all of the conquered land was returned to Finland, with only the western portion of the Rybachi peninsula being retained by the Soviet Union.[8]

Since Stalin would subsequently insist on the cession of the whole Petsamo area to the Soviet Union, the obvious question is, why did he return it to Finland when it had been occupied by the Red Army during the fighting? One possible explanation is that, by the time of the peace negotiations with Finland, Stalin realized that there would be a struggle between the Germans and the Western powers over Norway and that returning Petsamo to Finland would be a way to keep the Soviet Union out of any danger of direct involvement in such a struggle. He was prepared to assist the Germans at a critical juncture in the fight for Norway by allowing them to use a naval base on Soviet territory to support their assault on the important town of Narvik, but a Finnish territorial buffer between the Soviet Union and Norway was certain to keep any fighting at a distance.

As for an independent Finland, that was something Stalin at the time clearly preferred to a lengthy struggle to subdue an obviously re-luctant population. Once the war then under way between Germany and the Western powers was over or had entered a new stage, new opportunities might arise. And these opportunities would be more easily realized because of the territorial concessions already secured by the peace treaty, for the location of the ceded regions would make it difficult – indeed, practically impossible – for Finland to defend itself against any Soviet attack in the future.

The spectacular German victories in the north and west of Europe in April and May 1940 precipitated several steps by Stalin that fit in with whatever longer term ambitions and hopes he then held. Estonia and Latvia were annexed to the Soviet Union. At the same time, Stalin ordered the annexation of *all* of Lithuania, including the small portion that was to have become German. This Soviet ac-tion would lead to lengthy negotiations with Berlin, culminating in an agreement in early 1941. The Soviets agreed to pay Germany a sum identical to that which the United States had paid Russia for Alaska in 1867 – a land so much larger that if the Mariampole dis-trict had been located in it, hardly anyone would have been able to find it. Clearly Stalin's insistence that all three of the Baltic States were to be permanently incorporated entirely into the Soviet Union was a very high priority in his vision of the postwar world. It is true that the final agreement on the Mariampole district of Lithuania was a part of Stalin's strenuous attempt to appease Germany and open the way for the Soviet Union to join the Tripartite Pact. It would, however, have been possible for him to direct the Red Army to pay attention to the agreed demarcation line in Lithuania in 1940, just as he had ordered adherence to the demarcation line in Poland the year before. Alternatively, it would have been possible to shift forces to the agreed demarcation line after their initial movement, as had also been done in the Polish case. Stalin's insistence on the incorporation of the Baltic States and the importance he attached to it were to have further repercussions later in the war.

Stalin also pushed for additions to Soviet territory on the border with Romania. As in the partition of Poland, he had taken territory well beyond the borders of pre-1914 Russia. In the case of Romania, he demanded not only the territory Russia had held in the nineteenth century, including that taken from its Romanian ally at the end of the Russo-Turkish War of 1877–78, but beyond that all of the former Austrian province of Bucovina, which had been allotted to Romania by the 1919 peace treaty. The Germans succeeded in persuading the Soviets to reduce their demand to about half of that province but made sure that the Romanian government yielded to all other Soviet territorial demands. Furthermore, Berlin was willing to see the Soviets subsequently occupy some Romanian islands in the Danube. In this case as elsewhere, the Germans were quite willing to let the Soviet Union annex territory because they had already decided to attack that country in the following year and expected to take it all back very quickly.[9]

Because German planning for the invasion of the Soviet Union called for an alliance with Finland and Romania in that operation, German forces occupied Romania and Germany sent troops and supplies to Finland in the fall of 1940, thereby putting a halt to any further ambitions of the Soviets in regard to these countries at that time. Those ambitions may have included further steps against Finland; they certainly involved bases of some type in and control over Bulgaria. Complaints about Germany's violation of the 1939 agreement for Finland to belong to the Soviet sphere and emphasis on Soviet ambitions in Bulgaria would be central to the instructions Stalin gave to Vyacheslav Molotov for his conversation with the German leaders in Berlin in November 1940.[10]

Stalin's written instructions of November 9, 1940, contain important contemporary evidence on his thinking about the future. He expected further negotiations with the Germans after Molotov's talks in Berlin; Stalin assumed that the German foreign minister would make a third trip to Moscow. In the meantime, certain matters were to be resolved. Stalin was greatly concerned, and Molotov made this very clear to the Germans, about the shift in German policy toward Finland. Failing to recognize that the Germans had long before decided to attack the Soviet Union and expected Finland to be an ally in the invasion, Stalin wanted Germany to abide by the prior allocation of that country to the Soviet Union by removing its soldiers and stopping weapons shipments for the Finnish army. Since the Germans had at no time indicated a special interest in Bulgaria, Molotov was to explain the Soviet Union's interest in the establishment of bases in that country, along with its interest in the control of the Straits and general relations with Turkey, for Stalin clearly anticipated open access to the Mediterranean. Similarly, there were to be arrangements for the Soviet Union to have some yet to be defined access through Danish waters into the North Sea from the Baltic Sea. Now that the Soviet Union had a common border with Hungary because of its own annexation of eastern Poland and Hungary's annexation of the Carpatho-Ukraine, the Soviets wanted to have a clearer picture of the Germans' plans for Hungary as well as Romania. Furthermore, the Germans were to be informed about the Soviet Union's interest in Iran, though there is nothing in the record as to whether at this time Stalin already expected to annex the northwestern portion of that country.

At this point in the war, Stalin was expecting a possible peace between Great Britain and Germany and a possible peace between China and Japan. In regard to the former, Molotov was to suggest that the British return all of Germany's former colonies to her, leave Gibraltar and Egypt – presumably to Franco's Spain and Mussolini's Italy, respectively – but keep the rest of its current empire. At a time when communist parties around the world were calling for peace, this peace concept would also have left Germany in control of Austria, most of Czechoslovakia, Denmark, Norway, the Low Countries, and most of France. The Soviet Union had already recognized Italy's annexation of Ethiopia and Albania in 1939 and was thus in full agreement with Germany on the dispensation of those countries. In East Asia, Stalin visualized the Axis powers joined by the Soviet Union mediating a peace between Chiang Kai-shek's China and Japan. The settlement Stalin contemplated would leave Manchuria to Japan and in addition allocate to Japan the Dutch East Indies, since Germany was to retain control of the Dutch mother country of that enormous and rich colony.

The possibility of peace negotiations was actually not discussed in the Berlin talks – conducted on occasion in an air-raid shelter – any more than one other topic to which Stalin's instructions alluded.

On the future of Poland, the 1939 agreement with Germany was to remain in effect. That agreement not only had provided for a territorial division but also had stipulated that neither side would tolerate Polish nationalist agitation directed at the land acquired by the other.[11] It is important to note in this connection that the exchange of central Poland for Lithuania by the Soviet Union had in effect placed the majority of the culturally Polish portion of the population of prewar Poland under German control. More than half a year before Molotov's trip to Berlin, Stalin had issued an order that illuminates his view of the future of Poland.

On March 5, 1940, a few days before the signing of the Soviet-Finnish peace, Stalin had the Politburo approve the killing of practically all of the approximately 15,000 Polish officers and reserve officers captured by the Red Army in the preceding year and held in several special camps. This mass murder, generally referred to as the Katyn massacre after the location where several thousand of the corpses were discovered in 1943, needs to be seen as indicative of Stalin's view of the future of Poland and the Soviet Union's relations with any future Polish state.[12] Since the British and French had declared war on Germany in accordance with their pledges to Poland, they were likely to insist on some sort of Poland carved out of the German-occupied part of that country in any compromise peace. That Poland, if there ever were one, would thus be deprived of a significant portion of its potential elite. Furthermore, a small number of officers were carefully spared and would form the nucleus of a pro-Soviet Polish army that, appropriately, came to be called the Berling Army after one of those spared in the mass killing and later placed in nominal charge of a Polish force fighting on the Eastern Front. In the period between the mass killing in early April 1940 and the German invasion of the Soviet Union, this small group of officers could be held in reserve for any contingency. Such a contingency was to come far sooner than Stalin hoped or anticipated.

Stalin dismissed all warnings from his own intelligence and from both the British and American governments of the forthcoming German invasion as provocations. He tried very hard to join the Tripartite Pact, to make appeasing gestures toward the Germans, and to signal a willingness to make additional concessions in negotiations by a number of moves in the economic and financial sphere.[13] While Stalin's interest in joining the Tripartite Pact implied a willingness to go to war with the United States under certain conditions, he was unwilling to believe that the Germans would attack without prior negotiations – this although Germany by 1941 had attacked a whole series of neutral states without such negotiations. The German invasion, therefore, came as both a tactical and strategic surprise, with disastrous effects for the military position of the Soviet Union.

Having helped the Germans to drive the Allies off the European continent in the North, the West, and the South, Stalin now found himself in the terribly dangerous situation of being essentially alone in fighting against them in eastern Europe. The critical test would be whether, like Czar Alexander I when facing Napoleon, Stalin could keep effective control of the unoccupied portions of the Soviet Union and muster the vast country's human and material resources for the fight or whether, like the regime of Nicholas II in February 1917 and the Provisional Government in October 1917, he would lose his grip on the state and the country's people. At the end of July and in early August 1941, the substantial counterattacks of the Red Army on the central portion of the Eastern Front showed that the regime retained effective control of the Soviet Union. The hard initial blows had not dissolved the regime, as the Germans had

confidently anticipated. Whatever the subsequent details of the sav-
age fighting at the front and the swings of fortune, Stalin would remain in charge of a struggling but continuing government. He could
look to a future in which the Soviet Union either would be victorious alongside whatever allies German initiative provided or, alternatively, could make a separate peace with the Germans once the
latter had recognized on a large scale what the Japanese had learned
the hard way on a small scale, namely, that this was a country they
could not crush. How did Stalin see the world of the future in either
of these contingencies?

Stalin's vision of the future in case he was able to work out a
separate peace with Germany is very poorly documented. Unlike
the British after the winter of 1939–40 and unlike the Americans
from December 1941 on, Stalin was prepared to consider renewed
negotiations with the Germans at various points during the war,
most likely starting in the late fall of 1941 and continuing until
the summer of 1944.[14] The bulk of the relevant evidence on this
subject remains sealed in the archives of the Russian Federation.
From what hints there are, especially from the German side and in
the American intercepts of Japanese documents relating to their attempt to bring the Germans and Soviets together, it would appear
that Stalin's main interests were to end the fighting that was so terribly costly and to retain all or most of the Soviet territory held in
June 1941. In the first half of the war in the East, he may have been
willing to make some territorial concessions to the Germans, most
likely by yielding Lithuania to them. In the second half of the war,
his terms would have been harder and most likely would have included the transfer of central Poland from German to Soviet control. But until some substantial evidence on the subject is released,
all this must remain speculative.

The creation of the Free Germany Committee and the League of German Officers within the Soviet Union in the summer of 1943 suggests that if there were no possibility of negotiations with the Hitler regime, perhaps that government could be replaced in Berlin by one more amenable to a new agreement with Moscow.[15] What sort of terms such a replacement regime might have attained remains unknown and perhaps unknowable. The critical issue from the perspective of the Soviet dictator would in any case have been the end of fighting on the Eastern Front at a time when the Western Allies were certain to be continuing their fight with Germany. And in the meantime, the actual or implicit threat of a separate peace on the Eastern Front – as had happened in 1918 and 1939 – would cause the Western Allies to be more willing to make concessions to Soviet demands.

What sort of future did Stalin envision in case the Soviet Union continued fighting alongside its allies until Germany and the states associated with it had been defeated? The first significant evidence regarding this issue is to be found in Stalin's lengthy conversations about a possible alliance and an associated secret protocol with British Foreign Secretary Anthony Eden when the latter met with the Soviet leader repeatedly in Moscow during December 16–20, 1941.[16] As will become apparent, Stalin changed his mind on several points later in the war, but he was quite explicit about Soviet hopes and demands at this time, a time when the Red Army had turned the tide against the Germans on the Eastern Front and Japan's attack on Great Britain, the United States, and the Netherlands had removed any immediate danger to the Soviet Union from Japan.

On the issue of borders, Stalin was most insistent on recognition of the incorporation of the Baltic States into the Soviet Union. No subject took up more time in the discussions than this one, on which Eden insisted he had to consult his government and also had to consider the position of the United States. While Stalin at this time favored the annexation of East Prussia by Poland, not only did he want the Memel territory reincorporated into the Lithuanian Soviet Socialist Republic – and hence the Soviet Union – as a reversal of the retrocession of that area to Germany by Lithuania before the war, but he also demanded that the city of Tilsit (now Sovietsk) be detached from East Prussia as ceded to Poland and instead be added to the Lithuanian SSR, thus providing a bridgehead across the Niemen (now Nemunas) River for the Soviet Union. There was also the suggestion that additional territory, including the city of Königsberg, be under Soviet occupation for twenty years.

On the future of Finland, Stalin at this point said nothing about its domestic institutions. On the issue of borders and bases, his ideas went substantially beyond the terms of the March 1940 peace treaty with Finland. The border north of Leningrad and in the middle of the Soviet–Finnish boundary was to be that of the prior treaty, but there were two additional demands. The Soviet Union was to have undefined army and naval bases in Finland, and the Petsamo area was now to be annexed. Whether the demand for bases was, as in the case of the Baltic States, a preliminary to annexation of the whole country at some future date is unclear. When it finally came to a peace settlement with Finland, the Soviets exchanged their prior base at Hangö for one at Porkkala, but by then Stalin had assured his American and British allies that Finland could remain independent. If one asks why Stalin now demanded the territory around Petsamo that his army had occupied a year earlier but that he had then returned to Finland, one might speculate that for the Soviet leader the desirability of a common border with a postwar Norway outweighed the risks of involvement that had swayed him earlier. In addition, this expansion at the expense of Finland would cut that country off from access to the Arctic Ocean and provide better security for the Soviet port of Murmansk.

As for the border between the Soviet Union and Poland, Stalin talked about the border of June 1941, but also about the Curzon Line with possible modifications. The latter line, developed after World War I as a possible boundary, was somewhat more favorable to Poland than the border established by the German-Soviet agreements of 1939. There would be much further discussion of this issue during the balance of World War II, and this subject will be reviewed subsequently. The key point is that by December 1941 Stalin looked to a future border with Poland that would allow the Soviet Union to retain most of the land assigned to it by agreement with Germany but left open a little room for further discussion. At this time, Stalin appears to have recognized that Bialystok in the north and Lvov in the south were predominantly Polish in population, but he was prepared to have one but not both returned to Poland.[17] As already mentioned, Stalin expected almost all of East Prussia to be turned over to Poland, and although he could not commit his government, Eden indicated agreement with this concept.

Stalin insisted that the territory the Soviet Union had acquired from Romania in 1940 would again be Soviet. Furthermore, the Soviets were to be allowed military and naval bases in Romania. Stalin did not mention to Eden the great interest in a Soviet role in Bulgaria that he had instructed Molotov to take up with the Germans. Perhaps this was because, unlike Romania, Bulgaria had not declared war on the Soviet Union. He did, however, suggest that a piece of Bulgaria might be turned over to Yugoslavia and another piece be ceded to Turkey, which was also to obtain the Dodecanese

Islands and possibly a piece of the French mandate of Syria. Interestingly enough, Stalin at this time wanted Czechoslovakia restored to its pre-Munich borders, with the addition of some territory at Hungary's expense, subjects on which he would later change his mind. Hungary was also to return to Romania some of the territory it had acquired from Romania under Germany's tutelage. He wanted Greece restored to its prewar borders. Yugoslavia was to be restored, with some additions at the expense of Italy. Although Stalin subsequently turned strongly against the idea of confederations among some of the smaller states of east and southeast Europe, he expressed himself as still open on this issue in December 1941.[18]

For western Europe, Stalin suggested the restoration of the independence of Norway, Denmark, Holland, Belgium, and Luxembourg. France would be restored, but the Soviet leader made it clear that he did not expect that country to play any great power role in the future. This was presumably a reflection of his disappointment at its rapid collapse in 1940. Stalin proposed two modifications to the restored independence of all these states. He expected some special concessions to the Soviet Union in regard to transit through the straits from the Baltic into the North Sea, a point that Molotov had been instructed to bring up with the Germans in the preceding year. As for the other western European states, he was prepared to see British bases established in them – perhaps as a way to make his insistence on bases in Finland and Romania look more acceptable to London. Austria and Albania were to regain their independence as well, and presumably possess their old borders.

In view of the most recent developments in the war, it is not surprising that at this time and throughout the subsequent war years Stalin was especially concerned about the future of Germany, especially its possible military revival. However important the topic,

Stalin's view of what should be done was at this time evidently not particularly precise. The British record of the conversation reads, "As to Germany, I [Stalin] think it is absolutely necessary in order to weaken Germany to detach the Rhineland from Prussia, especially the industrial district. What should be done with it could be discussed afterwards; whether it was made an independent State or a protectorate, etc. I think this is the only guarantee which will ensure that Germany would be permanently weakened. Austria should be restored as an Independent State and possibly Bavaria also might be constituted an independent country."[19] Stalin mentioned but did not discuss with Eden the transfer of German territory up to the Oder River to Poland in addition to the cession of East Prussia. That possibility would eventuate in the new border created after the war; but although there have been assertions that Stalin had already offered the Polish Prime Minister Wladyslaw Sikorski a border on the Oder River, it is not clear that by December 1941 Stalin had definitely made up his mind on this issue.[20]

The British government was not willing to commit itself to Stalin's territorial reordering of Europe by a secret protocol, and its knowledge that the United States government was even less inclined to agree to anything of the sort strengthened it in this policy. There would, therefore, be a simple Anglo–Soviet alliance treaty with no secret protocol. This refusal of the Western Allies to agree to a secret protocol with territorial provisions appears to have had some influence on at least one of the modifications Stalin made in his own vision of the future after his meeting with Eden.

When Molotov was in London in May 1942 to work out the text of the Anglo–Soviet Alliance, he still referred to Stalin's support of the transfer of East Prussia to Poland.[21] It is not at this time clear precisely when Stalin altered his position on this issue. Most likely later in 1942 or early in 1943 he began to insist on the division of East Prussia in an entirely different manner. The Memel territory was still to be included in the Lithuanian SSR, but the whole northern half of pre-1939 East Prussia was to be turned over permanently to the Soviet Union. This would include the major port of Königsberg, now Kaliningrad, in the Soviet Union, while Poland was to be compensated for this change in plans at the expense of Germany by the city of Stettin, now Szczecin, on the west bank of the Oder River. Furthermore, the half of East Prussia that would be acquired by the Soviet Union was not to be and never was incorporated into the Lithuanian SSR. Instead it was to become – and is currently – a province (oblast) of the Russian Federation. If one asks for an explanation of this change in Stalin's view, the most likely answer is to be found in his insistence on the recognition by the British and American governments of the *de jure* incorporation of the Baltic States into the Soviet Union. As it became clear during 1942 that the United States and the United Kingdom, the latter under stiff American pressure, were not going to agree to this, Stalin saw in the creation of a province of the Russian Federation on the southwestern border of Lithuania a territorial form of security holding the three Baltic States firmly in the grasp of the Soviet Union.

On the question of the border between the Soviet Union and Poland, there was a lengthy series of negotiations both directly between those two states and between the Western Allies and the Soviet Union. These cannot be reviewed here in detail, but there are four aspects of the negotiations that must be mentioned because they shed light on Stalin's view of the postwar situation.[22] First, there was his insistence in talks with the Poles and with Britain and the United States that the Curzon Line must be the basis of the future border. He was prepared to agree to some modifications in favor of Poland. These involved primarily the area around Bialystok in the north and Lvov in the south. In the end, in the face of repeated efforts by Roosevelt and Churchill to secure both for Poland, it was the Bialystok region that Stalin was willing to yield to Poland. Although he agreed to a small shift in favor of Poland at the southern end of the proposed Soviet–Polish border, he was unwilling to have the city of Lvov – in spite of its majority Polish population – included in postwar Poland.

It is conceivable that in his insistence on retaining Lvov Stalin was influenced by the possibility that its cession would also involve returning the oil-producing area of Borislav-Drohobych to Poland, a point repeatedly mentioned by President Roosevelt. Such a territorial arrangement would make Poland less dependent on the Soviet Union for its oil supplies. More important, almost certainly, was the very substantial Ukrainian population in the rural areas around Lvov. Stalin wanted all Ukrainians to be under the rule of Moscow, a policy that, as will be examined subsequently, also influenced his insistence on a major cession of territory by Czechoslovakia. As the largest nationality in the Soviet Union after the Great Russians, and one that was of enormous economic importance to the state, the Ukrainians were a people about whose loyalty there might be doubts that Stalin was determined to erase. In the Bialystok region, on the other hand, Poles were undoubtedly the overwhelming majority in the rural land as well as the urban center, especially after the Germans had murdered all the Jews living there.

A second aspect of the negotiations over the Soviet–Polish border was the increasing connection between this and another issue: the extent of the German territory that would be ceded to Poland in addition to East Prussia or the southern half of that area. Some in the Polish government-in-exile hoped for expansion westward, becoming increasingly insistent on what came to be called the Oder-Neisse line. Though not as large as the lands between the 1939 Soviet–Polish border and the new one Stalin proposed, this hitherto German area was economically more valuable because it included the whole Silesian industrial and mining district as well as the rich agricultural lands of central and lower Silesia. The concept that this was a way of compensating Poland for its territorial losses in the East came to play an increasing role in discussion of the issue. Furthermore, if, as was widely assumed, Danzig would be turned over to Poland and Stettin on the west bank of the Oder was ceded by Germany, Poland would have a coast and harbors on the Baltic Sea that were far more substantial than those of the prewar years. In addition, Stalin could be certain that the new western border of Poland would have a twofold effect favorable to the Soviet Union. Germany would be greatly weakened by this vast loss of important territory, and postwar Poland would be dependent on the Soviet Union for its security in the face of any German revisionist aspirations, ensuring that Poland would be unlikely to join with Germany in any anti-Soviet alignment.

The third aspect of these projects to move Poland westward was the sometimes implicit but often explicit assumption that all or almost all Germans living east of the new Polish–German border – as well as those in the northern half of East Prussia – would be relocated to whatever remained of Germany at the end of hostilities. The Germans had for years denounced the efforts of the peacemakers of 1919 for their attempt to adjust Europe's boundaries to the population. They instead advocated and during the war applied the notion that one first drew boundaries and then adjusted the population to them. This procedure was now to be applied to the Germans, and on a massive scale. It was increasingly assumed by all Allied leaders that there could not be any German minorities in central or eastern Europe outside the postwar borders of Germany. The Germans in Poland as well as those in a restored Czechoslovakia and the other countries of southeast Europe would be transferred to Germany and replaced by other settlers. Those who had been in Czechoslovakia had shouted loud and long that they wanted to go "Heim ins Reich" (home into the Reich). They would now get their wish – though not in the way they had anticipated.[23]

The fourth – and in many ways perhaps most important – aspect of Stalin's view of the future of Soviet–Polish relations involves the anticipated domestic situation of the Poland that had been moved westward. The saving of a small number of Polish officers from the mass killing in 1940 has already been mentioned. They were to provide the nucleus of a new Communist, Polish military force that would fight alongside the Red Army. Those Poles recruited within the Soviet Union under the auspices of the Polish government-in-exile were allowed to leave with their families via Iran to join British forces in the Middle East. These soldiers ended up fighting in Italy, and in the meantime the situation of their home country changed dramatically. A new Polish Communist Party was organized to replace the one that Stalin had dissolved before the war. Its leadership was promised that the Soviet regime would break relations with the government-in-exile, something Stalin did in the spring of 1943, using as an excuse the response of that government to the discovery of the corpses of thousands of Polish officers at Katyn. What was called the "Union of Polish Patriots" became the Communist government of postwar Poland, installed first in Lublin and subsequently in Warsaw. To make certain that the government-in-exile in London could not play any role in postwar Poland, Stalin had the Red Army stop across the Vistula River from Warsaw during the

Polish uprising there in 1944. His preference was for the Germans to crush the uprising of elements loyal to the London Poles. Subsequently, his own forces, in a lengthy and bloody campaign, would destroy the remnants of the Armia Krajowa, the Polish underground army that had fought the Germans since 1939 and was loyal to the government-in-exile. And it would be to the newly created and established Communist regime in Poland that the territorial concessions regarding the Curzon Line and the massive transfer of formerly German territory would be made.[24]

As for the free elections that were to follow quickly upon Poland's liberation, these would not be held until 1988 – more than forty years later. While Poland, unlike the Baltic States, was not to be incorporated into the Soviet Union, it was to be ruled by a government installed by Moscow and dependent upon it, its military forces under the command of a Red Army marshal. In this way, Stalin would control his new Western border completely and weaken Germany, whatever happened to the industrial area in the Ruhr and Rhineland. The insistence on a Poland totally dominated by the Soviet Union has to be seen partly as a way of expanding Communism as an ideology, partly as a way of increasing the power of the Soviet state, and partly as a form of insurance on Stalin's part against the possibility of any German revival as rapid as that which had followed Germany's earlier defeat in 1918.

It is of great significance that the removal from Germany of its major area of agricultural surpluses and the driving of its inhabitants and those of the industrial centers of Silesia into the rest of the country would preclude adoption of the plan for Germany's future that Roosevelt and Churchill favored. That, however, is story best examined in the context of the Western leaders' views of the postwar world. Of perhaps even greater long-term significance was the extent to which Stalin's policy on the Polish issue damaged the relations of the Soviet Union with Britain and the United States. Since both London and Washington tried hard to make this point clear to Stalin at the time, he evidently preferred to sacrifice whatever chances there might have been of good relations with his wartime allies in the future to his policy toward Poland. The breach between the wartime allies was most obvious to the public in Britain and the United States when Stalin, in the face of insistent requests, refused to allow airplanes from bases in England and Italy to land at Soviet bases while aiding the rebels in Warsaw and when he in other ways showed his desire for the Germans to crush the Polish uprising. For the historian it is clear that whatever concessions Stalin might have been willing to make in regard to the future independence of Finland in order to satisfy the preferences of his allies, on the future of Poland there would be not the slightest shift to accommodate the preferences of the British and Americans – to say nothing about the preferences of the people of Poland.

Stalin's limited flexibility when it came to the future of Finland can be seen not only in his willingness to defer to the preference of Churchill and Roosevelt that the country remain independent but also in the negotiations with Finland for a separate peace in 1944. As Stalin had told the British and the Americans, he was prepared to exchange the Soviet base at Hangö for Petsamo. This proposal was included in the terms offered to the Finns in April 1944. The Finnish government turned down the Soviet peace terms at that time. After the Soviet summer offensive of that year broke the Finnish front and it was becoming increasingly obvious that Germany was rapidly losing the war, the Finns once again sought peace. This time the terms offered to them in September – which they felt obliged to accept – included both the cession of the Petsamo area and a Soviet base at Porkkala instead of Hangö.

There would be one other significant territorial change demanded by Stalin during the war in addition to the incorporation of the Baltic States, the boundary changes with Finland, Poland, and Romania, and the annexation of the northern half of East Prussia. The incorporation of much of eastern Poland into the Soviet Union automatically created at the southern end of the new boundary a common border with Czechoslovakia. Already in 1942 leaders of the Polish government-in-exile anticipated that this development and the Soviet reincorporation of northern Bucovina from Romania were likely to lead to a Soviet demand for the Carpatho-Ukraine from a reborn Czechoslovakia.[25] This is exactly what happened. The Czechoslovak government-in-exile was obliged to agree to the loss of its easternmost province at the end of the war.[26]

The Czechoslovak government probably gave in on this question for fear of even more extensive Soviet demands, such as the incorporation of Slovakia into the Soviet Union in a manner analogous to that of the Baltic States. From Stalin's point of view, it appears most likely that there were three factors that together led him to insist on taking this territory from an ally. In the first place, the newly acquired land was to be included in the Ukrainian SSR. The substantial Ukrainian population in the Carpatho-Ukraine was under no circumstances to be left outside the Soviet Union as a possible focus for Ukrainian separatist agitation. Second, the annexation of this area provided the Soviet Union with a common border with Hungary and thus placed it in a better position to exert pressure on that country (and invade it in 1956). And third, this pressure was implicitly augmented by the fact that the territory annexed included key passes through the Carpathian mountains and thus automatically placed the Red Army in a more favorable position toward southeast Europe as a whole.

During the war, most likely in its latter years, Stalin developed additional territorial ambitions that were for the most part not realized, but they do provide significant insights into the sort of postwar world he would have preferred to see. These expansionist hopes focused on Greece, Turkey, Iran, and Japan. Although he had called for the restoration of Greece to its prewar borders and agreed to its allocation to Great Britain in his spheres-of-influence agreement with Churchill, he requested a base at the port of Alexandroúpolis on the northern shore of the Aegean Sea. He expected Turkey to allow Soviet bases on the Straits and to cede the northeastern portion of the country to the adjacent Armenian and Georgian Soviet Socialist Republics. Following upon the joint British–Soviet occupation of Iran in August 1941, Stalin evidently entertained hopes of annexing the northwestern part of that country. The details of these aspirations for Soviet expansion cannot be reviewed here, as they were thwarted by American and British opposition, but the raising of the demands is of relevance to a survey of Stalin's hopes for the postwar situation.[27]

These demands for additional territory and bases indicate that Stalin looked to further expansion of Soviet control in two directions. On the one hand, there was the desire to control a direct route to the Mediterranean and to weaken any obstruction of that aim by Britain and Turkey. In addition, the territorial aspirations for parts of Turkey and Iran suggest a desire to increase the Soviet Union's role in the Middle East.

In East Asia, Stalin's expectations are only partly clear. He had been prepared to yield the special position of the Soviets in Manchuria to the Japanese and, as already mentioned, was willing for Japan to retain Manchuria in a compromise peace with China. With the signing of the Soviet–Japanese Neutrality Treaty of April 1941, he anticipated a period of friendship between the two countries.[28] During the fighting with Germany, he promised the Americans and British that the Soviet Union would enter the war against Japan after the defeat of that country. It was becoming obvious that Japan would be crushed, and Stalin's view of that country shifted toward an anticipated military confrontation. Now he expected that the Soviet Union would regain control of Port Arthur and Dairen as well as a special position in a Manchuria returned to Chinese control. On the mainland of Asia, Outer Mongolia was to be independent of China and, presumably, under Soviet control. Stalin further expected to have the Soviet Union play a major role in a postwar Korea freed of Japanese control.

As for the new borders that were to be drawn, the Soviet Union was to regain the Kurile Islands and the southern half of Sakhalin from Japan. Beyond this, there were more extensive ambitions, but these are in need of further research. In any occupation of Japan, the northern island of Hokkaidō – possibly along with the northern portion of Honshū – was to become a Soviet zone, but Stalin's ambitions appear to have extended beyond such a role. The seizure by Soviet forces of several small islands off the coast of Hokkaidō, their annexation, and the expulsion of the Japanese inhabitants from them point to further hopes on Stalin's part. It is this seizure of what had always been Japanese territory that has prevented the signing of a peace treaty between Russia and Japan; it is inconceivable that the islands were seized and annexed without Stalin's explicit authorization.[29] Perhaps Stalin hoped that the island of Hokkaidō could become a permanent part of the Soviet state, perhaps he had other ideas, but there is simply no accessible reliable evidence to decide this question.

The other major issue in East Asia that Stalin had to consider was the relationship of his country to the Chinese Nationalists under Chiang Kai-shek and the Communists under Mao Tse-tung. Material support for the Nationalist government in its fight against Japan had been reduced in the face of the urgencies created by the German invasion, but official relationships remained in spite of some friction. At the Yalta Conference, the concession to demands by the Soviet Union for a return to its prior special rights in Manchuria was, in effect, paid for by Stalin's commitment to exclusive recognition of the Nationalist regime. Neither this agreement nor the subsequent Soviet stripping of Manchurian industrial facilities endeared Stalin to the Chinese Communists. His recommendation that the Communists work with Chiang was also not well received.[30] As the situation in the Chinese civil war developed during the last stage of the Pacific War and the immediately following years, Stalin moved from advocating partition of the country to full alignment with Mao, but that is another story.

If Stalin's perception of the future of Japan remains shrouded in doubt, there are some very clear expressions of his about the future of Germany, though in this case also there were changing or conflicting preferences. It is clear that Stalin did not expect France to play any significant role in the future containment of revived Germany. He had nothing but contempt for that country because it had folded so quickly, and he considered its position as a major empire and world power at an end. And he had nothing favorable to say about Charles de Gaulle as a possible agent of French revival.[31] He would eventually agree reluctantly at the Yalta Conference to allowing a zone of occupation in Germany for France, but only as long as that zone was carved out of the parts of Germany assigned to Britain and the United States. The weakening and the restraining of Germany in the future would have to come about by other means.

The transfer of East Prussia and all German territory east of the Oder-Neisse line has already been mentioned. The loss of the industrial area of Silesia – including its coal mines – would certainly weaken Germany substantially. Stalin was agreeable to the demand but never completely convinced of the necessity for Germany's unconditional surrender.[32] He also went back and forth on the question of a permanent dismemberment of Germany, originally favoring it but dropping the concept as the Western Allies did so. He was, however, very clear on two points. First, Germany must be disarmed and controlled lest it regain strength and initiate another war in twenty years.[33] Like all others at the time, he was enormously impressed by Germany's rapid recovery from the defeat of 1918 and its willingness to try again. And again, like most others, he failed to attribute this to the strong, not weak, position that Germany had been left in by the peace settlement of 1919.[34] Second, he wanted substantial reparations to help rebuild the Soviet Union, which had been so terribly ravaged by the fighting and by the scorched-earth policies of both sides. This issue would work out very differently than Stalin anticipated, but the point that needs to be made is that during and immediately after the fighting he was prepared to make some concessions on other issues to obtain industrial facilities and other forms of reparation in kind from all the zones of occupation, including those of the Western powers.[35]

Shortly before the German surrender, a Soviet-sponsored group of German Communists and individuals aligned with them was flown to Berlin to provide the nucleus of a regime that would be subservient to Moscow and might influence events even outside the zone of occupation assigned to the Soviets. There is, however, still no solid evidence about Stalin's real long-term hopes for Germany, and it is by no means impossible that the incomplete planning for the occupation may reflect a policy of opportunism rather than one of clearly established and defined goals.[36] Stalin was undoubtedly concerned about the possibility that there might be a revival of Germany with British and American backing, but ironically it would be precisely his own policies that eventually produced such a development.[37]

A very significant instrument that Stalin saw as possibly serving as a mechanism to restrain Germany in the future was a new international organization. Since the Soviet Union had had the unique experience of being thrown out of the League of Nations, the whole idea of an international organization was one that Stalin approached with great caution. Several of the difficulties that would arise in the negotiations for the establishment of the United Nations Organization were probably the product of Soviet suspicions and concerns about facing a hostile majority in any international structure. Nevertheless, Stalin not only agreed to Soviet participation when, in October 1943, the three major allies met in Moscow in their first conference but also would subsequently make concessions to enable the project to go forward. In this process, of which some details will be recounted below, the primary concern of Stalin appears always to have been the potential role of any organization in coping with renewed German aggression.[38] Searching for the best way to deal with Germany, Stalin originally favored Churchill's concept of regional associations as primary and the worldwide organization as secondary, abandoning this view as the British came around to the American one, which reversed the priorities.[39]

The two demands raised by the Soviet delegation at the Dumbarton Oaks Conference in regard to the preparation of a preliminary draft of a UN Charter should be understood as reflections of

Soviet concern about facing a hostile majority. The call for each of the sixteen Soviet Socialist Republics to have a separate vote in the United Nations Assembly may have been in part a way to off-set the imagined control of the votes of the British dominions from London but reflects that concern only in part and was primarily design to assure the Soviet Union a substantial number of votes.[40] At the Yalta Conference, Stalin agreed to compromise substantially on this point, insisting on and obtaining separate membership only for the Ukrainian and Belorussian Republics.

Soviet insistence on a veto power by the great powers on all matters, including procedural issues, is also best understood as deriving from suspicion as a result of prior experience. It is worthy of note that both the American and British governments in the months between the Dumbarton Oaks and Yalta Conferences independently came to the conclusion that the participation of the Soviet Union in the international organization was so important that they were prepared, if necessary, to give in on this issue. It turned out that they did not have to, because Stalin agreed at Yalta to a compromise according to which veto power was restricted to substantive issues.[41] Both Churchill and Roosevelt were pleased not to have to make a concession that they had been willing to make if absolutely necessary. On the other hand, nothing that the Americans or the British could do would persuade the Soviet leader to join the International Labor Organization or the World Bank and the International Monetary Fund.[42] The Soviet leader's obstinacy in regard to the latter two international organizations is deserving of further research, assuming the relevant archival material exists and is eventually made accessible.

There was one other aspect of the planned international organization on which Stalin, with obvious reluctance, made a concession, in this case to President Roosevelt. As will be elucidated in more detail in Chapter 8, Roosevelt was very interested in having China recognized as a great power and as one at least theoretically on a par with the other three, the United States, Great Britain, and the Soviet Union. The Soviet leader, like Winston Churchill, thought this a ridiculous and unrealistic concept. But Roosevelt was insistent, and both other leaders decided to give way to his preference.[43]

It should be noted in this connection that Stalin did not expect any substantial postwar aid from the United States. While the leaders of the United States thought it probable that the Soviet Union, like Britain, would look for such assistance – and perhaps on a larger scale than Britain because of the enormous destruction of the war – Stalin clearly did not think along these lines. Unlike the British, Stalin did not raise the issue with the Americans during the war, only mentioning it to Ambassador Averell Harriman when the latter was leaving his post in January 1946.[44] Certainly Stalin's one lengthy discussion of his postwar economic and trade plans during the war was focused on trade (exports from the Soviet Union were to pay for imports) and on his desire for a large merchant marine and navy.[45] As already mentioned, Stalin was very interested in massive reparations in kind from Germany and also insisted on reparations in the peace made with Finland in 1944. Presumably under his instructions, the Soviets removed enormous quantities of industrial equipment from Manchuria in 1945, but the Soviet leader evidently expected to rebuild his country's economy on the basis of the areas under his control.

The reluctance of Stalin to ask for reconstruction assistance from the United States should probably be seen in the context of his view of postwar relations with the United States and Great Britain in general. The available evidence suggests a high level of suspicion combined with an assumption of hostility. As he explained to the Comintern leader Georgi Dimitrov in January 1945, the Soviet Union was then allied with the "democratic faction of capitalists" but in the future would be opposed to them also.[46] Already during the war, Stalin clearly suspected that the British might very well consider doing what he himself repeatedly thought about, namely, working out a compromise peace with Germany.[47] It was certainly in connection with this suspicion that he was always concerned about the possible implications of Rudolf Hess's flight to Britain in May 1941 and his imprisonment by the British thereafter – and that after the war the Soviet government insisted that if Hess was not to be executed, he not be released from prison until his death.

Stalin's expectation of postwar enmity between the Soviet Union and Great Britain is also the explanation for the change in his policy on the subject of the establishment of a Jewish state in Palestine. Until some time in 1944, most likely the summer of that year, Soviet policy had always opposed Zionism whether inside or outside the Soviet Union. Beginning in that summer, a new policy emerged. Within the Soviet Union, Zionist activity continued to be banned, and soon after there was a systematic assault on Jewish cultural and other institutions. But at the same time, in international affairs the Soviet government began to favor a Jewish state in the British mandate of Palestine. It also allowed the emigration of Jews from areas under Soviet control in the expectation that these Jews would find a way to get into Palestine legally or illegally. It was the expectation of Stalin that the agitation for and eventual formation of a Jewish state in Palestine would serve to undermine Great Britain's position in the Middle East. Not long after the establishment of the state of Israel, Stalin's policy would again change, this time to extreme hostility, but at least for a critical few years the Soviet Union pursued a policy designed to strengthen the Jewish presence in Palestine and to assist in the creation of a Jewish state there in order to make trouble for the mandatory power.[48]

In other respects, Stalin had hoped to obtain British agreement to a division of Europe along the lines outlined to Eden in December 1941, with the Soviets in the east, the British in the west, and a reduced and controlled Germany and possibly some associations of smaller states in the middle. When, primarily in response to American objections, the British refused to go along with this and insisted on a straight alliance treaty instead, the Soviets proceeded to sign alliance treaties with several of the governments-in-exile and to develop their own government for postwar Poland. As the war on the Eastern Front turned more and more in favor of the Soviets, it became clear that the Red Army would decide what diplomacy had failed to accomplish. Under these circumstances, Stalin agreed with Churchill in October 1944 on a spheres-of-influence agreement that to all intents and purposes recognized a British claim to control of Greece in exchange for Soviet control of the rest of southeast Europe.[49] The peoples of that region would exchange German for Soviet domination. It is impossible to say which one turned out to be worse for them, but in any case the independence that they had attained in the years before 1939 was abruptly and brutally ended for decades by the war.

How did Stalin envision the future relationship between the Soviet Union and the United States? In the year preceding the German invasion of the Soviet Union, Stalin had shown an interest in joining the Tripartite Pact of Germany, Italy, and Japan.[50] This interest, which was not reciprocated by the Germans, who had already decided to attack their Soviet neighbor, is of relevance to the question of Soviet–American relations. Article III of the pact obligated the signatories to assist each other if a country not involved in the war in Europe or Asia attacked any one of them. Since Article V explicitly exempted the Soviet Union's relationship with the Tripartite Pact powers from the provisions of Article III, the threat of war implied by Article III was obviously directed against the United States and was so interpreted by all at the time. Stalin's repeated efforts to move forward negotiations for the Soviet Union to join, in the face of silence from Berlin, reflects a general hostility toward the United States. This would not be substantially and basically altered by the fact that the German invasion forced him into a temporary working partnership with the United States. Any comparison of the reports of German diplomatic and military representatives in the Soviet Union on their treatment during the years of the Nazi–Soviet Pact with the reports of American and British representatives in the Soviet Union during the years 1941–45 makes it obvious that Stalin preferred his former associate and instructed his underlings to behave accordingly. Although full evidence on the subject is not available and probably never will be, the broader perspectives of the Soviet leader are also reflected in the greater allocation of Soviet intelligence resources to spying on his wartime allies than on his wartime enemies.

Stalin's view of the United States was both uninformed and greatly influenced by his Marxist views. He was always suspicious of what in orthodox Marxist terms was called "reformism" – a label that fitted the New Deal generally and Roosevelt personally all too well. He was, therefore, most suspicious of Roosevelt's attempts at developing a good relationship, assumed that the president's anti-colonialism was simply a scheme to allow the United States to replace Britain as an imperial power, and expected that postwar relations with the United States would be strained and poor.[51] On some issues that did not appear essential to him, Stalin was prepared to make concessions to the American leader. The future independence of Finland and a nominal major power status for China in the United Nations Organization appear to belong in this category. But on issues he considered really important, no amount of blandishment could move the Soviet leader. Whether it was the question of leaving Lvov to Poland or joining the World Bank, no efforts by Washington or personal pleas by Roosevelt could budge Stalin.[52]

As for the development of atomic weapons, Stalin was well informed by Soviet espionage of the advances of the Western powers but did not move beyond committing laboratory resources to committing industrial resources until after – with his encouragement – the Americans had dropped the first A-bomb on Hiroshima. He was encouraged in this policy by the knowledge that the Germans were not making any substantial progress in this field.[53]

As Stalin looked to the future of his own country and the additional lands that were coming under Soviet control in east and southeast Europe, he certainly had some serious concerns in addition to his expectation of poor relations with Britain and the United States. The establishment of what he called "friendly" regimes in Poland, Hungary, Romania, Bulgaria, Czechoslovakia, Yugoslavia, Albania, and East Germany was certain to be a lengthy and difficult process. He well knew the hostility to Communism and the Soviet Union of the majority of the population in each of these countries. The result was that the Communist regimes imposed on these countries were all the more repressive, a fact that hardly made them less unpopular. Churchill's wartime belief that Poland would be spared the process of being made into a Communist state if it made the territorial concessions Stalin demanded was retroactively made dubious by the developments in Czechoslovakia, where the government had agreed to such demands. The evolution in Yugoslavia and Albania would take a form that Stalin certainly did not anticipate in 1945.

Inside the Soviet Union, there was the dramatically obvious problem of recovering from the devastation and human losses of war, a problem that certainly contributed to Stalin's insistence on reparations in kind from Germany and its satellites as well as the retention for labor of large numbers of prisoners of war. Extraordinarily but unconsciously like Hitler, Stalin had long before the war developed and even initiated gigantic schemes for the rebuilding of Moscow along lines that would befit it as the capital of the world socialist system. Like the Germania of Hitler's imagination, Moscow was to be the site of the world's largest assembly hall. If Hitler insisted that the bridge over the river Elbe at Hamburg was to have more square feet of surface than the Golden Gate Bridge in San Francisco, Stalin approved a project that would make the statue of Lenin on the Palace of Soviets stand eight meters higher than the top of the Empire State Building in New York. Together with other buildings of equally monstrous proportions, the Palace of Soviets was to symbolize the triumph of the ideology to which Stalin was sincerely dedicated.[54]

There was, it must be noted, great concern on Stalin's part about the impressions gathered outside the Soviet Union by returning forced laborers deported by the Germans, by the returning Red Army prisoners who had survived mass death in German hands, and by Soviet soldiers who had seen parts of central Europe. Expectations of relaxation of rigid controls and a better future on the part of the population of the Soviet Union certainly presented a major challenge to Stalin.[55] Primarily at the insistence of a most remarkable individual female aviator, Marina Raskova, he had been persuaded to authorize women in combat air force formations; but in spite of their part in the Soviet war effort, not to mention the hundreds of thousands of women who worked in arms factories, fought and died in the Red Army, and in other ways contributed to victory, the return to a male-dominated social system was entirely in accord with Stalin's preference.[56]

In the face of these challenges, Stalin had some very great advantages. His leadership of the country in a terrible war had ended in spectacular victory, great territorial gains, and an internationally recognized great power status for the country. The horrendous conduct of the Germans had made Stalin appear a benign ruler by comparison – surely an extraordinary accomplishment and one retroactively emphasized by the real tears shed by so many in the country when Stalin died in 1953. For the first and only time in its history, the Communist regime had not only admirers outside the country but also the willing if not enthusiastic support of the vast majority of its own population. What Stalin, his assistants, and his successors would do with the legitimacy that the successful defense of the country had provided them would be a long and sad story.

6. Winston Churchill

Prime Minister Winston Churchill walks with a guard and members of the Anglican clergy through the ruins of Coventry Cathedral, which was bombed by the Germans in November 1940. Library of Congress, Prints and Photographs Division, LC-USZ62-16191.

U NLIKE THE LEADERS DISCUSSED IN THE PRECEDING CHAP-
ters, Churchill had not been the head of his government
when Britain entered the world war. Born in 1874 into the British
upper class, he had first served in the Liberal cabinet that had initiated Britain's move toward an early version of the welfare state, had
lost his position at the head of the Admiralty because of his association with the British failure to open the passage into the Black
Sea at Gallipoli, and had subsequently shifted to the Conservative
Party. As chancellor of the exchequer in the 1920s, Churchill had
ironically played an important role in the establishment of fiscal procedures that contributed to Britain's disarmament. Breaking with
the Conservative Party on the issue of India – to be reviewed subsequently – he had isolated himself further by his support of King
Edward VIII in the abdication crisis of 1936. It had been this self-
created isolation that had detracted from the impact of his calls for
rearmament in the crises created by Hitler's Germany.

Churchill was called by Prime Minister Neville Chamberlain to
join the government as First Lord of the Admiralty when Britain
declared war on Germany in September 1939. It was from this office
that he moved to the position of prime minister in May 1940. Both

of the major political parties, the Conservatives and the Labor Party, would have preferred Lord Halifax to assume the position at that time, but he made it clear that he did not think that in a war crisis the country could be led from the House of Lords. The reason for Labor's preference is related to the issue of home rule for India, the issue over which Churchill had gone into the political wilderness in the 1930s and to which there will be occasion to return in the discussion of Churchill's views on the postwar world.

During his term in the cabinet, from September 1939 to May 1940, Churchill had devoted himself to the current problems of the navy and had also from time to time involved himself in other military and diplomatic issues of current interest to him in the conduct of the war. He had not been involved in any detailed discussion of or planning for the postwar world. This does not mean, however, that he did not have general views on the subject. It will be easier to understand the evolution of Churchill's vision of the postwar world during his years as wartime prime minister if those broader perspectives with which he entered the highest office are reviewed first.

Almost immediately upon his assumption of the office of prime minister, Churchill was confronted with military disasters even greater than the German victory in Norway that had catapulted him to the top. The crushing and rapid defeat of France, evident by the third week of May, appears to have temporarily suggested to him the possibility of a peace with Germany if that country would settle for a return of its pre–World War I colonies and a predominant role in central Europe, but there was really no likelihood that Hitler would agree to anything like that.[1] By the last days of May and the first days of June, Churchill was clear in his own mind that Britain would have to fight on until victory was attained. He was strengthened in this conviction by the successful evacuation of the bulk of the British Expeditionary Force from Dunkirk, the support of the cabinet, and a hardening of British public opinion, which rallied to his determined and eloquent leadership.

Whatever defeats British arms suffered thereafter – and there would be many of them – Churchill never wavered on this issue. As shown by the secret shipment of the country's gold and foreign exchange and securities reserves to Canada in the summer of 1940 as well as preparations for guerilla warfare in the British Isles if occupied by Germany, he meant to continue fighting even if the home country fell to a German invasion. Stalin's projection onto the government in London of his own interest in a separate peace with Germany never had any basis in reality, for the government under Churchill's leadership looked only to a victory over the Axis. But what about the world after that victory had been attained?

Although Churchill did not develop precise ideas about the future of Germany for some time during the war, he had a clear opinion on one point when he became prime minister. His experience in the cabinet in the winter of 1939–40 and the spring of 1940 had convinced him that Germany must be utterly crushed this time and that there could be no reliance on internal opponents of the Hitler regime. He knew of the feelers that those who claimed to be interested in overthrowing the Nazi system had extended during that period, and he realized that instead of carrying out a coup against Hitler, many of these very individuals had first planned and then led the invasions of five neutral countries. Whenever in subsequent years there seemed to be approaches of a similar kind, he always harked back to this experience and the failure of all British efforts to encourage the self-proclaimed plotters. If the latter actually carried out a coup against the Hitler regime, then one would see, but in the interim there would be silence from London.[2] Only a complete defeat of Germany would preclude a third German attempt at world domination and secure Britain from a German threat the way prior British victories had staved off the threats from Spain and France in earlier centuries. It was not for nothing that Churchill was descended from the first Duke of Marlborough and had devoted much of his time in the 1930s to writing a multivolume biography of the Duke who had played a central role in the defeat of the France of Louis XIV. It was, after all, in the palace at Blenheim, named for one of the Duke's great victories, that Churchill had been born.

During the soundings from real or imaginary German opponents of Hitler in the winter of 1939–40, the London government had made it absolutely clear that any peace settlement must restore independence to Czechoslovakia and to Poland, although there had been no precision as to their boundaries. Now that the Germans had overrun an additional six countries, it was always Churchill's view that their independence also had to be restored. It was as obvious to Churchill that there could be no peace in Europe unless the eight countries subjugated by Germany by the summer of 1940 regained independent status as it was obvious that only a total German defeat could lead to such a situation on the continent.

Although on this issue the evidence on his thoughts before becoming prime minister is not entirely clear, he was expressing his expectations about postwar Europe in such detail as early as August 1940 that they should be seen as a reflection of his thinking when assuming office. He looked forward to a Europe kept at peace by five great powers – Great Britain, France, Italy, Spain, and Prussia (sic) – who would work with three groups of smaller states in northern and central Europe and the Balkans. Britain would serve as intermediary to the New World; there would be a court to settle disputes, and there would also be an international air force to keep countries in line. There was no reference to the Soviet Union, which was then still allied with Germany, or to other parts of the globe. Churchill also held the opinion that there should be a fair distribution of raw materials and no vindictive settlement with the defeated.[3] On all these questions, Churchill's views would evolve during the following years, but this starting point will help in understanding those changes.

From his early years in India as well as his general view of the centrality of British control of India to the preservation of the British Empire, Churchill had been of the opinion that there could be no real relaxation of control there by London and by its representatives in Delhi. His views on this issue, expressed in a private letter in 1922, never changed.[4] They had been a key element in his break with the Conservative Party over its willingness to allow substantial change and, several years later, to pass the 1935 Government of India Act over his endless and vehement opposition in Parliament. These same views would dominate his perception of imperial and colonial issues through the whole war.

This was one point on which Churchill was absolutely set from the day he became prime minister and from which he never deviated the slightest bit. Great Britain would keep its empire intact, and no one, especially no American and no inhabitant of any of the colonies, was going to change that. As he explained in public in a speech in the House of Commons on November 10, 1942, "I have not become the King's First Minister in order to preside over the liquidation of the British Empire."[5] Not all members of the coalition cabinet over which Churchill presided agreed fully with him on the rejection of any outside interference or supervision, but he himself never wavered on this point.[6]

This objection to any infringement on the continuation of the British Empire had a number of implications for Churchill's policies and concepts during the war that need to be mentioned. As he made clear as soon as the point was raised, the call for people to be governed by rulers of their choice contained in the Atlantic Charter that he and President Franklin Roosevelt signed in August 1941 was certainly not to be applied to Britain's imperial possessions.[7] Furthermore, to preclude the establishment of unfortunate precedents, the same thing was to hold for the colonial possessions of other Allied powers like France, Belgium, and the Netherlands, who were all, in Churchill's view, to have their colonies restored to them if any had been occupied or seized by enemy forces during hostilities. All the European colonial empires were to emerge intact from the war. Especially in regard to the return of French Indo-China to France, this was to provide an additional point of friction with President Roosevelt, who, as will be discussed subsequently, was certain that the colony should under no circumstances be returned to French control.[8]

Still another aspect of Churchill's determination to maintain the imperial system was his preference for converting the mandates under League of Nations supervision that had been acquired from Germany and the Ottoman Empire after World War I into ordinary unsupervised colonies – just the opposite of Roosevelt's belief that all colonies should be converted into trusteeships, his term for the mandate system.[9] It was in part to provide a basis for the change Churchill wanted that he argued for the annexation of the formerly Japanese-controlled mandated islands in the Pacific by the United States – just as Roosevelt insisted that they become trusteeships and not be annexed.[10] There was one exception to Churchill's position on the mandates, and that was in regard to the possible future of Palestine and other mandates in the Middle East; this will be discussed below.

The fixation on the restoration of the British Empire would greatly influence Churchill's perception of how Britain should contribute to the war against Japan when victory over Germany finally was coming into sight. The British campaign to recover Malaya and Singapore for Britain while recovering the Dutch East Indies for Holland, which he insisted on despite the preference of most British military leaders for fighting alongside the Americans in the Pacific, has to be seen at least in part as a means of recovering from the terrible blow to Britain's prestige and military situation that the surrender of Singapore had been.[11]

It was, in fact, almost certainly in connection with the disaster to British arms and prestige caused by the rapid Japanese conquest of Malaya that Churchill wanted a small but strategically important *addition* of territory to British control. He wanted the Thai portion of the Kra Peninsula taken from Thailand and added to Malaya to provide a land connection between the British colonies of Malaya and Burma.[12] While in the context of the time this was no doubt a reaction to the failure to conduct operation "Matador," which had originally been designed to preclude a Japanese advance overland to Singapore by a British occupation of the Kra Peninsula, the whole concept of expanding the colonial empire by annexing part of Thailand shows the prime minister's thinking to be anchored firmly in the world of the previous turn of the century.[13] Although the concept of annexing part of Thailand to British Malaya was never raised at the end of the war, when Churchill had been driven from office, it is surely worth mentioning as a significant clue to the way in which Churchill saw the postwar world and Britain's role in it.

This was especially true of his view of the future of India. He had gone into the political wilderness in the 1930s rather than go along with the Conservative Party's support of further steps toward eventual dominion status for India. His lengthy and bitter fight against the 1935 Government of India Act both isolated him in British politics and revealed his implacable insistence on the maintenance of the older imperial system.[14] Nothing changed in this regard during the war. He distrusted the people of India.[15] He was not prepared to make substantial concessions to Indian demands during the war since he believed that the London government had already gone much too far in that direction before the war, and he resented the obviously opposite views of President Roosevelt on the subject. This was shown especially dramatically in the great crisis in India in the spring of 1942 as Japanese forces approached the border of India. He was simply not about to agree to substantial changes in the system of British control of the jewel in the British imperial crown.[16]

The fact that Chinese Nationalist leader Chiang Kai-shek advocated independence for India only increased Churchill's dislike for him and his disdain for Chinese aspirations.[17] He was not about to return Hong Kong before the time specified by treaty. There was in his mind some possibility of negotiations after the war in regard to the territory on the mainland of China that had been added to the original Hong Kong island colony, but he was adamant on the main issue.[18] He always thought Roosevelt's view of the future of China as a major power ridiculous. During the Cairo Conference, when Churchill met Chiang for the only time, he remained doubtful about China. Lord Moran, Churchill's personal physician, commented in his diary that while Roosevelt thought of the future importance of four hundred million Chinese, Churchill "thinks only of the color of their skin; it is when he talks of India and China that you remember he is a Victorian."[19] Long after the war, Moran commented again in his diary, "It would seem that he has scarcely moved an inch from his attitude towards China since the day of the Boxer Rebellion [of 1899–1901]."[20] There is an extraordinary discrepancy between Churchill's antiquated view of imperial and racial questions, on the one hand, and his steady and acute interest in the latest developments in weapons development and scientific research, on the other.

While Churchill had little but disdain, heavily tinted with racial preconceptions, for the Chinese and their leader, he held entirely different views of Britain's other major allies. Whatever periodic differences on specific questions he had with President Roosevelt, there was never any doubt in his mind of the importance of good Anglo–American relations during and after the war for the future of both countries and for the peace of the world.[21] He may well have placed more emphasis on sentimental attachments between the two countries than the facts warranted, but his view of the postwar world always included a major role for the United States in close alignment with the United Kingdom. If there was any concern about the long-term policy of Washington, it was more about the possibility of an American relapse into isolationism, as occurred after World War I, than over any excess of American worldwide ambitions.[22] As already indicated, there were plenty of specific issues on which the two leaders differed greatly, but none of these reduced Churchill's interest in cooperation with the United States during the war or in the postwar world.[23]

In regard to future relations with the Soviet Union, Churchill's view might best be described as one of hope tempered by doubt. He

was entirely aware of the importance of the Soviet role in defeating
the Axis and directed that all possible efforts be made to assist the
ally that the Germans had forced to Britain's side.[24] Although Stalin
always grumbled that Britain was not doing enough to send direct
aid and to open a second front in the West, Churchill pushed for
the delivery of as much aid as possible and, whatever his hesitations
about a cross-channel invasion, was absolutely committed to a max-
imum military effort. And when Stalin complained too vehemently,
Churchill could always – and did occasionally – remind the Soviet
leader that it had been his policy of helping the Germans to drive
the Allies off the European continent in the North, West, and South
that had placed his country in the unenviable situation of having to
fight them very much by itself in the East. In addition to Churchill's
basic opposition to Communism as an ideology and dictatorship as
a form of government, there were two further factors that impinged
on his formulation of policy toward the Soviet Union in regard to
postwar relations.

In the first place, the British prime minister was very much aware
of the fact that Britain's military power was stretched to the limit
and its economic position in the alliance sustainable only because
of American aid. His willingness to make extensive concession to
Stalin's policies was influenced by his recognition of his country's
waning power: the sooner concessions were made and arrangements
worked out, the more favorable these would be compared with what
might be attainable later. As a result of this perception, he would repeatedly run directly counter to Roosevelt, who saw his own country steadily growing in strength and was therefore of the opinion
that postponing issues was preferable because then the United States
would be in a stronger bargaining position.

Two issues on which the contemporary evidence on the positions of the two leaders is quite explicit may serve to clarify the situation. When attempting to work out a rapprochement with Moscow in the hope of weaning the Soviet Union away from Germany in the fall of 1940, Churchill had been willing to recognize the Soviet annexation of the Baltic States. He was held back from such a step only by vigorous objections from Washington. In 1941–42, in the negotiations for a formal Anglo–Soviet alliance, the same issue arose. Again it was Roosevelt's objections that held the British government back from *de jure* recognition of the annexation of the three Baltic States.

A somewhat similar difference involved the division of Germany into occupation zones. Roosevelt had made clear his preference for the western and eastern zones to meet in Berlin. Afraid that the Red Army would halt at the Soviet Union's June 1941 border and invite the Western powers to complete the defeat of Germany essentially by themselves, the British drew up a zonal division map that placed Berlin deep inside the Soviet zone of occupation. In this case, by getting the Soviets to accept their line – which became the border between West and East Germany – the British were able to have it their way, with the two powers jointly persuading the Americans to accept their map.[25] Ironically, Churchill was coming around to Roosevelt's view of the preferred borders in the spring of 1945, and his disillusionment with Stalin induced him to argue in vain for American troops to remain deep inside the zone allocated to the Soviets, hoping to use this as a means of exerting pressure on Stalin.[26] By that time there was no chance of American agreement, even though the issue fell to Truman rather than Roosevelt to decide. The relevant agreements on zones had already been signed, and the United States was eager for the participation of the Soviets in the escalating fighting against Japan.

There was, however, in the second place, never any doubt in Churchill's mind that the Soviet Union would play a major role in the postwar world and that it was in Britain's interest to try to make the relationship between the two countries as smooth as possible. His interest in a system of spheres of influence clearly dividing Europe, to be discussed subsequently, has to be seen as motivated by his desire to reduce friction and competition between the two countries. Similarly, his willingness to make a major concession to the Soviet point of view in regard to the great power veto in the United Nations Organization, also to be reviewed later, has to be seen as a sign of the importance Churchill attached to the participation of the Soviet Union in the new international structure.

The other ally figuring significantly in Churchill's perception of the postwar world was France. He had been shocked by the collapse of France in 1940, but he could never envision a future situation in Europe in which a revived France did not play a major role. His original sponsorship of Charles de Gaulle has to be seen in this context. Whatever frictions subsequently developed between Churchill and the Free French leader, who did his best, or worst, to demonstrate his independence by being as difficult as humanly possible, the British prime minister always looked forward to a renewed major role for France.[27] Far from coveting pieces of the French colonial empire, as some French officials imagined, Churchill strongly favored the full revival of France's colonial role, a point especially obvious in his arguments with Roosevelt over this very issue. It is true that there was endless friction between the British and Free French over the mandate of Syria, but its inclusion in the British Empire was never an aim of Churchill.

The interest of Churchill in a major role for France in the postwar world was particularly obvious in his consistent advocacy of a zone of occupation for France in Germany. Perhaps influenced by the experience of America's 1923 withdrawal from its zone of occupation in Germany after World War I, not only did he want France to have a zone this time, but he also wanted it adjacent, at least in part, to the American zone so that French forces could take over this zone if the Americans withdrew again. It would take a lot of persuasion by him and by members of the American delegation to the Yalta Conference to secure Roosevelt's agreement to a French zone of occupation in Germany, but the very insistence of the British on this point is indicative of the importance they attached to it.

Not surprisingly, Churchill thought a lot about the postwar future of Germany. Like all his contemporaries, he was very much influenced by the fact that Germany had made such a rapid military recovery after World War I and had insisted on initiating another great conflict so soon after the horrors of the last one. His refusal to consider a compromise peace with the Hitler government and his unwillingness to deal with internal opponents of the Nazi regime unless they struck against that regime first on their own have already been mentioned. But what form did he think Germany's defeat should take, and what did he think ought to be done with Germany after its defeat? Churchill gave considerable attention to both of these questions and developed his own answers to them.

In cabinet deliberations, Churchill was always clear on the subject of Germany's defeat. There would be no repetition of the armistice arrangement that had ended World War I. If Germany were to be reoriented for readmission to the society of civilized nations after its descent into barbarism, then complete defeat and occupation would be necessary. Although he did not use the term "unconditional surrender" before the January 1943 Casablanca Conference, that was always implicit in the policy he advocated.[28] When the words "unconditional surrender" were to be used publicly at his meeting with Roosevelt at Casablanca to reassure domestic opinion after the arrangement made with Admiral Darlan for the surrender of French Northwest Africa and to reassure Stalin when it became obvious that there could not be a cross-Channel invasion in 1943, Churchill obtained the agreement of the London cabinet to the use of the term. He would have been prepared to exclude Italy from the application of this policy, but the cabinet insisted on its application to all the Axis powers.[29] Whenever questions arose thereafter about any modifications or detailed explications, Churchill was always against such action. Not unreasonably, he pointed out that an occupation of the whole country and permanent removal of large portions of its pre-1937 territory were unlikely to make surrender more attractive to the Germans.[30] It is worth noting in this connection, since it is generally overlooked in discussions of the "unconditional surrender" policy, that all internal German attempts to overthrow the Hitler government came *after* the public announcement of that policy and that none had occurred in the ten years of Nazi rule preceding the deliberately staged public call for such an end to hostilities.

Although Churchill did not want Germany to be some kind of pariah nation into the indefinite future, he wanted the strictest controls imposed on it. He repeatedly voiced his belief that Prussia and the south German states should be in separate nations in the future, but his general perspective is best summed up in his own repeatedly utilized phraseology: Germany should be "fat but impotent."[31] It was this view – that Germany should be able to provide its people with a relatively high standard of living but be unable to threaten its neighbors – that led him to support the proposal of United States Secretary of the Treasury Henry Morgenthau for the removal of heavy industry from Germany and a shift to agriculture so that the country would resemble Holland and Denmark, other European states that had had a high standard of living before the war but had achieved this status without any heavy industry. And it was this view that led him to accentuate the deindustrialization phrases in Morgenthau's proposal when it was submitted to him and Roosevelt at the Quebec Conference in 1944.[32]

There can be no doubt that Churchill's preference was along these lines, and he held to it for months.[33] What led him – like Roosevelt – to abandon the concept was that it was too soft on the Germans, not too hard, as asserted by those who failed to look at the map, which showed the majority of the land in the East between the 1939 and the 1945 borders left to Germany. Germany could be shifted toward a more agrarian-based economy only if it retained the bulk of its eastern agrarian lands; if these were detached from it and their population transferred to the remainder of the country, such a project would become impossible. The evolution of British policy toward an acceptance of the detachment from Germany of its eastern lands and the removal of their German population has to be understood in the context of British policy toward the Soviet Union and Poland, a subject that will be discussed next. It was clear to Churchill and others in London at the time that one could either try to shift some five million Germans from industry to agriculture or take vast agricultural lands away from Germany and move an additional five million or more Germans out of them into the remainder, but one could not do both.

To understand the attitude of Churchill toward Germany's eastern border, one most distinguish between two aspects of this issue:

the future of East Prussia and Danzig, on the one hand, and the border between contiguous Germany and Poland, on the other. Whatever Churchill's reservations about making formal commitments to
postwar borders during the war, primarily because of his concern
about Roosevelt's opposition to a repetition of the World War I
"secret treaties," his perception of what was to be done about East
Prussia and Danzig was a product of the incredibly stupid German
propaganda of the interwar years. Germans had lived on both sides
of an area with a predominantly Polish population for some six or
seven centuries, and only in 1772 had they been territorially tied together by an East–West corridor created by Frederick the Great in
the First Partition of Poland. Nevertheless, German governments of
all varieties never ceased their loud complaints about the return to
Poland – by the peace treaty of 1919 – of much, though not all, of the
land taken by Prussia in 1772 and 1793. If Germans could not live
on the other (eastern) side of Polish area, they, not the Poles, would
have to move. Although it is hard to determine a date, very early in
the war Churchill and his government concluded that East Prussia
and Danzig would be turned over to Poland after the war and that
the Germans living in these territories would have to be resettled in
the rest of Germany.[34] It is unclear whether Churchill or Stalin or
Roosevelt came to this conclusion first, but their unanimity on the
position that these areas should under no circumstances remain part
of Germany must be regarded as the last great triumph of German
propaganda against the Treaty of Versailles.[35]

The issue of the border between Poland and the eastern parts
of contiguous Germany, that is, the issue whether the 1939 border should be changed, was in Churchill's eyes very much sub-
ordinated to the future *internal* situation of Poland and the relationship of Britain and Poland with the Soviet Union. Because of

Stalin's previously noted insistence on the 1941 western border of the Soviet Union, with only small adjustments in favor of a restored independent Poland, Churchill increasingly inclined toward a very substantial westward expansion of Poland at Germany's expense. Although long unwilling to commit Britain formally on border questions, primarily out of deference to Roosevelt, he indicated at the Teheran Conference and thereafter a growing willingness to agree to a massive shift of the German–Polish border. It was his hope that the cession of very substantial German territory to Poland might make the Polish government-in-exile in London more amenable to the cession of much of eastern Poland to the Soviet Union – as the latter demanded. This, in turn, would, in Churchill's eyes, make possible a resumption of relations between Moscow and the Polish government-in-exile and the eventual return of the latter to Poland. Thus he hoped to see a truly independent Poland between the Soviet Union and a smaller Germany as opposed to a Poland ruled by a Communist government controlled by and dependent upon the Soviets.[36]

It will never be known whether Churchill's expectations would have been realized if the London Poles had agreed to his views. This author is inclined to think that there was no such possibility in the face of Stalin's preference for a Communist regime in Warsaw and his numerous steps preparing for such an outcome. This analysis is reinforced by the fact that the yielding of territory by Czechoslovakia to the Soviet Union did not spare that country from the imposition of a Communist regime. But whether or not Churchill's hopes were realistic, the critical point is that both in the hope for a resolution along the lines he preferred and in the face of the reality that the Red Army would move through Poland, however defined, into the center of Germany, the British leader and his government came to accept the idea of a new border on the line of the Oder and Western Neisse Rivers. And beyond this, they came to accept both the transfer of all Germans out of the lands turned over the Poland and the cession to Poland of Stettin on the western side of the Oder River as "compensation" for the northern part of East Prussia, which, including the port of Königsberg, was allocated to the Soviet Union, with only the southern part being allocated to Poland.[37]

Although the context was somewhat different, Churchill and his government also agreed to the expulsion of more than three million people of German cultural background from a restored Czechoslovakia.[38] In eastern Europe, all territorial transfers were to be accompanied by population shifts. The Germans had objected vehemently to the 1919 attempt to adjust Europe's boundaries to the population and in World War II had substituted their preferred procedure of drawing boundaries and then moving the population to fit. Now that procedure would be applied to them.

To return to the question of the German–Polish border, it will now be obvious why in the winter of 1944–45 Churchill, like Roosevelt, abandoned the concept of reorienting Germany toward agriculture. With all of Silesia and much of Brandenburg and Pomerania to be turned over to Poland and over eleven million Germans to be driven from their homes into a substantially smaller Germany, the German population could either starve, be fed indefinitely at the cost of Allied taxpayers, or be allowed to earn its living by a controlled but slow industrial recovery. The British and American people would not tolerate either of the first two options, so it would be the third that would necessarily be pursued. Beyond his thoughts about separating Prussia from south Germany, Churchill went back and forth on the subject of dismembering the country. For a while he thought that dismemberment was compatible with the reparations that Stalin sought, but in the last months of the war he began to have doubts on this point.[39]

Churchill's doubts about reparations and the zonal division of Germany in the spring of 1945 must be seen in the context of his evolving perception of relations with the Soviet Union in general and Stalin in particular. As previously mentioned, he wanted all possible aid sent to the Soviets for their part in the fight against Germany and its allies. He hoped that Stalin could be persuaded to be more generous territorially toward Poland and that territorial concession to Poland at Germany's expense would promote a renewal of relations between Moscow and the Polish government-in-exile and also pave the way for the latter's return to Warsaw. Neither of these hopes was realized. He came to conclude, in spite of repeated disappointments, that he could establish a firm working relationship with Stalin during the war as a prelude to decent Anglo–Soviet relations in the postwar world. He was willing to work out a spheres-of-influence agreement with Stalin in the fall of 1943 and did so in 1944; and he was most pleased by Stalin's adherence to the portion of the agreement that allocated Greece to the British sphere.[40] In view of the great importance that Churchill attached to postwar British influence in Greece, this was a matter of special importance for his assessment of Stalin's intentions.[41]

Churchill continued to be hopeful in spite of the failure to reach an agreement on Poland. He was positively enthusiastic about the prospects for good relations immediately after the Yalta Conference.[42] Soon thereafter, however, he became more and more doubtful that Stalin would abide by the agreements made there and turned to the harsher line mentioned above. But in spite of this, he wanted to try to work with Stalin in the future, discouraged talk of a western European military alignment to counter the Soviets, and assumed that the terrible destruction suffered by the Soviet Union would keep it from making atomic weapons – weapons he had wanted kept secret from the Soviets – for three years after the end of the war.[43] There is good evidence that Churchill remained hopeful about the future of Anglo–Soviet relations until the end of his administration in July 1945.[44]

Churchill had clear ideas about other specific issues with implications for the postwar world. He was certain that Emperor Haile Selassie would again rule an independent Abyssinia (Ethiopia) liberated by British armies from Italian control.[45] In Europe, Austria would again be an independent state in its 1938 borders. It would thereby serve as a barrier to future German expansion into southeast Europe and might become a member of some type of confederation of smaller states.[46] It was his hope that Britain would be in a position to exert some influence on postwar Italy, and he favored a monarchy for it as well as other countries as a barrier against the establishment of dictatorships.[47]

Churchill was an early supporter of the concept of punishing Nazi war criminals once information on atrocities reached him from open sources and the decodes of intercepted German radio communications.[48] He was, however, opposed to an international tribunal and preferred punishment by execution for those who would be publicly listed as war criminals. This position was long shared by the cabinet in London and only abandoned in the spring of 1945 in the face of American insistence on trials, seconded by the Soviet and French governments. Graciously giving way on the issue, the Churchill government then invited its major allies to a conference in London to draw up the charter for what came to be the international tribunal at Nürnberg.[49]

In accordance with his generally sympathetic attitude toward the aspirations of the Zionists, Churchill favored the establishment of a Jewish national home in the British mandate of Palestine. He appears to have been favorably impressed by the so-called Philby Plan, which proposed the creation of an independent Jewish state in a confederation of independent Arab states led by Ibn Saud of Saudi Arabia. Such a project, from Churchill's point of view, would accommodate the hopes of the Zionists and provide a refuge for surviving Jews from Europe, make that unit dependent on British military support, secure the northern approach to the Suez Canal, and create a broader Arab confederation that would be under British influence. As it became obvious that Ibn Saud was not prepared to play the role this plan assigned to him, Churchill turned back to the concept of partitioning the Palestine mandate into Jewish and Arab states, with some specific places remaining under British control, a concept that had been put forward by the Peel Commission in 1937. Churchill was, however, in favor of allocating a larger share of the mandate to the Jewish state. He wanted the Jewish state to include the Negev in the south, and he considered the possibility of some kind of additional extensions of land for Jewish settlement to be attached to the Jewish state by taking a portion of the former Italian colonies. He dropped all such ideas upon the assassination of his good friend and colleague Lord Moyne, the British minister resident in Cairo, by Jewish extremists in November 1944. His support of Zionist hopes against the steady and vehement opposition of British military, colonial, and diplomatic circles ended at that time.[50]

On the broader issues of Europe's postwar organization, Churchill had some general ideas that changed somewhat during the war. Early in his term as prime minister, he was still something of an admirer of the League of Nations. Then he envisioned a United States of Europe, with Britain as the link to the New World.[51] As already mentioned, he envisioned a collaboration of major European states, favored Germany dividing into at least two countries, and foresaw some sort of international air force to maintain the peace. He did not warm to Roosevelt's view that four major world powers should act as the globe's policemen, in part because this elevated Russia and China to positions he preferred they not hold. With a vision that remained Eurocentric, he also thought of confederations of smaller European states. Increasingly he came to believe in some form of a united Europe in which Britain would protect the smaller members of the union, especially against any revival of German aggression. At all times during the war, however, he was opposed to the drawing up of detailed plans for any new structures to be created after victory.[52]

On the general issue of a postwar international organization, Churchill long held to the opinion that the primary focus should be on the formation of a regional council of Europe, a council of Asia, and any other such regional councils as might be desired. The United States was to be associated with the European regional council, something Roosevelt was determined to prevent, as it would reawaken the opposition to direct involvement in European affairs that had played such a large role in the American rejection of the League of Nations. For Churchill, some international association drawing together the various regional councils was really an afterthought and not of particular importance. Since this was the exact opposite of Roosevelt's concept of a truly international United Nations Organization within which there might be regional associations if that were desired, Churchill slowly came around to the

American concept and agreed to the outline for such a structure as developed at the Dumbarton Oaks Conference in 1944.[53] While Churchill favored the idea of an international air force, Roosevelt opposed that idea and again had his way.[54]

On the topic of membership in the new international structure, Churchill decided that India must have its own representation, as it had had in the League, and for this reason he supported the Soviet insistence on at least some of the Soviet Socialist Republics having their own separate memberships.[55] As already mentioned, he wanted the system of mandates established after World War I abolished in favor of outright colonial possession. Churchill was, therefore, initially opposed to the concept of trusteeships and a Trusteeship Council, but eventually he gave way on the issue rather than break with the Americans and refuse to ratify the charter of the UNO, which included a Trusteeship Council.[56]

What about the future domestic development of the United Kingdom itself? Devoted as he was to the great past of the British Empire and its capital, Churchill certainly wanted and expected the major buildings damaged during the war to be restored to their former glory, but there is no evidence for concepts going beyond the obviously needed repairs. Churchill was initially opposed to wartime discussion of postwar social reform for fear of breaking up the coalition of the major parties that had been formed under his leadership and that he wanted to hold together until victory had been secured.[57] In part as a reflection of his own role as a Liberal earlier in the century, in part because of domestic pressures, Churchill changed his perspective on the broader question of postwar planning. He came to argue for a new election when the fighting ended so that a new government – which he expected to lead but in the event did not – could adopt measures to widen opportunities, ensure full employment, and generally expand the system of social insurance that he had himself helped inaugurate at the beginning of the century.[58] The government that replaced Churchill's after the election of July 1945 would depart radically from his view on both colonialism and a national home for Jews in Palestine, but on the issue of domestic policy it would go far beyond any concepts of reform and social insurance that he had ever envisioned.

7. Charles de Gaulle

General de Gaulle, accompanied by General Mast, saluting as the band plays Marseillaise outside the summer palace of the bey of Tunis, Carthage, Tunisia (June 1943). Library of Congress, Prints and Photographs Division, LC-USW3-036299-E.

HOWEVER HIGH HIS HOPES AND AMBITIONS BEFORE WORLD
War II, it is highly unlikely that the thought of being the personal leader of France was central to the thinking of the French general who came to symbolize French resistance to Germany. Born in 1890 to a middle-class family in northern France, Charles de Gaulle early aspired to a military career. He began as a private, then went to the special and prestigious military academy of Saint-Cyr. He served in World War I and spent time as a prisoner of war in Germany. In the interwar years, de Gaulle moved up in rank and also became an advocate of a way of using armor that differed from that favored by the French high command, namely, massed employment of tanks in independent units as opposed to their integration with the infantry as a form of support.

De Gaulle's refusal to accept the defeat in France in June 1940 as marking the total defeat of his country made him into the leader of what came to be called the Free French movement. The realities of the situation placed him in a position that depended on British military, political, and financial support, on the one hand, but that he certainly intended to assert as entirely independent, on the other. The result of this was that the British government, and especially

Winston Churchill, looked to him to revive a French military effort alongside the British effort while at the same time becoming increasingly exasperated by the calculated rudeness with which he insisted on going his own way.

Once the United States was drawn into the war, his relationship with that country and its president would be similar in many ways to his acerbic relations with the British and their prime minister. Although the rebuilding of a significant French army was absolutely dependent on equipment provided by the United States,[1] de Gaulle found innumerable ways to affront the American government, from annoying Secretary of State Cordell Hull in the uproar over the French islands of St. Pierre and Miquelon to an especially rude withdrawal of a prior agreement to meet President Roosevelt in Algiers after the Yalta Conference.[2]

Looking to the future, de Gaulle did indeed stress the significance of good relations and common policy toward Germany for France and Great Britain.[3] Nevertheless, after Germany attacked the Soviet Union, he considered himself and his movement less dependent on Great Britain now that there was a new major ally.[4] As he explained in his memoirs, he actually felt closer to the Soviets than to his other allies.[5] Since this was certainly not a reflection of any ideological affinity for the Soviet regime, it must be seen as something of a return to the Franco–Russian alignment of the years before and during World War I. In October 1943, he explained to the American ambassador to the Soviet Union, Averell Harriman, that after the war France and the Soviet Union would be the major European powers since neither could depend on Britain or the United States. His belief that both of the latter would concentrate on their own affairs and ignore European developments was most likely shaped by his experience of the years between the two wars, somewhat the way his perception of future Franco–Soviet relations was influenced by prior events.[6]

The precise form that de Gaulle's view of the postwar world took during the war is difficult to explain because his wartime papers, unlike those of the pre- and postwar years, are closed to research.[7] On one subject at least the evidence is clear and overwhelming. De Gaulle was absolutely insistent that all French colonial possessions were to be returned in full sovereignty to France.[8] His own territorial base for much of World War II was made up primarily of those French colonies in West Africa that had rallied to his side in the summer of 1940. It is not unreasonable to assume that this very fact, in addition to his absolute belief in the past and future grandeur of France, influenced his thinking about the future of the country's colonial empire. In this context he was invariably insistent on the maintenance of French control of what was then called French Indo-China, which in his thinking presumably included the territories ceded to Thailand during the war.[9]

In spite of promises to the inhabitants of the French mandate of Syria in 1941, de Gaulle was determined not to allow that mandate assigned to France out of the ruins of the Ottoman Empire to become independent. He was concerned that Turkey, to which France had ceded a small portion of the mandate before the war, might want to acquire more of it – a suspicion that we now know to have been correct. Furthermore, he thought that the British had designs on the French mandates of Syria and Lebanon, a point on which he was undoubtedly wrong. The shelling of Damascus by French artillery *after* it had been liberated from Vichy French control and turned over to the Free French presumably disabused of their hopes any who at the time believed the prior promises of independence.[10] It should be noted that de Gaulle not only suspected British designs on

Syria but also on the French-controlled island of Madagascar in the Indian Ocean, again with no basis in reality.[11] In these and possibly other instances, de Gaulle revealed a suspicion of British colonial expansionist ambitions of a half century earlier that is eerily like Churchill's fixation on the same period, though Churchill had expansionist designs only on a piece of Thailand and no thought of taking over any part of the French colonial empire.

This fixation on the imperial past is also evident in de Gaulle's rejection of the Atlantic Charter of August 1941, with its renunciation of territorial expansion on the part of the signatories. Such a policy of returning to the territorial status quo of 1939 was unacceptable to de Gaulle, both in the colonial field and in Europe. In the colonial field, he clearly wanted to annex the southern portion of the Italian colony of Libya to French Equatorial Africa. In Europe, he expected to annex to France not only a piece of Italy and the Saar region from Germany but also much or all of the German territory on the left bank of the Rhine.[12] De Gaulle's view of the future of Germany will be examined further, but first something must be said about his territorial ambition with regard to Italy.

In view of the lack of relevant evidence, there is currently no way to tell whether the leader of the Free French expected to enlarge the French colonial empire at the expense of Italy's beyond a part of Libya, something that might theoretically have been possible in northeast Africa. There is, however, dramatic evidence as to his expectation of annexing a portion of northwest Italy to metropolitan France. De Gaulle's effort to seize and retain for France the Valle d'Aosta in 1945 brought on a confrontation with the new American President, Harry Truman, one that deteriorated into a dispute of unprecedented ferocity. In the face of Truman's threats, de Gaulle backed down, but his very insistence surely reflects a strong commitment to achieving territorial expansion at Italy's expense.[13]

Since the portion of Libya that de Gaulle hoped to annex contained only one oasis and was otherwise desert, of which France already held a vast amount in Africa, and the Valle d'Aosta consisted primarily of mountains and glaciers, of which France also already had a substantial quantity, there is an obvious question here. What was de Gaulle thinking when he was so insistent on these two hoped-for annexations? The answer to this must be speculative, but it looks to this historian as a sign of de Gaulle's mental world again being that of a prior era. If you won a war, you took land and colonies from the defeated, just as you expected to lose such territory if you lost a war. That in these two cases the areas that he expected France to acquire would contain nothing of substantial inherent value would be irrelevant in such a framework. The fact that they were adjacent to the French homeland in one case and to a French colony in the other sufficed. That the Americans and British stood in the way of such territorial expansion only deepened de Gaulle's dislike and disdain for them.

Since de Gaulle felt close to the Soviet Union, it should come as no surprise that, as he saw the future, there was no reason to object to the Soviet Union returning to its June 1941 borders. And because he accepted inclusion of eastern Poland in the Soviet Union, de Gaulle was prepared to see Poland expand westward at Germany's expense to whatever extent the Poles might want. He was interested in the revival of Poland's independence but beyond that appears to have had no interest whatever in the boundaries of the countries of eastern Europe.[14] The position the leader of the Free French took favoring the rearrangement of the prewar boundaries in eastern

Europe that Stalin wanted was undoubtedly linked to his expectation of Soviet support for his preferred rearrangement of the borders in western Europe. In the postwar years, de Gaulle would very substantially change, if not almost reverse, his wartime policy preference; here, however, it is his wartime views that must be examined.

During World War II, de Gaulle was certain that France must, above all, obtain security from any revived Germany in the future. He saw the menace of Germany as not restricted to the immediate situation, for he believed that the German people as a whole and not only the Nazis had adopted the wrong approach to the world after World War I.[15] In his eyes it was German militarism and not only Hitler that had to be eliminated.[16] As long as the Germans were in occupation of France and until there was a substantial Allied landing in France, he wanted the French population to avoid incidents with the occupation forces that would provoke massive reprisals by the Germans. He was pleased that the French Communists finally turned against the Germans in the wake of the German invasion of the Soviet Union, but he was not in accord with what he saw as premature attacks on Germans within the country.[17] Furthermore, when the British and Americans did stage the invasion in June 1944, the Free French leader made as many difficulties as possible for them because they had not consulted him beforehand, as he had expected. Once he saw himself hailed by the population of French territory liberated by the Allies, however, he looked to the implementation of his hopes for a future that would be entirely different from the arrangements that those same allies had insisted on, including those in the 1919 peace treaty that were against French preferences.

This time the main features of the peace settlement of 1919 as it affected the relations of France to Germany would be reversed.

That prior arrangement, with its continuation of a unified Germany and a Rhineland left to that country, had made it possible for the Germans to invade France for the third time in seventy years. In the future, there would be no unified Germany and there would not be a German Rhineland. The territory on the left bank of the Rhine would become a separate unit under French control. Whatever was left of German territory after the eastern portions had been turned over to Poland would not be one country. There might be a loose confederation of states, of which several in the southwest were expected to be under French influence. And the whole area would be under occupation first and under supervision later. There was to be a substantial part of residual Germany as the French zone of occupation as well as a French sector of Berlin. In subsequent years, the French would be able to play a significant – and generally obstreperous – role in the system of supervision that de Gaulle expected to be established. In this fashion, France could be made secure against any future German attempts to invade any of its neighbors or to dominate Europe, since there would be no Germany in the pre-1914 sense. Furthermore, French military forces would be at the least on the Rhine along its whole length and most likely further east.[18] As he came to recognize the interest of the Soviets in the Ruhr, especially in connection with the question of reparations, he shifted to advocacy of joint control of that important industrial area east of the Rhine by France, the Soviet Union, Great Britain, and the United States but in any case intended that it never again be part of united Germany.[19]

It should be noted that there was a difference of enormous significance between any changes in Germany's western borders as perceived by de Gaulle as well as Churchill and Roosevelt and those changes in the East envisioned by all the Allies. Although the contemporary documents are silent on the issue, it is simply assumed in all of the planning that the local population of any lands taken away from Germany in the West would remain where it was unless some individuals moved on their own initiative. The support of Churchill and Roosevelt for detaching the Saar area and placing it under some form of French control never implied a displacement of the local population. There is also nothing in de Gaulle's wartime and postwar comments to suggest that he thought differently on this question in regard to the Saar area or the very large additional lands he expected to detach from Germany in the West.

When Germany's eastern borders were under discussion, however, the assumption, sometimes implied and sometimes explicit, always was that any local population of German nationality or background would be moved out into whatever remained of Germany and would be replaced by others. It was this fundamental difference in the wartime perception of border changes and its implementation in the immediate postwar years that would make it possible for the Saar area to be returned to Germany a decade after the end of the war as French policy changed, while the parts of pre-1939 Germany in the East that came under Polish and Soviet administration in 1945 were almost completely denuded of their German population long before the new boundaries came to be recognized internationally as permanent.[20]

If one asks, what was to happen inside the French Empire and inside France after the war, there are at least some indications of de Gaulle's hopes and expectations. He was not prepared to break with his allies over the issue of extending the French empire into additional territory.[21] There was to be, on the other hand, no real change in the colonies remaining under or restored to French control. A special conference was called for by de Gaulle in the fall of 1943 and was held at Brazzaville in what was then French Equatorial Africa in January–February 1944. With the Free French leader present in person, it was made absolutely clear to all that there would be no evolution toward autonomy or self-government. No Africans were invited to participate. The prewar colonial system was to remain essentially unchanged.[22] Some of the African colonies and New Caledonia in the South Pacific had, in effect, been France in the years 1940, 1941, and much of 1942 in de Gaulle's eyes. They would continue to be parts of France into the indefinite future. It is perhaps worth noting that on this issue, like that of policy toward Germany, de Gaulle would change his views dramatically in the 1960s.

As a sidelight on de Gaulle's unshaken belief in the colonial rivalry with Britain, it should be noted that he provided shelter in France for the Grand Mufti of Jerusalem, who had spent much of the war in Germany. It had been the hope of the latter that German or Italian rule would displace the British in the mandate of Palestine and that they would kill all the Jews living there, as Hitler had personally promised him. The Mufti fled to France at the end of the war in the correct expectation that the French would provide him shelter from the extradition sought by the British. As the Mufti had also hoped, de Gaulle subsequently enabled him to escape.[23] While Stalin wanted to undermine Britain's position in the Middle East by shifting from opposition to support of a Jewish national home in Palestine, de Gaulle hoped to accomplish the same objective by assisting the extreme Arab nationalist element in the mandate. The possibility that such an action might undermine the French as well as the British position in the area – and especially in the mandates of Syria and Lebanon that he was determined to keep – does not appear to have occurred to the French leader.

What were de Gaulle's views about the internal situation in France itself? Fears were repeatedly expressed by de Gaulle's opponents among French exiles and by President Roosevelt during the war that he expected to establish himself as a dictator in the country. Even if these concerns were stimulated by de Gaulle's general personal demeanor, they do not appear to have been well founded. The available evidence suggests that there were two major aspects to de Gaulle's thinking about the domestic future of France. One was that the chief executive needed to have a more central and authoritative position in the government and that the political parties would continue to operate but be less influential. This view may well have been a product of his experiences in the French Third Republic of the 1930s, with its perpetually shifting cabinets. The other facet of his perception of the future was a recognition of the likelihood that social concerns would be of enormous importance and probably central to the political situation in the future, a position one might not expect from a military leader but on which he was surely correct.[24] De Gaulle was especially interested in establishing his own firm control of the country in the immediate aftermath of the fighting, partly to make certain that there would be no American–British military government. He was, therefore, prepared to leave in place a considerable proportion of the administrative and police apparatus that had been there before liberation, even if many of those in position had collaborated with the Germans during the occupation.

Unlike World War I, in which the physical devastation both from the fighting itself and from deliberate destruction by the Germans had been enormous, the damage from World War II was substantially less, even if considerable in some areas. Nothing

suggests that de Gaulle had any intention of going beyond the necessary reconstruction of damaged buildings and areas, and he was certainly not about to alter the appearance of the Paris he had reentered
to popular acclaim in August 1944. The grandeur of the French capital was already an established fact; the city needed no architectural
monstrosities of the sort Hitler, Mussolini, and Stalin had in mind
for their capitals.

If de Gaulle had specific views on a future international organization other than that France would play a major role in it, there is
no evidence to that effect. At the Conferences of Dumbarton Oaks
and San Francisco, the French delegations worked with the others without pushing for any special position other than that France
would again, as in the League of Nations, have a permanent seat on
the Council. Since this came to be assumed by the British, Americans, Soviets, and Chinese, there was no cause for concern here.
Whether de Gaulle, like Churchill, would have preferred for the
mandates that had been assigned to France after World War I to
be converted into colonies rather than become trusteeship territories is not known. As long as the areas involved remained under
full French control, the question does not appear to have received
much attention from de Gaulle. It needs to be kept in mind in this
connection that it was the French B Class mandate of Cameroon
that had been one of the very first portions of the French Empire
to declare for de Gaulle. Even if a contributing motive for this had
been the fear that the area might be returned to German control,
the important point is that it was in Africa that the Free French
movement had acquired its first real territorial base. The leader who
personified that movement was unlikely to forget that fact.

From the perspective of de Gaulle, the most important points
were that France was again free of German occupation and could

hope to assert its independent role in Europe and the world. A truncated, occupied, and hopefully disunited Germany could not threaten France in the forseeable future. The Soviet Union appeared to be a reliable ally on the other side of Europe. The colonial possessions of France had all been returned to control from Paris. In France itself, de Gaulle was the great hero, an ironic situation given even greater strength by the early postwar development of the myth that most of the people of France had been resisters all along and had only waited to acclaim the conquering liberator on his return to the country.

8. Franklin D. Roosevelt

President Franklin D. Roosevelt reviewing American troops, Casablanca, Morocco (January 1943). Library of Congress, Prints and Photographs Division, LC-USW33-027834-ZC.

F RANKLIN DELANO ROOSEVELT WAS BORN INTO A PATRICIAN
New York family in 1882. He entered politics as a Democratic
state senator in New York and became the second man in the Department of the Navy in the administration of President Woodrow
Wilson. After his defeat as the vice-presidential candidate of the
Democratic Party in the 1920 election, he suffered a serious polio
attack. While still recovering from that, he was elected governor of
New York, was reelected to a second term, and then won election
to the presidency in 1932. In 1936 he was reelected. In 1940, in
the world crisis resulting from Germany's great victories in western
Europe, Roosevelt created something like a coalition government
before being reelected to an unprecedented third term. It was during this third term that the country was thrust into the war by the
decisions of Japan, Germany, and Italy.

Any review of President Roosevelt's vision of the world after
World War II must begin with the way in which his experiences
in and after World War I affected his perspective. There will be repeated references in this chapter to aspects of the "lessons" he believed he had learned, but certain points have to be made clear at
the beginning. Unlike the majority of Americans, who had come to

believe by the late 1920s and early 1930s that it had been a mistake for the United States to enter what was then called the Great War, Roosevelt had been in favor of an earlier entrance and did not share the opinion that the United States should have stayed out altogether. He had also thought it a mistake to grant Germany an armistice in 1918 rather than fight on until Germany surrendered unconditionally, but on this issue, like the preceding one, he had kept quiet at the time as a loyal member of the administration of President Wilson.

He had been a supporter of the 1919 peace settlement, including the League of Nations, and had suffered his only electoral defeat when running for vice-president of the United States on the Democratic Party ticket in 1920. Not surprisingly, he believed that it was the American repudiation of the peace settlement and his political party that had contributed to the dangerous international situation that the country faced during his time as president.

It had been Roosevelt's hope that the United States could keep out of another war with Germany by assisting the Allies to defeat the Axis powers. That meant initially helping France and Britain and, from the summer of 1941, assisting Britain and the Soviet Union. He hoped that by lengthy negotiations, to which he devoted an enormous amount of his own time, the Japanese could be delayed from entering the wider war on Germany's side long enough to allow the authorities in Tokyo to see that Germany was likely to lose rather than win and was therefore not worth joining. This tactic came within two weeks of working, but the Japanese took the plunge before they could assimilate the lesson of German defeats on the Eastern Front and in North Africa in the last days of November and the first days of December 1941. With Germany and Italy hastening to go to war with the United States, the only remaining possibility was to restrain Germany's European satellites from joining in. For half a year the president had the State Department try to persuade the governments of Hungary, Romania, and Bulgaria to withdraw their declarations of war. Only in June 1942 did Roosevelt give up and ask the Congress to declare war also on these countries, which absolutely insisted on fighting the United States.

In the face of the determination of Japan, Germany, Italy, and their associates to go to war with the United States, Roosevelt was equally determined that this would be the last time that they did so. If this was not the most important objective of the president for the postwar world, it was certainly very high on his agenda and would stay there as long as he lived. The demand for the unconditional surrender of the Axis powers was designed to make certain that Americans would not have to fight Germany a third time and the other countries a second time. The evidence is clear that this was Roosevelt's view from December 1941 on.[1] The United Nations Declaration of January 1, 1942, issued from Washington, called for a "complete victory."[2] Though the words "unconditional surrender" were not used in this document, that was certainly implied.[3] The public proclamation of the demand for unconditional surrender did not come until the Casablanca Conference of January 1943. It was openly announced with great emphasis at that time for both domestic political and international diplomatic reasons, but the policy itself was the president's from December 1941.[4]

In Roosevelt's view, the failure to make such a demand in 1918 had contributed to the German arguments that they had not really been defeated and/or that they had stopped fighting on the basis of promises that had not subsequently been kept by the Allies. No one was going to make that kind of argument in the future as a way to persuade the Germans or Japanese that they might do better the next time. Roosevelt resisted all arguments supporting a modifica-tion of the unconditional surrender policy in subsequent years.[5] In a speech on August 25, 1943, at a time when the Allies had re-cently won great victories, Roosevelt reassured the peoples of the Axis about their fate after unconditional surrender but insisted that surrender would have to come first.[6]

Like Churchill and Stalin, the experience of Germany starting another world war so soon after its prior defeat left Roosevelt im-pressed with the danger that in another twenty years the Germans might try again. Such a contingency had to be prevented if at all possible. In Roosevelt's view, that meant surrender first and substan-tial precautions thereafter. Because of the descent into barbarism that accompanied Germany's insistence on another world war, only when major changes had been made in the thinking of Germany's population under strict supervision could any German state or states rejoin the civilized world.

What kinds of precautions did the president believe should be taken after Germany had surrendered and was occupied by the Allies? Roosevelt was not in favor of the preparation of extensive and detailed plans for the future of Germany. As he put it in a mem-orandum of October 20, 1944, "I dislike making detailed plans for a country which we do not yet occupy."[7] If this was his view the day before American troops seized Aachen, the first large German city occupied by the Allies, it obviously characterized his approach earlier in the war. That does not mean, however, that there were not a number of issues on which the president had quite definite ideas.

From an early date Roosevelt believed that substantial territory should be taken from Germany, especially in the East. The un-believably stupid German propaganda of the interwar years had convinced Roosevelt – as it had Churchill – that East Prussia was to be taken from Germany and turned over to Poland, most likely together with Danzig. He would subsequently agree to the partition of East Prussia between the Soviet Union and Poland, but there was under no circumstances to be a return to the situation of prior centuries, when Germans had lived on both sides of Poles. The Germans had declaimed endlessly against the Versailles concept of adjusting boundaries to people and had insisted instead on adjusting people to new boundaries. The Germans living in East Prussia would have this German principle applied to them. Furthermore, the president was agreeable to substantial but not precisely defined portions of German Silesia also to be assigned to Poland. While these territorial changes would come to play a role in Roosevelt's view of the future eastern as well as western borders of Poland, they must be seen in the first place as part of what he believed should happen to Germany.[8]

In addition to these external territorial changes, the president repeatedly considered a major internal territorial change: the "dismemberment" (as it was called) of Germany into several separate states. This project was discussed in Washington as well as London and Moscow during the war, only to be abandoned in theory but adopted in practice. No theoretical division of Germany into a set number of separate states was ever worked out and agreed upon either within any of the three major Allies or between them. Nevertheless, in practice the allocation of supreme power to the commanders-in-chief in each of the zones of occupation by the leaders of the Allies would actually make for a division of Germany, at first into four and then for decades into two states. Roosevelt had quite concrete ideas on this subject, and those ideas greatly influenced American strategy in the European war.

Starting in 1942, Roosevelt had stated his preference for American troops to enter Berlin first, and in 1943 he had sketched out a division of Germany into occupation zones, with the American and Soviet zones meeting at Berlin and with the British taking up a zone in the south.[9] Since the British government obtained Soviet agreement to a division that placed Berlin deep inside the Soviet zone, that foreclosed this particular issue, though Roosevelt argued from the fall of 1943 to the fall of 1944 for an American zone in the northwest rather than the south of Germany. This aspect of occupation zone allocation was eventually worked out in a new agreement,[10] and in early 1945 the president was persuaded to agree to an occupation zone for France carved out of the territory allotted to Britain and the United States.[11] This issue is reviewed below in connection with Roosevelt's views on the future of France. The critical point is that his belief in the need for an American presence in the center of Europe dovetailed with his and his advisors' insistence on an invasion of northwest Europe across the English Channel. This was both the best way to defeat Germany and simultaneously the way to ensure the United States a role in the postwar disposition of Germany and of European questions in general.

Whatever the external and internal boundaries of Germany after that country had surrendered unconditionally, there were also some internal changes that Roosevelt believed essential to keep the Germans from starting still another big conflict. Based in part on his views of Germany from the time before he became president, Roosevelt was certain that any future Germany should be allowed no aircraft, no uniforms, and no marching.[12] It was the president's concern about a future possible threat from Germany that led him, like Churchill, to agree with the concept of transforming

Germany into a country rather like Holland and Denmark, with a high standard of living but no heavy industry, as suggested by his Secretary of the Treasury and friend, Henry Morgenthau. Most of the literature on this subject has ignored the relevant maps and echoes the propaganda of Joseph Goebbels instead. A change of Germany in the direction of what Churchill called "fat but impotent" required the retention by Germany – whether in one state or several – of much of its eastern agricultural area. If, however, the whole territory east of the line of the Oder and Western Neisse Rivers was taken away and the Germans living there were pushed into the remainder of the country, such a project would become impossible. One could either try to shift some five million Germans from industry into agriculture *or* drive some additional six or seven million Germans out of their homes in the agriculturally important parts of the country into the remainder, but one could not do both.

In view of Stalin's insistence on the Oder–Western Neisse border, the Morgenthau plan had to be dropped as too soft on the Germans, not too hard as some still imagine.[13] This abandonment of Roosevelt's preference in the face of Soviet insistence did not mean that his view of Germany had fundamentally changed. His approval of harsh directives for the occupation in March 1945 shows that his view that the Germans should not starve but must accept the fact that they had been defeated and were responsible for their own sad situation had in no way changed.[14] The whole country would be occupied by the Allies. The unconditional surrender at the end of the fighting, this time signed by leaders of the German armed forces instead of civilians who could be blamed for defeatism by military figures afterwards, would come after Roosevelt's death. By that date the German surrender was obviously very near – and American troops were in the center of Germany and of Europe, as Roosevelt had wanted.

As for planning for the peace in general terms, Roosevelt wanted that done in the Department of State. This was quite different from President Wilson's establishment of an agency outside the State Department for the planning of the World War I peace treaties. Other agencies would be called on for membership and expertise, but the lead was to be taken by State.[15] The president had his own view on many subjects, but he wanted any detailed planning to be coordinated by a staff housed in the State Department, an approach that his secretary of state certainly appreciated. And this insistence very much affected his handling of the second subject he believed had not been handled properly at the end of World War I. This time the State Department would be very much involved in the planning of a new international organization.

If one mistake that Roosevelt believed had been made at the end of World War I was the failure to insist on Germany's unconditional surrender, another very big one, very much in his mind because of its link to his own 1920 candidacy, had been the American repudiation of the peace settlement and of the Democratic Party – the party identified with the settlement. Central to this was the issue of an international organization to preserve the peace. Whatever the merits and defects of the League of Nations, Roosevelt had no doubt that the refusal of the United States to participate in it had greatly reduced the chances for its success. A new international structure would be needed after World War II. The president was determined that such a structure should grow out of the alliance against the Axis along lines developed at State, that it should include the major powers, that the American public should become accustomed to the idea of playing an active role in it, and that such an organization should be supplemented by a series of specialized organizations that would assist both in their fields of activity and also contribute to more harmonious international relations. Although all four of these aims were interrelated in his mind and in their implementation during the war, it may be simplest to review his ideas about them and the steps he took toward their implementation one at a time.

At Roosevelt's meeting with Churchill at the Atlantic Conference of August 1941, the president still thought it best to postpone public discussion of a future world organization, presumably for fear of arousing too much opposition at home. As urged by Undersecretary of State Sumner Welles, he already looked toward a new structure but one that would depend on power rather than formal structure.[16] Very early, however, at least by the fall of 1941, Roosevelt was thinking of an association of the four major powers to keep the peace, a concept that he referred to as the "Four Policemen."[17] These four, in his thinking, always meant the United States, Great Britain, the Soviet Union, and China. The future role of France as seen by Roosevelt is discussed subsequently. A critical issue for examination in this context is the president's view of China as one of the great powers, a concept that others, especially Churchill, found extremely difficult to accept.

There is substantial contemporary evidence that the future role of China as a major world power was a significant element in Roosevelt's vision of the postwar world. Whether he really had long favored the end of extraterritorial rights by other powers in China, as he subsequently claimed,[18] he certainly saw to it that they ended during the war, as was explained in Chapter 4. Over and over Roosevelt insisted during the war that China, after a period of reconstruction, would play a major role in world affairs. He saw it as a future counterweight against any effort of the Soviet Union to dominate Asia once Japan's military power had been crushed. With the agreement of Hull, he wanted China associated with the October 1943 Moscow Declaration. He held to this general perspective in the face of strong objections from Churchill and the less vehement reluctance of Stalin.[19] As the new Australian Minister to Washington reported on the president's views after their first meeting in his diary, "He said that he had numerous discussions with Winston about China and that he felt that Winston was 40 years behind the times on China and he continually referred to the Chinese as 'Chinks' and 'Chinamen' and he felt that this was very dangerous. He (Roosevelt) wanted to keep China as a friend because in 40 or 50 years' time China might easily become a very powerful military nation."[20] Eventually both Churchill and Stalin would yield to Roosevelt's insistence on China's formal status, but more to please him than out of a change in conviction.[21]

Although the president was by no means prepared to specify details about a new international organization, he was happy to have originated its name and was willing to share his concept of the four policemen with both the British and the Soviets early in the war.[22] At some time in the early years of the war, he thought that no others should have armaments at all, but he dropped that idea. He was at all times opposed to Churchill's idea of giving primacy to a European council of some sort, with American participation, since he was certain that any such arrangement would again arouse the strongest opposition in the United States. There could be regional associations within the United Nations – and he always thought of the countries of the Western Hemisphere in this connection – but the main structure was to be an international one. He was influenced in this not only by the experience of 1919–20 but also by the advice of Sumner Welles, whose judgment the president respected.

Roosevelt was dubious about the concept of an international police force but believed that the new organization should be able to call on the major powers for armed forces.[23]

Before the Quebec Conference of August 1943, he agreed to Hull's draft of a four-power agreement for a new postwar organization, obtained Churchill's agreement there, and then sent Hull to Moscow in October to secure Stalin's assent.[24] It should, therefore, not be surprising that he returned to the subject when for the first time he met with Stalin at Teheran later that year.[25] The United States and the Soviet Union had both been absent from the League of Nations in its formative years; Roosevelt wanted to make sure that this situation would not be repeated. In addition to urging his allies to agree to a new organization for the postwar world, Roosevelt simultaneously worked to build up public support for such an organization in the United States, especially in the Senate, where the prior effort had failed. He was obviously extremely sensitive on this point and devoted considerable time and effort to make sure that there would be substantial support in the country long before the issue was likely to come to a vote.[26] In the winter of 1943–44, Roosevelt and his advisors discussed the details of the proposed new organization, and the president obviously was very much interested in these.[27] It may be seen as a sign of his concern that he paid such attention to the details in this case, for his usual practice was to leave the finer points to others. Micromanaging was simply not his style.

When the issue of the extent to which each of the major powers with a permanent seat on the Security Council of the planned new international organization could exercise a veto over procedural as well as substantive matters came to the fore at the Dumbarton Oaks Conference and in subsequent months, Roosevelt became very much involved in this question. Although he wanted the veto reserved for substantive matters so that no power could keep the Council from at least discussing an issue, both he and Churchill, independently of each other, came to a significant conclusion. Both were of the opinion that the participation of the Soviet Union, which insisted on a right to veto procedural matters, was so important to the successful establishment of the United Nations Organization and the future peace of the world that each went to the Yalta Conference prepared to yield on this issue to Stalin if necessary. At that meeting, Stalin came around to their point of view, and the fact that neither Churchill nor Roosevelt had been obliged to make the concession that they had been reluctantly willing to make has to be seen as one factor in their feeling of satisfaction with the conference in its immediate aftermath.[28]

One further issue that greatly interested Roosevelt was the need for speed in setting up the new organization. He was of the opinion that the delay in actually forming the League of Nations at the end of World War I had been a mistake.[29] The pressure from the United States for both the preliminary meeting at Dumbarton Oaks and the formal organizing meeting in San Francisco to take place already during hostilities has to be seen as a result of Roosevelt's concern over this question, even though he himself had died before the second of these meetings could be held. And again in order to avoid what he believed was a mistake made by President Wilson earlier, Roosevelt made sure that the American delegation to the San Francisco Conference included prominent Republican as well as Democratic Party members.

The United Nations Organization was by no means the only postwar structure in which Roosevelt was personally interested. Knowing in general terms of the destruction and suffering caused by the war, Roosevelt played a major role in the establishment of an international relief organization, what came to be called UNRRA, the United Nations Relief and Rehabilitation Administration. He was concerned that the task was so large that private charities, however helpful, simply could not be expected to cope, as had largely been true in World War I. On the other hand, he did not want the United States to carry the whole burden alone, however large its share might have to be. With these views, he played a major part in setting up UNRRA, had the basic instrument for it signed in the White House, and insisted on appointing his former lieutenant governor and successor as governor of New York, Herbert Lehman, as its first head, even before the end of the latter's current term of office as governor.[30]

Roosevelt clearly wanted the UNO to be supported in its work by a whole range of international functional organizations that would contribute to better international relations and thus help maintain the peace. He was interested in what came to be the Food and Agriculture Organization.[31] He wanted the United States to join the International Labor Organization and to assist in the development of other forms of international economic cooperation.[32] Having become president after years of economic turmoil in the world and during the Great Depression, Roosevelt was especially interested in the establishment of mechanisms to prevent the kind of economic warfare and dislocation that had preceded the war and, in his opinion, had contributed to its coming. It was in this context that he asked his personal friend and Secretary of the Treasury, Henry Morgenthau, to take the lead in the international negotiations that led up to the Bretton Woods Conference that established the World Bank and the International Monetary Fund.[33] Afraid that the dollar would replace sterling as the key international currency,

Churchill initially had doubts and delayed action but eventually came around.[34] The Soviets were doubtful about the whole project from the start and refused to join the new institutions in spite of every American effort to bring them around. Clearly Stalin wanted no part of what he appears to have thought was some capitalist plot – but his rejection of a project close to Roosevelt's heart also reduced the chances of any American consideration of assisting the Soviets with their massive task of postwar reconstruction.[35]

Another field in which Roosevelt had quite definite views about postwar developments was in the field of international air travel. He favored competition not only within each country but also on international routes. He foresaw a dramatic change in the way in which the great distances in the Pacific would effectively shrink with future technological developments in aviation. Furthermore, he was especially concerned about the rights of American airlines to fly international routes in essentially open competition with other countries' airlines. On this subject, there would be enormous difficulties with the British, who feared that American advances in air transport during the war would put their own airlines at a severe disadvantage in future competition. These issues were ironed out after very heated debates at the Civil Aviation Conference in Chicago in November–December 1944, with both Roosevelt and Churchill actively involved in instructing their delegations. The compromise reached satisfied neither side entirely, but the basis for the postwar world travel system was laid at that time – and the British would discover that they could operate quite successfully within it.[36]

If Roosevelt was as interested as the evidence shows in the creation of a new international organization to help maintain peace as well as a host of subsidiary international agencies to supplement and support the United Nations Organization, how did he see the future place of the United States in the world? There was never any doubt in his mind on two subjects. He was confident that the strength of the country would grow as it built up its military power during hostilities and that the possession of atomic weapons, whose development he personally pushed forcefully at all times, would provide an adequate margin of strength once the country demobilized its armed forces, as he correctly assumed that it would.[37] He was equally certain that the country should under no circumstances annex any territory. He had signed the legislation under which the Philippines were to become independent, and while the war initiated by Japan caused postponement of independence for the islands, Roosevelt never had the slightest doubt that independence would come as soon as possible. It was the other side of this fundamental anticolonialism attitude of Roosevelt that would lead to his greatest difference with Churchill. If the United States was not to acquire any colonies, what about the colonies of others?

Throughout the war Roosevelt held to the view that colonialism was, and most certainly should be, a fading institution. Whatever the problems and faults of the American occupation of the Philippines, he saw the process toward its independence not only as the correct path but also as something of a model for the colonial empires of others. Since the British empire was by far the largest, and India constituted its most populous element, he had no doubt that India should move toward independence and hoped that the crisis there in the spring of 1942, as the Japanese army approached India's border, would help the process along. He quickly discovered that Churchill was essentially unyielding on this question. The president felt unable to take dramatic steps against an important ally in the military crisis, but he left no doubt about his views, sent a mission to India that shared his views, and generally let it be known that he favored independence for the subcontinent.[38]

During the war, he repeatedly expressed his preference for the end of colonialism, whether British, French, Dutch, or other.[39] He felt strongly that the French should not be allowed to return to French Indo-China, made certain that the French army units being equipped and organized for participation in the Pacific War were under no circumstances to be utilized there, and only began to change his mind on the issue when the Japanese displaced French control by their coup in March 1945.[40] He tried unsuccessfully to persuade Churchill to return Hong Kong to Chinese sovereignty early, with the provision that it become a free port, a concession to which Chiang was prepared to agree.[41] His personal meetings with the Sultan of Morocco and King Ibn Saud were designed to demonstrate his anticolonial sentiments – and were certainly so interpreted by the annoyed French and British governments.[42]

An aspect of the president's view of the future was especially obvious in regard to the fate of what must be seen as a residual legacy of the League of Nations: the mandate system established by the 1919 treaties and placed under a form of very tenuous League supervision. In direct opposition to Churchill's view that the mandates ought to be converted into colonies, Roosevelt wanted them converted into trusteeships on the road to independence under a far stricter and more intrusive supervision than had ever been assigned to the League.[43] It was in fact his belief that not only should the former mandates become trusteeships but also that the colonial possessions of all the European powers should become trusteeships, with the explicit or, if necessary, implied assumption that in ten or twenty years they too would attain independence.[44] In the final analysis, he could push through the trusteeship concept just for the former mandates, and American negotiators at San Francisco had to settle for a situation where other colonies would become trusteeships only by the voluntary agreement of the colonial masters – which was most unlikely. No one, however, had any doubts about the president's strongly held views on the subject.[45]

Ironically, the persons who found the president's attachment to the trusteeship principle most difficult to understand included many of his own political and military advisors. They believed, in many instances very strongly, that the United States should annex the former Japanese mandated islands in the Pacific that were being taken from the Japanese in bloody battles during the war and that they considered essential to the security of the United States in the postwar years. Repeatedly they argued that the United States should add them to its totally owned possessions in the Pacific, like Guam and Wake Island. In this position, they were invariably supported by the British, who no doubt saw this as a useful precedent for their own policy, since the islands in question had been Japanese mandates. Roosevelt would have none of this. He repeatedly and emphatically informed his military and political subordinates that the United States was not about to annex anything anywhere. The islands that had been mandates of Japan would become trusteeships of the United States, with the implicit, and occasionally explicit, assumption that they would move toward independence, though possibly with leased American bases of the sort that the United States had acquired in British territories like Bermuda under the destroyers-for-bases deal of 1940.[46] In the face of strong arguments to the contrary from inside the administration and from Great Britain, as president and commander-in-chief, Roosevelt would have his way on this issue, and Harry Truman, when president, would adhere to this clear policy preference of his predecessor.

Whatever the differences between Roosevelt and Churchill on the question of mandates and colonies, the president not only expected to continue working effectively with the British prime minister during the war but also looked forward to a future in which Great Britain would continue to play an important role. His initial assumption that Britain would be one of the "Four Policemen" and then a permanent member of the Security Council of the UNO reflects this perspective. He expected the continuation of some sort of partnership in the field of atomic weapons, though he did not anticipate a maintenance after hostilities had ended of the Combined Chiefs of Staff system. This structure, created right after the United States had been drawn into the war, had worked very effectively in the coordination of the military efforts of the two powers and would be needed in the immediate postwar transition period but hardly thereafter.[47] As the roles of the United States, the Soviet Union, and Great Britain shifted during the course of the war, Roosevelt was increasingly inclined to pressure Churchill on issues of military strategy where they differed – like the invasion of southern France. In Churchill's view, the president seemed to be more willing to accept the strategic views of Stalin, an inclination that the British prime minister very much resented. Nevertheless, Churchill and Roosevelt continued to respect one another highly and to work in basic harmony.

As already mentioned, Roosevelt expected that there would be a British zone of occupation in Germany, though he would have preferred both a different border with the Soviet zone and a geographical reversal of the expected American and British zones. Roosevelt's views on the future of Japan are examined below. Although the evidence is not absolutely clear, it is safe to assume that he expected that Great Britain would also have a zone of occupation there.

While this had not been settled in detail by the time Roosevelt died, the assumption was that there would similarly be a British zone in Austria.

There were other British policies in addition to Britain's colonial stance on which the American president had his reservations. As an advocate of low tariffs in domestic American politics and as a strong believer in the need to open the channels of world trade symbolized by the reciprocal trade agreements pushed by Secretary of State Cordell Hull, Roosevelt very much wanted the British system of imperial preferences weakened, if not abolished. His strong interest in Article VII of the master Lend-Lease agreement with Britain, which dealt with this question, certainly needs to be understood in this context.[48] He was by no means reluctant to pressure the British government on an issue that had long been close to his heart.

Although Roosevelt, like Churchill, was a self-confident patrician, he had a very different outlook on the social issues of the past, present, and future. He thought of Britain as far too rigidly structured socially and expected, correctly as we now know, that there would be a shift to the left in Britain during and after the war. He therefore hoped to develop ties to the British Labor Party in a way not entirely unlike his development of ties to Churchill earlier in the war, when the latter was a member of the government of Neville Chamberlain.[49] It is not clear whether the Labor Party's anticolonial stand influenced him in this regard, but it would certainly not have diminished his hopes for that party's advance to power, which came three months after his death.

Roosevelt was one of the few American presidents – if not the only one – with a real interest in Canada and some familiarity with it. His ties to that country's wartime prime minister, William Lyon Mackenzie King, were unprecedented. If this relationship facilitated the growing independence of Canada in international affairs, the deployment of American troops to the Southwest Pacific at a time when Britain was unable to defend Australia and New Zealand from the advance of Japan led to an even more dramatic shift in the outlook of the governments and people in those portions of the British Commonwealth. Seeing themselves dependent on the United State in their time of greatest peril, the peoples and governments in Australia and New Zealand looked increasingly to the United States as the bulwark of their security in the future.[50] The role of Great Britain in the world of the future that Roosevelt anticipated – one in which Britain's colonies became independent states and its Commonwealth members asserted their full independence – was a subject that Roosevelt did not puzzle over any more than anyone else at the time.

What about the future relationship with the other major ally of the United States, the Soviet Union? Roosevelt had no doubt about the character of its government, having described it as a dictatorship as bad as any other on earth at one of the few public gatherings where his comments were met with booing.[51] He had kept the London government from recognizing the Soviet annexation of the Baltic States in 1940 and would do so again during the 1941–42 negotiations for an Anglo–Soviet alliance.[52] He knew that the Soviet Union was carrying the main burden of the fighting in the war and did what he could to help this critical ally. Just as he had Hull work on the subject of international trade and Lehman on relief, so he put his close assistant Harry Hopkins to work on getting supplies to the Soviet Union.[53] The concern that the Soviets might either collapse or make a separate peace with Germany haunted him as it did Churchill. How did Roosevelt see the future place of the Soviet Union? There was never any doubt in his mind that it would be one of the major powers and that its cooperation would be essential if new wars were to be avoided. His willingness to concede to the Soviets their preference on the question of the veto if that were necessary to obtain that country's participation in the United Nations has already been mentioned. On the questions of the future borders of the Soviet Union and its possible control of the countries of eastern and southeastern Europe, the president had a series of interrelated views that require review in detail.

As just stated, he opposed any recognition of the annexation of the Baltic States. He expected Finland to retain its independence, though he does not appear to have been especially interested in the details of any boundary settlement between it and its Soviet neighbor.[54] The Soviet border in Europe in which Roosevelt was, by contrast, very much interested was that with Poland. He was not willing to recognize the 1939 line that the Soviets had worked out with Nazi Germany, and he pressured the British not to accept it either. Since he favored the assignment of East Prussia to Poland as well as some additional gains for Poland at the expense of German Silesia, he thought that the Polish government in exile could agree to the cession of some lands in the East to the Soviet Union, but he argued strongly himself and through his ambassador in Moscow for the Poles to retain Lvov and also perhaps the nearby oil fields.[55] He adhered to this position right through the Yalta Conference but could not persuade Stalin to agree. As explained in Chapter 5, Stalin did agree to a small shift of the 1939 line at the southern end of the border with Poland but insisted on retaining Lvov. Roosevelt's ideas about the Soviet borders with Romania and Czechoslovakia remain unknown, and the Soviet demand for the cession of Turkish territory did not come until after Roosevelt's death. In East Asia, the president believed that the southern half of Sakhalin as well as the Kurile Islands should be returned by Japan to the Soviet Union. Other aspects of his opinions on the future of East Asia will be reviewed in the context of his thoughts about China, Korea, and Japan.

Roosevelt had several other major concerns about the role of the Soviet Union in the future. He was sure that in the course of military operations the Red Army would overrun most of east and southeast Europe and that as a result, in addition to reannexing the Baltic States, the Soviets would in effect control the countries there in the postwar years. While he hoped that the Yalta Declaration on Liberated Countries might moderate Soviet policy in these states,[56] he was never very confident on this point. Repeatedly he pointed out to those he met that there was nothing except a third world war that could prevent Soviet domination of east and southeast Europe and that this was simply not a realistic prospect. There was only the hope that over a period of years the Soviet Union itself would evolve on more moderate lines and ease its hold on the countries taken under its control.[57] He objected to the allocation of percentages of British and Soviet control in southeast Europe of the sort Churchill and Stalin agreed to in October 1944, but he was not about to advocate war with the Soviet Union to prevent it from annexing or dominating what it intended to annex or dominate. Not a happy prospect, especially for the peoples directly affected. It was, after all, the insistence of Germany on starting a second world war that had ended the independence of these countries in the first place. Another world war was unlikely to increase their happiness – or that of anyone else.

The other two worries of the president concerned the implications of Soviet great power strength for a Europe without a strong Germany, on the one hand, and an Asia without a strong Japan, on the other. It was the first of these concerns that led him to rethink policy toward France. This topic is reviewed in more detail below, but the president's reversal from envisaging a disarmed France to one that had substantial military forces was tied to his concern about a Soviet Union faced with an essentially defenseless western Europe.[58] Similarly, his constant advocacy of a major role for China in the postwar world was in part due to his belief that there needed to be a counterweight to the Soviet Union in East Asia after the defeat of Japan.[59]

While Roosevelt was worried about future domination of east and southeast Europe by the Soviet Union as well as its possible danger to other countries in Europe and Asia, he was always sensitive to the real security concerns of a Soviet Union that had suffered a terrible invasion. His insistence on completely disarming Germany, reducing its size, possibly dividing it into several states, and in any case keeping it under Allied occupation for some time was intended to assure the Soviets that there would not again be an invasion by Germany.[60] In accordance with his proclivity for raising all manner of ideas, he toyed with several rather extraordinary notions that he believed might make the Soviet Union less inclined toward aggression and more satisfied with its international position. On the one hand, he considered the idea of some sort of internationalization of the railway across Iran to the Persian Gulf to ensure the Soviets would have a route to the ocean; on the other, he toyed with the notion of providing the Soviet Union with free ports on the North Atlantic coast of Norway.[61] Nothing would come of either scheme, but they deserve mention as a reflection of the president's strong belief that a satisfied Soviet Union might be a more comfortable neighbor for the United States as well as for all others on the globe.

Roosevelt's vision of the future position of China has been mentioned repeatedly. He assumed that it would be a major power once it recovered from the ravages of war. The territory taken from China by Japan, especially Manchuria and Formosa (Taiwan), would certainly be restored to China, though there was an interest in the possibility of an American base on Formosa.[62] As mentioned in connection with his meeting with Chiang at Cairo, Roosevelt expected Chinese participation in the occupation of Japan. Since Korea was also to be released from Japanese control, Roosevelt anticipated that there would be a period of trusteeship for it on the road to independence and expected China and perhaps the Soviet Union to act as trustees.[63] His ending of extraterritorial rights in China and his failure to persuade Churchill to agree to an early return of Hong Kong have also been mentioned. As the position of the Chinese Nationalist regime of Chiang Kai-shek became obviously weaker during the war, a fact shown dramatically by the failure of Chinese resistance in the face of the Japanese 1944 Ichigo offensive, Roosevelt was increasingly interested in having the United States develop some sort of relationship with the Chinese Communists.[64] He thought that Chiang's position could be strengthened by getting the Soviet Union to focus its policy in China exclusively on the Nationalists, and his agreements with Stalin at Yalta on East Asia were designed with this end in mind.[65] It is too often forgotten that this policy succeeded temporarily but was subsequently aborted by the collapse of the Nationalist regime. Whatever happened in East Asia, Roosevelt until his death remained convinced of the long-term significance of China and expected that country to share in the occupation of Japan when victory over that country had been achieved.[66]

The other ally about whose future Roosevelt had definite ideas was France. His general opposition to colonialism and its implications for the French colonial empire have already been mentioned.

While originally in favor of the future disarmament of France, he changed his mind during the war, as also mentioned, and not only came to play a major role in pushing the rebuilding of the French army during the war but also expected that process to continue.[67] He was dubious, to put it mildly, about de Gaulle, and the latter did everything possible and impossible to reinforce the president's negative opinion.[68] Although all his life Roosevelt was a Francophile who maintained his knowledge of the French language, he very much doubted that the country would regain its status as a great power "for at least 25 years."[69]

As a practical matter, Roosevelt expected the French to continue to control northwest Africa for years to come even if his meeting with the Sultan of Morocco showed that this was hardly the arrangement he preferred.[70] As the situation in liberated France appeared to develop in a calm and democratic direction, without either the chaos or the de Gaulle dictatorship that had earlier worried him, Roosevelt slowly moved toward a more positive view of France's future role. In November 1944 he agreed to France becoming a member of the European Advisory Council, which was supposed to play a role in developing plans for the continent's future.[71] That organization never played the major role anticipated for it, in part because of Roosevelt's own attitude toward it, but here was a symbol of a new future and a revived role for the country that had collapsed so dramatically in 1940.

Given the continued stability in France that winter, Roosevelt was persuaded by his advisors to reverse himself on other aspects of the future position of France. At the Yalta Conference, he consented to a seat for France on the Allied Control Council for Germany and also agreed that France should receive occupation zones in Germany and Austria.[72] He did not live to see the French government utilize its position on the Control Council to counter American policy in postwar Germany, but it is unlikely that he would have been surprised. Since he had originally agreed to Henry Morgenthau's plan for the future of Germany, which included a substantial territorial cession to France in addition to the return of Alsace and Lorraine, it is safe to assume that he was willing to have the Saar area turned over to French control at the end of hostilities. Roosevelt's effort to meet with de Gaulle after the Yalta Conference, though rudely thwarted by the latter, certainly illustrates the president's slow turning from his negative view of the future of France to one more in keeping with his own earlier essentially pro-French attitude.

With these perspectives on the future of the United States' main allies, how did Roosevelt see the future of its wartime enemies other than Germany? His view of Italy has to be examined first. The prior discussion of Roosevelt's great emphasis on the concept of trusteeships for colonial territories heading for independence will serve to explain his views of the future of Italy's colonial empire. Abyssinia (Ethiopia) had already been liberated by British forces and would regain its recently lost independence. The rest of Italy's African colonies would become trusteeships on the road to independence as well. There appeared to be no need to discuss the return of Albania to independence and the transfer of the Dodecanese Islands to Greece. What about Italy itself?

Like Churchill, Roosevelt would almost certainly have been willing to exempt Italy from the demand for unconditional surrender had not the British cabinet insisted on its inclusion when the demand was to be announced publicly at the Casablanca Conference. After Italy did surrender, Roosevelt generally sided with the more liberal elements in the internal bickering among Italian politicians. As for the future of the monarchy, it was his view that the Italian people should decide that themselves.[73] It is certainly likely that

domestic American politics influenced the president in his generally more generous attitude toward Italy than Germany, but then
the Italians had arranged to dump Mussolini and the Fascist Party,
unlike the Germans, whose enthusiasm for Hitler appeared to be
undiminished. As the United States took steps to assist with the
rehabilitation and reconstruction of the country, it was likely that
Italy would turn more toward the United States than Britain in
the future, but it is by no means clear that this was Roosevelt's
intention.[74] Roosevelt never could quite figure out why Italy had
declared war on the United States, any more than he could understand why Hungary, Romania, and Bulgaria had, and he never was
as concerned about the possibility of its launching a war of aggression again in the future as he was about the potential for Germany
or Japan to start another such war.

There was never any doubt in Roosevelt's mind that Japan would
have to surrender unconditionally and be occupied by Allied forces,
with China as the fourth power instead of France. The plans for the
invasion of Japan were submitted to his successor, not to him, but
there is no reason whatever to believe that Roosevelt's decisions
in the final stages of the Pacific War would have been any different than those actually made by President Truman. The way to defeat Japan was essentially similar to the road to final victory over
Germany.

There were, however, critical differences in Roosevelt's view of
Japan and his view of Germany. He registered the dissimilarity between a German public that had turned to National Socialism and
had become increasingly enthusiastic about it, on the one hand, and
the series of coups, assassinations, and provoked incidents by which
the militarists had shot their way to power in Japan, on the other.
While Japan, therefore, was to lose all imperial acquisitions gained

since its war with China in 1894–95, there is not the slightest indication that Roosevelt ever contemplated for Japan the sorts of territorial amputations imposed on Germany – at least to a considerable extent with his approval. Similarly, Roosevelt at no time considered dividing Japan into several separate states, a strategy very much part of his thinking about the future of Germany. The literature that attributes all manner of racist sentiments to American leadership in World War II has conveniently and consistently ignored the fundamentally positive view of Japan held by Roosevelt and his advisors as compared with their perspective on Germany.[75]

Since American strategy looked to the defeat of Germany before that of Japan, the president was less involved in the planning for Japan's future, but the basic outlines were laid down while Roosevelt was still alive. Surrender, as already mentioned, would be followed by four-power occupation, on the assumption that the Soviet Union would have joined in the war against Japan. The possibility of retaining the emperor, at least in the transition period, was also contemplated.[76] Although the evidence on this is not clear, Roosevelt may well have thought of this very controversial issue the way he did about the monarchy in Italy: let the people decide what they wanted once unconditional surrender had taken place. Although it is difficult to establish the extent to which the president was consulted about the planning for the occupation of Japan, that planning clearly reflected Roosevelt's broad differentiation between Germany and Japan: a raw deal for the former and a new deal for the latter.[77] The long-term implication clearly was an essentially territorially undiminished Japan back on the track toward a democratic structure at home, accompanied by a moderate foreign policy in a peaceful world and by good relations with the United States. The president's assumption appears to have been that such a development was likely to occur substantially sooner with an essentially intact Japan in East Asia than with a greatly reduced Germany in Europe.

Roosevelt did not have many specific views on other countries. As indicated, he expected East Prussia and extensive additional former German territory to be turned over to a revived Poland, and he tried hard but unsuccessfully to retain Lvov for Poland. He assumed that the other countries occupied by Germany during the war would regain their independence and that Austria would also be reestablished with its prewar borders. Because of the obvious internal problems of Yugoslavia, Roosevelt at one point thought that it might have to be divided into a Serb state and a Croat state and that a plebiscite might be necessary, but this was no certain project.[78] In any case, he assumed that there would be substantial American troops in Europe for only a few years after the end of hostilities, a prediction that only Stalin's authorization for North Korea to invade South Korea in 1950 would invalidate.

A very specific issue of a different sort on which Roosevelt had a firm opinion was the issue of punishing war criminals. In October 1941, before American participation in the war, the president had, like Churchill, denounced the German practice of shooting hostages.[79] In August 1942 he stated publicly that war criminals would have to stand trial in the very countries that they now occupied, and he made it clear later that year that he wanted public warnings of forthcoming trials to discourage war crimes but that there would be no mass shootings or reprisals.[80] Under these circumstances, it is easy to understand his approval of the inclusion of a statement on war crimes and trials to be issued by the meeting of Allied foreign ministers in Moscow in October 1943.[81] In spite of the views of some of his advisors, like Secretary of State Cordell

Hull, and the clear preference of the British government for summary executions, Roosevelt always held to the concept that those accused of war crimes, however awful, ought to be tried by tribunals of some sort.[82] His successor held to this view and, in agreement with the French and Soviets, imposed it on the reluctant British.

One might say that Roosevelt's opinion on the future of Palestine was in a way another side to his insistence that war criminals be brought before tribunals. He had followed the process of German persecution of Jews on the basis of extensive reports and had been the only chief of state to withdraw the American ambassador from Berlin on the occasion of the pogrom of November 1938. Convinced by the Zionist leader Chaim Weitzmann at their meeting in February 1940 that, for Jews, there was no real alternative to Palestine as a place of their own, he came to accept the project called the Philby Plan, outlined in the chapter on Churchill. From Roosevelt's point of view, this project for an independent Arab confederation under Ibn Saud and the creation in it of a Jewish state in Palestine had a double advantage. It would provide a place for the survivors of the mass killing of Jews by the Germans and for any others who wanted to move to Palestine as a place to settle, and at the same time it was consistent with his belief that the mandates carved out of the Ottoman Empire should move toward independence.[83]

The project Roosevelt favored was impossible to implement because Ibn Saud rejected it when the president urged it on him at their meeting after the Yalta Conference. His basic conviction that there should be a "free and democratic Jewish commonwealth in Palestine," as he expressed it, remained unshaken.[84] In view of the large number of Jews then living in Arab countries, the president appears to have thought of a population exchange of some sort.

As he explained his position to Undersecretary of State Edward Stettinnius after his reelection to a fourth term in November 1944, "Palestine should be for the Jews, and no Arab should be in it."[85] Ironically, this was almost the very day on which Churchill abandoned his support for the creation of a Jewish state in a partitioned Palestine upon the assassination of Lord Moyne, but Roosevelt did not know that. He had wanted a provision for religious freedom included in the initial proclamation of the United Nations in December 1941.[86] In one way or another, the subject was always with him.

Another area in which the president had a continuing interest was Central and South America. He had taken a whole series of steps to try to alter the relationship of the United States with countries that frequently, and with good reason, viewed the United States with apprehension and distrust. There is no reason to doubt that what had come to be called the "Good Neighbor Policy" was to be continued. The fact that almost all the countries of the Western Hemisphere had joined the United States and Canada in the war could be seen as in part the fruit of that policy – and Roosevelt himself certainly thought so. There were, and were likely to continue to be, major troubles in the relationship of the United States with Argentina, but that was more of an exception than is often realized. The largest country, Brazil, had sent soldiers to fight alongside those of the United States in Italy, and the most immediate neighbor, Mexico, had contributed a small air force contingent to the war effort. All signs pointed to a continuation of a degree of hemispheric solidarity, occasionally troubled but nevertheless solid in any crisis brought about by an outside challenge.[87]

What about the domestic situation in the United States? Roosevelt had no doubt that the United States would dramatically reduce the huge military forces it had mobilized and would reconvert its industrial capacity to peacetime production. With the memory of the problems of World War I veterans, culminating in the bonus march on Washington and its dispersal by troops, there had been much discussion of what to do to assist the vastly greater number of veterans returning from service this time. The GI Bill of Rights, as it was called, with its provisions for college support, housing loans, and special unemployment benefits, had been enacted by the Congress and signed by the president on June 22, 1944. An increasing number of the prewar New Deal measures, like Social Security, a legal minimum wage, deposit insurance, and the Tennessee Valley Authority, had become an accepted part of the American scene, but there was not likely to be anything new added to the earlier measures. The election of November 1942 had brought massive Republican gains in both houses of Congress, and the president was fully aware of the fact that a coalition of Republicans and Southern Democrats controlled the Congress and would easily block any new initiatives in the field of social legislation. There is no reason to believe that in these circumstances he gave much consideration to the possibility of further social reform.

In the prewar years, the appearance of Washington itself had changed as the result of the construction of large buildings to accommodate the personnel of new and enlarged government agencies. During the war, there had been not only additions to these buildings but also the construction of the huge Pentagon on the other side of the Potomac River. Roosevelt, however, had no grandiose plans for future buildings in the nation's capital. For himself, he wanted only a plain stone placed in front of the new National Archives building. It is there today, at the corner of Pennsylvania Avenue and Seventh Street, but almost no passersby notice it. Instead, tourists visit the elaborate memorial to Roosevelt constructed decades later in the park along the Potomac, where children now pat the bronze statue of his dog next to the statue of the president.

Roosevelt was aware of the changes in the situation of African-Americans in the country and had tried to push the armed services, especially the navy, to employ more African-Americans in positions other than mess stewards, but without much success. In part under the influence of his wife, Eleanor, he had reversed the position of the last Democratic administration in Washington, that of Woodrow Wilson, on the general attitude of the federal government on matters of race from support for segregation to opposition to it. The practical implementation of such opposition, however, was only in its initial stages. Here was an enormous problem on which much of the effort would fall to Roosevelt's successors.[88]

During the war, Roosevelt, like other World War II leaders, had led a country in which women were increasingly drawn into industrial work to satisfy the demands of the war effort as more and more men entered military service.[89] To a substantial extent, though not as much as in the Soviet Union and Britain, women were also enrolled in the military itself. In one important way, however, Roosevelt's position on the role of women in society differed from that of the other leaders at the time, and this difference predated the time when the United States was drawn into the conflict. Having relied on her already when he was governor of New York, Roosevelt had appointed Frances Perkins to be Secretary of Labor in 1933 as the first woman ever to serve in the Cabinet. She remained in that position until shortly after Roosevelt's death in April 1945.[90] Here was a clearly visible symbol of a new perspective on an issue on which Roosevelt was ahead of many of his contemporaries – including all the other leaders covered in this book.

By temperament and inclination, Roosevelt was an optimistic person. He was always certain that victory would come to the Allies. And if any one or more of the Allies dropped out voluntarily or were forced out because of Axis victories, then the United States would defeat Germany, Japan, and their associates by itself. He was determined that this time the United States would play an active and constructive role in the postwar world, and he had worked hard during the conflict to prepare the American people for that eventuality. Military strategy had been oriented toward achieving a complete victory and placing American forces in a strong position to influence the settlement to come. That settlement would prevent the recurrence of the catastrophes Roosevelt had seen twice in his lifetime so that the peoples of the earth could live in peace as they moved toward the better and freer life that he confidently expected.

9. THE REAL POSTWAR WORLD

M ORE THAN HALF A CENTURY AFTER THE END OF WORLD
War II, it is possible to see how postwar developments came
to reflect the hopes of World War II leaders or to confound them.
Perhaps no figure of the war would be more disappointed by subsequent developments than the man who insisted on war in 1939,
Adolf Hitler. It was not simply that Germany was utterly defeated
instead of victorious, as he had anticipated. Far from conquering vast
stretches of land for German agricultural settlers, Germany would
lose not only the same pieces of land that had been lost by the
peace settlement of the prior great conflict but also large parts of
pre-1939 Germany, including much of its most important agricultural land (as well as mines and industry), where Germans had made
up the overwhelming majority of the population for centuries. Furthermore, in addition to the Germans fleeing or being driven out
of the areas ceded to Poland and the Soviet Union, several million additional people of German cultural background were driven
out of Czechoslovakia and other countries of central and southeast Europe. Instead of lots more *Lebensraum*, the German people
had very much less – and Germany now had to accommodate an
additional eleven million people within its reduced boundaries. In

recent years, Germany has also welcomed tens of thousands of people of German background who decided to move from the former Soviet Union and from Poland to Germany.

Several further population changes either had taken place by 1945 or would occur soon after. On the one hand, there were the enormous casualties of war. The most recent careful study of the subject concludes that the German military had over 5.3 million deaths in World War II, almost three times the number lost in World War I, out of an only slightly larger population.[1] On the other hand, the halting of the killing of handicapped Germans by the Allies certainly saved the lives of tens of thousands of seriously wounded German soldiers who would have been killed by their own government. They could expect no easy life but could be there for their families and receive some additional support as the country's economy recovered. Ironically, as that recovery moved forward in the West German Federal Republic formed out of the three western zones of occupation, there turned out to be a serious shortage of workers. Smaller than before and more crowded than ever, the country began to import workers from Turkey, Yugoslavia, and elsewhere. Formerly hysterical about the presence of half a million Jews, it now drew in several million Muslims.

The German anticipation of killing all the Jews in the mandate of Palestine and other portions of the Middle East has turned into its opposite. Hundreds of thousands of European Jews who survived the mass slaughter of Jews by the Germans during the war moved to Palestine and played a significant role in the establishment, defense, and development of a Jewish state there. About seven hundred thousand Jews from Arab states – Jews whom the Germans once had expected to kill – also fled to the new Jewish state of Israel and came to constitute a major portion of its Jewish population.

The only reason they are not on the verge of becoming a majority of the Jews in Israel is that over the last twenty years hundreds of thousands of Jews from the former Soviet Union – Jews whom the World War II German invasion had not reached – have also moved to Israel. During those same years, substantial numbers of Jews from the former Soviet Union have also moved to Germany and now constitute the majority of the Jewish population (of approximately 100,000) in that country, an ironic reversal of Hitler's hopes and plans.

While postwar Germany (first West Germany and then the re-united state) has made a substantial effort to compensate Jews for losses suffered under the Nazi regime, it has not as yet produced a similar policy for the Roma and Sinti (gypsies). The survivors in Germany and those persecuted elsewhere still await a policy on the part of German authorities. Other categories of victims, like those forcibly sterilized, also await new policies.

Perhaps the change in Germany that would disappoint Hitler even more than those already mentioned is the change in the German public's political and social mentality. The overwhelming majority of Germans have become accustomed to living in a parliamentary democracy and at peace with their neighbors, and they expect both conditions to continue into the indefinite future. For most Germans, whatever criticisms they have of their local, state, or national governments, it is the policies, not the nature of the government, that they believe should be changed. Similarly, while they may not always like their neighbors, the very idea of going to war with them has become inconceivable to most Germans. In a prisoner-of-war camp after the war, Field Marshal Ritter von Leeb noted in his diary the things Germany would have to do somewhat differently in order to win the third world war against the same enemies, a contingency he evidently took for granted.[2] It would be very difficult to find substantial numbers of Germans now who would find that prospect desirable or even conceivable.

One of the few developments in postwar Germany that would have met with at least qualified approval from Hitler has been in the field of religion. Large numbers of Germans have formally left the Catholic and Protestant churches and have ceased paying church taxes. This is true for people in both the eastern and western parts of the country. In German hotels, the Bible that is provided for travelers generally contains only the New Testament – a posthumous triumph of sorts for the Germanic Christians who advocated this policy in their effort to remove traces of Judaism from their neo-pagan form of Christianity.

As for the issue that Hitler always considered of supreme significance, the ability of the Germans to feed themselves from the products of their own soil, the change in Germany and Europe is as dramatic as the changes already mentioned. The agricultural problem of the countries of western and central Europe lies in the production of agricultural surpluses. Subsidies under the European Union's agricultural program are designed to help its farmers cope with surpluses and to keep out too much food imported from outside the Union. There was certainly hunger in Germany in the immediate postwar years, but it was no worse than elsewhere on the continent, and food rationing ended earlier than in England. Certainly there are people in Germany who are poor and at times hungry, but any suggestion that they displace farmers in the Ukraine or the northern Caucasus would not find many enthusiastic volunteers. As for the absence of a colonial empire in central Africa, it would be even more difficult to locate any German advocate of such a project.

Today's German military hardly see themselves heading forth to conquer other countries. Their government may send them to NATO- or UN-sponsored police or peace-keeping missions outside Germany. There is, however, none of the enthusiasm for war that made even an opponent of Hitler who lost his life because of that opposition express delight at the prospect of an invasion of Poland in 1939.[3] Whatever the occasional frictions about trade and immigration issues, Germany's sponsorship, at the insistence of Chancellor Helmut Kohl, of Poland in its attempt to join NATO suggests a dramatic reversal of prior Prussian and German policy, which looked toward the elimination of Poland and the simultaneous drawing of Russia as far into central Europe as possible.

Like the imperial expansion efforts of Japan in East Asia, German aggression in Europe had brought enormous advantages to the Soviet Union. In spite of terrible human losses and physical destruction, the Soviet Union had emerged from its ordeal not only freed of the invader but also in a position to exert control over substantial additional territory from East Germany to Bulgaria. The settlement at the end of World War I and the ensuing upheavals had pushed the Soviets away from central and parts of eastern Europe. Having once done what they could to assist the Bolsheviks in their effort to take over Russia, the Germans totally failed to recognize that one of the great advantages of the peace settlement for Germany had been that it provided a substantial buffer between themselves and the regime they had helped install in Moscow. As discussed below in the review of what happened to Stalin's empire, the countries of east and southeast Europe who lost their independence to the Soviet Union as a result of Germany's insistence on war only regained it decades later. Like the French before them, the Germans have given up thinking of marching to Moscow. The peoples between Germany and Russia have had to pick up where their lives and their development were halted in World War II.

Mussolini's dreams of a Mediterranean empire have evaporated as effectively as Hitler's dreams of world domination. The colonies in Africa acquired by prior Italian governments have moved toward independence, as have the two countries that Mussolini actually annexed: Ethiopia and Albania. The islands in the Aegean seized from Turkey in 1912 have been ceded to Greece. There are few signs that large numbers of Italians are greatly upset about these losses of land once under Italian control. The United States prevented de Gaulle from annexing a small portion of northwest Italy to France. There were small territorial losses by Italy to the former Yugoslavia, but the city in that general area that was most in dispute, Trieste, remained with Italy, ironically because the New Zealand forces deployed in the Allied campaign in Italy were able to reach the city before the Yugoslav partisans of Marshal Tito.

The great change in Italy has been a substantial industrial development that provides the very economic base that the country lacked when its leaders, especially Mussolini, attempted to project a great power policy on hopelessly inadequate economic foundations. While substantial poverty remains a feature of the country, there are probably few Italians who believe that this situation could be remedied by seizing territory in Africa or sending an army to fight on the plains and in the mountains of southern Russia. Similarly, while the political system of parliamentary democracy restored in postwar Italy may not always function to the general satisfaction of the population, there is little inclination to end rather than try to improve this political structure. The Italian public ended the monarchy by a plebiscite; this may be the one feature of the country that fits with Mussolini's ambitions, even if accomplished in a way he would have most vehemently rejected because of his objection to any and all manifestations of democratic governmental procedures.

Italy's colonial empire had provided homes for a very tiny number of Italians and jobs for a few more. It had, however, been a drag on the Italian national budget before Mussolini took over the government, and it was even more of a drag during his tenure of power. The fighting into which he had plunged the country bankrupted the economy, which, as mentioned above, had been inadequate to sustain a major military effort in any case. Without the drain of colonial expenses and of wars that the country could not afford, Italy has become a moderately wealthy country. There are certainly poor people in Italy, especially in its southern portions, but the standard of living is quite substantially higher than in the heyday of fascism.

Had the Axis powers triumphed, Italy would doubtless have been allowed some of the crumbs of a victory won primarily if not exclusively by her European ally. Nothing in the record suggests that while living in Germany's shadow – even with a larger slice of Africa – the people of Italy would have been particularly happy. They would, quite justly, have remained apprehensive about their powerful northern neighbor, by whose exertions and grace they would have acquired additional territory to police in the face of local populations who both despised and hated them. As for Mussolini's dreams of ending such Christian religious holidays as Christmas, finding a supporter of that notion in today's Italy would be a difficult task indeed.

Like Hitler and Mussolini, Tojo Hideki saw his ambitions for a greater Japanese empire dashed by defeat. Before entering the Japanese cabinet, he had been very much involved with Japan's expansionist drive as chief-of-staff of the Kwantung Army, the Japanese force stationed in Manchuria. Now that territory seized from China, as well as prior conquests at the expense of China, Russia, and Germany, along with the land of Korea, were lost to Japan. The dreams of an enormous further expansion from India and Siberia to Australia and substantial portions of the Western Hemisphere were also shattered. Alaska and Hawaii, instead of coming under Japanese control, became the forty-ninth and fiftieth states of the American Union. The oil wells, tin mines, and rubber plantations of Southeast Asia remained exactly where they had always been, with their products shipped to Japan by others, something the Japanese themselves had proven unable to do adequately during the war.

Certainly the most significant result of Japan's failed attempt at imperial expansion was the extent to which it halted the consolidation of China under the Nationalist government and thus paved the way for the triumph of the Communists in the world's most populous country. The Japanese coup staged in what was then French Indo-China in March 1945, that is, after Tojo's fall from power, started a period of decades of further upheaval as the French attempted to reassert their authority and later the United States tried to stabilize a democratic regime in the southern portion of the area.[4] The three states into which the area was divided after the war, Vietnam, Laos, and Cambodia, all experienced decades of instability and death.

In defeat, Japan, unlike Germany and Italy, lost only minuscule pieces of its original territory: several small islands off the coast of Hokkaido that were seized by the Soviet Union in 1945 and still remain in disputed between Japan and the Russian Federation. Like Germany, the whole country was occupied, but without zonal divisions. The presence of a British Commonwealth Occupation Force (BCOF) in the western portion of the main island of Honshu did not substantially affect the administration of the country as a unit.

With the emperor retained and a Japanese administrative apparatus remaining in place, even if purged and under American control, the country was spared long-term division because of its surrender before invasion.

A new constitution and massive reforms imposed by the American occupiers empowered political parties previously outlawed or pushed into insignificance, provided for land reform and female suffrage, and ensured an independent labor movement. With proportionately far fewer casualties and less destruction than Germany, Japan revived economically more rapidly than its major wartime ally. In effect, the country picked up where the military adventurers had hijacked the government at the beginning of the 1930s. A major long-term change in Japanese society overturns one of the original arguments for expansion. With its aging population, Japan needs not colonial territories for settlement by a burgeoning population, but substantial numbers of immigrants if there is to be any hope of sustaining the people's standard of living. A society that has prided itself on homogeneity will have to learn very new ways indeed. Perhaps Tojo would have been pleased to see two members of his wartime cabinet, Kaya Okinori and Kishi Nobusuke, enjoy high office again, but as representatives of a political party, not as officials in the replacement single party structure he had designed. The only aspect of the postwar changes that Tojo would have found unobjectionable was the maintenance of the position of the emperor, even if it has been substantially modified.

Some of the hopes of Chiang Kai-shek had been realized even before the war's conclusion. All extraterritorial rights in China had been ended, and China's status as one of the world's great powers had been formally recognized by the allocation of a permanent seat on the Security Council of the new United Nations Organization.

It was also clear that the territories taken from China by Japan were all about to be returned to Chinese sovereignty. It was dramatically obvious that one of these territories, Manchuria, had been largely looted of its industrial installations by the Soviet Union during the short period when it had been under Red Army control. This loss was at least somewhat offset by the seizure of whatever the Japanese had built up in the parts of China that their army had occupied since 1937. Hong Kong was not returned to China early, as Chiang had hoped. Similarly, China's position in Outer Mongolia and Mongolia itself was not reestablished. There would be no role for Chiang's regime in connection with Korea, which, liberated from Japanese control, was divided into two separate areas by the United States and the Soviet Union, with the two zones becoming – and still remaining – separate states.

The most important way, however, in which the Chinese leader's hopes were thwarted was by a civil war that followed upon the end of fighting against Japan and that finally, after years of combat, ended in the defeat of the Nationalists. Weakened from the outside by the aggression of Japan and from the inside by a combination of corruption, unwise political policies, and a military policy that depended upon the United States to defeat Japan without a major reorganization and participation of Chinese armies, the Nationalists were driven from the mainland by Communist forces. From Taiwan, which had been restored to China on Japan's defeat, Chiang could claim to be the legitimate ruler of all of China, but only in the United Nations Organization could that claim be other than a fiction for some years. While this development precluded a role for China in the occupation of Japan – a subject about which Chiang had always had reservations – Taiwan, on the one hand, and the mainland Communist regime, on the other hand, moved in directions that resembled Chiang's hopes and fears more closely than anyone might have anticipated. The Communists established a regime that was more repressive and corrupt than anything that critics of the Nationalists had ever commented on, while Taiwan moved, with fits and starts, to be sure, in the direction of a modernized democratic society.

It looked at first as if many of Stalin's aspirations and hopes had been realized. The crushing defeat administered to the German invaders and its brief intervention in the war against Japan ensured the Soviet Union a major role in Europe, Asia, and the world at large. The boundary with Finland, with its cutting off of Finland from the Arctic Ocean, which Stalin had insisted on, has remained in effect, though his successors decided to give up the base at Porkkala after Stalin's death. It looked for a while as if the Soviet leader's hopes for a dominant position in central, east, and southeast Europe would also be realized. The borders were those that Stalin had wanted, and the Red Army ensured the maintenance of the Communist systems installed under Stalin's supervision. Revolts in East Germany in 1953 and what looked like a rejection of Communism in Hungary in 1956 could be crushed. Similarly, what looked like a turn in the wrong direction in Czechoslovakia was easily ended by invasion in 1968. Finally, it looked as if the triumph of Mao in China showed that the belief that history was moving in the direction of a universal triumph for Communism was as well-founded as its faithful adherents assumed.

There were, however, fundamental miscalculations at the base of the Soviet leader's expectations. The Chinese Communists had not appreciated the Soviet Union's backing for the Nationalists, Stalin's recommendation for a partition of China rather than an effort at complete conquest, and the looting of Manchuria of its industrial facilities. Furthermore, Mao, unlike Chiang, raised questions about those territories taken from China in the nineteenth century and now important parts of the Soviet Union.[5] The Soviets' seizure from Japan of several small islands off the northern coast of Hokkaido has proven an impediment to good relations with Japan. The establishment of a client state in North Korea led to a war that Stalin authorized for this state to launch in an effort to seize South Korea but that in turn dramatically altered American military policy in Europe, where it was feared a similar event might take place.

In Europe, also, developments failed to live up to Stalin's expectations. In the face of what was happening in eastern Europe and the resulting fear of future Soviet actions, the countries of western Europe joined with Canada and the United States in a military alliance, NATO (North Atlantic Treaty Organization), to defend themselves. It was precisely Stalin's authorizing North Korea to invade South Korea that led to a major reorientation of strategy by the United States. The original plan had been to evacuate what small forces there were on the continent until a major invasion of the sort that had been launched on June 6, 1944, could liberate western Europe from the Red Army, as it had once liberated the same area from the German army. This was replaced by a plan that called for a force to defend near the border between West and East Germany, including a significant American contingent and a substantial one from a rearmed West German Federal Republic.

The popular support that successful defense against Germany had provided the Soviet regime slowly evaporated in subsequent decades. In the face of hopes by the public that conditions in the country would be relaxed, the system did not, perhaps could not, adjust. As the waning of ideology and continued deprivation and oppression ate away at the central regime's legitimacy, it began to fall apart at the fringes. Even while Stalin was alive, Yugoslavia under Marshal Tito's leadership asserted its independence. At the end of the 1980s the new empire that Stalin had created in eastern Europe began to dissolve, followed by the colonial empire created by the Romanov rulers in prior centuries. It is probably not a coincidence that the shift from the first of these two processes to the other began as the Baltic States, which had been independent between the two world wars, reasserted their independence – only to be emulated by other Soviet Socialist Republics. The northern half of former German East Prussia, now the Kaliningrad oblast of the Russian Federation, remains as an isolated reminder of the concept Stalin once pushed in order to hold the Baltic States firmly within the Soviet Union. Perhaps the most dramatic sign of the failure of Stalin and his successors to make something substantial of the victory of 1945 is the contrast between the colossal and successful Soviet offensives on the Eastern Front in World War II and the pitiful showing of the Russian army in its campaign against the independence movement in tiny Chechnya.

The transfers of territory from Poland, Czechoslovakia, and Romania to the Soviet Union remain in effect today, but these areas are now included in the western successor states that have broken away from Stalin's structure. The border between Poland and Germany insisted on by Stalin also remains in effect, but reunified Germany and Poland appear to be on the way toward a reconciliation that few would have anticipated. The international organization to whose creation Stalin contributed his part has hardly been concerned with the issue that he had thought would be one of its most important functions: keeping the Germans from starting another war and especially another invasion of the Soviet Union.

Certainly Stalin's hopes of a weakening of Britain by the dissolution of its colonial empire and the end of its influential position in the Middle East have been realized, but hardly in the way he had desired. A few of the new states emerging from the British Empire have experimented with Marxist concepts and in some cases have seen significant Soviet involvement in their military and political development. Over time, however, most have moved in other directions, and only Cuba, Vietnam, and North Korea remain wedded to the past – with as many of their people leaving as can find a way to do so. Stalin's expectation that the facilitation of Jewish immigration into Palestine and, for a short but critical time, support for the state of Israel would both weaken British influence in the Middle East and lead to the establishment of a satellite state there has also failed to be realized. The British position eroded anyway, and as soon as it turned out that Israel would not follow the Soviet model, Stalin himself turned to support the Arabs in their attempts to destroy the Jewish state – attempts that have not succeeded up to now.

If Stalin's world has disappeared and most of his hopes have been dashed by postwar developments, at first glance the same thing has happened to the world that Winston Churchill anticipated. The great empire in which he had grown up and that he expected to restore to its former glory has largely vanished. His immediate successors presided over the independence of India, and it was during Churchill's own return to office in the early 1950s that the process of decolonization of Britain's empire in Africa began with the change of the former British colony of Gold Coast into the independent state of Ghana. The ties holding together the Dominions in the British Commonwealth have loosened rather than tightened in the years since 1945. Other European colonial empires that

Churchill had also hoped to preserve dissolved almost as rapidly as the British one, sometimes violently, sometimes peacefully. At home in the United Kingdom, the Labor government installed a welfare state that, with few exceptions, has remained characteristic of the country ever since. These developments at home and abroad probably made a major contribution to Churchill's depressed spirits in the last years of his life. He had had bouts of depression in prior years, but the episodes became more frequent and prolonged.

It would, however, be inaccurate to focus only on the areas where Churchill's hopes were disappointed and ignore those where his aspirations were fulfilled, even if not always in quite the way he would have liked. The England he loved may be changed, but it most certainly retained its independence and the parliamentary institution that was central to his thinking. The countries of western Europe had their freedom restored to them by Allied victory, as Churchill very much wanted. The fact that relations with France in the postwar years were often troubled would hardly have surprised him. The continuation of good relations with the United States was indeed very close to his heart. The emergence in Germany of a parliamentary democracy that maintained good relations with its neighbors was certainly something he always had hoped for. That both Italy and Japan moved in somewhat similar directions was also in line with Churchill's preference. The movement toward European unity was something he himself had talked about a good deal, even if he was not prepared to delve into details. The emergence of the Cold War disappointed but did not surprise him. The new international organization was one to which he was committed. The emergence of an independent Jewish state in Palestine was certainly in accord with his own hope.

The move toward a comprehensive welfare state in the United Kingdom itself was one that he had resisted, but this is a far more complicated issue than appears at first sight. As a member of the Liberal Party cabinet early in the twentieth century, he had helped lay the foundations of a welfare state himself. A patrician isolated from the daily struggles and cares of ordinary people, he never grasped that the Labor Party that he so vehemently opposed in the 1945 election and that drove him from office was basically a social democratic rather than a socialist party. Because of his combative nature, he pictured its members as vastly more radical than they were, a sign of his failure to sense the reality of the time that is all the more astonishing in view of his excellent relations with the Labor Party's leaders in his wartime cabinet. Perhaps in this regard, as in his adherence to the imperialist concepts of the late nineteenth century, there remained that discrepancy between his active interest in the latest technology, on the one hand, and his continued dedication to the bygone world of his youth, on the other. It could be argued that in some ways his adherence to older values was just as well. It was his dogged devotion to the principles of that era that made him stick to a course of defiance in 1940 and maintain a total devotion to saving the world from the evils of Nazi domination. By so doing, he accomplished an extraordinary feat and provided the Britain he loved with what may well have been its last defining contribution to modern history.

Charles de Gaulle held to certain of his wartime visions of the future but changed others quite dramatically, certainly more than any of the other leaders who lived into the postwar years. It was possible for him to obtain a zone of occupation in Germany and in Austria and to secure for France a permanent seat on the Security Council of the United Nations Organization. The domestic upheavals in postwar France may have upset but hardly surprised him in view of his experience of prewar France. There appeared at first to be a return of the imperial role that France had played in Africa, Southeast Asia, and elsewhere. But in this regard, as well as in his policy toward Germany, de Gaulle would reverse himself in the postwar period.

Although for some time the French government utilized its position in the occupation of postwar Germany to make certain that all attempts to create administrative structures for the whole country were aborted, de Gaulle himself came around to the view that reconciliation with Germany would be better for France than an endless attempt to keep Germany as divided as possible. As the leader of those who refused to accept the idea that France had been completely defeated in 1940, he could never be accused by anyone of being pro-German or of having collaborated with the Germans during the war. The critical need of France, protection against still another German invasion, could be secured by friendship at least as effectively as by any other means. And it was this protection that had been and continued to be de Gaulle's central aim. As for France's continued troubles with Britain and the United States, they suited de Gaulle, who did what he could to increase rather than ameliorate them. His hopes for long-term good relations with the Soviet Union, on the other hand, proved entirely unrealistic. Ironically, it was in the French sector of Berlin that a big new airport was developed as part of the effort of the Western powers to thwart the Soviet blockade of West Berlin in 1948–49. It might be said that the truest form of homage that the French people paid to de Gaulle in the postwar years was the growing myth that almost all Frenchmen had resisted the Germans and had identified with his movement.

President Roosevelt did not live to see the end of the war, but by April 1945 the victory of which he had always been confident was clearly in sight. The way had already been cleared for the formal establishment of the United Nations Organization, and he had done all he could to make certain that this time the Senate would ratify the UN Charter – as it did by a vote of 89 to 2 on July 28, 1945.[6] Roosevelt also did not live to see the completion of the project to build atomic bombs, but he had been informed in December 1944 that the first ones would be ready in the summer of 1945. Since by that time it was clear to the American leaders that neither Germany nor Japan was close to having such a weapon, and since Roosevelt and Churchill had agreed to try to keep the atomic bomb secret from the Soviet Union, there could be the belief, perhaps illusion, that the rapid demobilization that was certain to follow victory would still leave the United States with a monopoly over the most powerful weapon then existing.

Whatever the details, the postwar world would see the United States in a very powerful position, as Roosevelt had wanted and expected, and this was true in spite of the massive reduction in its armed forces, a reduction only reversed in response to the invasion of South Korea, as already mentioned. The reconversion of American industry to peacetime production similarly moved forward roughly in the way that Roosevelt had anticipated. And the millions of returning veterans would be reintegrated into American society partly through the benefits of the GI Bill, which, as a result of its educational grants, greatly increased social mobility in the country and prevented a repetition of the agonizing prewar debate about a bonus. The reduction in barriers to the advancement of women and African-Americans that had started during the war would continue and later accelerate – certainly developments Roosevelt would have been happy to see. His steps to enlarge the system of national parks and monuments and in the field of conservation – one field in

which he followed his famous predecessor from the same family –
can be seen as precursors of the environmental movement in the
United States.

The invasion of northwest Europe, which Roosevelt insisted on
based on the idea that American forces would then be able to drive
into the heart of Germany and play a major role in forcing unconditional surrender and simultaneously acquire a base for a major American role in postwar Europe, accomplished both goals. Germany
surrendered unconditionally – though four weeks after Roosevelt's
death – and has shown no inclination to take the path of aggression again. The surrender took place under circumstances in which
American military forces were in the middle of Europe. The lines
were not as far east as Roosevelt had wanted and as Churchill, re-
versing his earlier position, preferred at the last moment, but in any
case they were far enough into the center of the continent to allow
the United States to play a major role in the postwar settlement.[7]

The hope for the free elections promised the peoples of east and
southeast Europe at the Yalta Conference was dashed, and so was
Roosevelt's hope that over the years the harsh system of Stalin's dictatorship would moderate. Whether the president's hope was realistic or not, that is, whether the Soviet system was capable of internal
reform and adjustment, perhaps along the lines that Czechoslovakia
attempted in 1968, is impossible to know. Instead of amelioration,
rigidity led to collapse. The fact that this occurred without a third
world war would certainly have gratified Roosevelt, who had expressed himself as above all averse to such a war as the way to secure the freedom of those who had exchanged German for Soviet
domination.

By his regularly approving the promotion to the highest military ranks of Americans of German ancestry, even of German birth,

during the war, Roosevelt had shown that far, from thinking the Germans incurable, he looked forward to the return of Germany to the civilized world. His instructions for the occupation, however modified in subsequent years, pointed the way to a new orientation for that country. Similarly, his advocacy of trials for accused war criminals paved the way for the trials that indeed took place and provided the basis for new ways of dealing with atrocious acts. By the time of Roosevelt's death, planning for the future of Japan was still mired in confusion, but the general thrust of the policy was clear. It is obvious in retrospect that the overall goal of American policy was to reintegrate Japan into a normal international order as a peaceful state with an internal structure that was more democratic – and that is what happened.

If relations with the Soviet Union would prove as troubled as the president feared on the basis of his last heated exchanges with Stalin about the possible surrender of German forces in Italy, the expectation that good relations with Britain would continue was realized. That the relationship with the France of de Gaulle would continue to be difficult was dramatically demonstrated right after Roosevelt's death in the clash between de Gaulle and the new president, Harry Truman, over France's attempt to annex a piece of northwest Italy.[8] The president's hopes for good relations with China were dashed by the victory of the Communists in the civil war that followed the Allied victory over Japan.

It was perhaps on the question of colonial empires that Roosevelt's hopes were realized more completely and much more rapidly than he had envisioned. The trusteeship system that he had insisted be applied to the mandates of the League of Nations was so applied. Over the years, these areas moved to one form or another of independence. The same system was applied to the African colonies taken from Italy by the victors, with the same results. Even more significant and in accord with Roosevelt's preference, the major colonial possessions of all the European powers moved toward independence. While in many cases this process was accompanied by violence, sometimes between the colonial population and the imperial power, sometimes between segments of the colonial population, and sometimes both, the process took considerably less time than the president had anticipated. And this process involved not only the colonies of the countries that had participated in the war, like Britain, France, Belgium, and Holland, but also the colonies of Spain and Portugal, which had remained neutral. Tiny pieces of the old empires do continue to exist, for example, the French islands in the South Pacific that provide France a place to test nuclear devices. On the other hand, the decolonization process came to lands in the Caucasus and Central Asia that Russia had colonized in the decades during which the west Europeans were partitioning Africa, South and Southeast Asia, and the islands in the Pacific.

The fact that in some instances a former colony or trusteeship became divided into two or more states, as happened with the British colony of India and the Belgian Mandate of Ruanda-Urundi, or that two were merged into one, like British and Italian Somaliland, would not in any way slow down the process that Roosevelt considered both good and inevitable. That the effort of the UN to create two states, one Arab and one Jewish, out of the British mandate of Palestine was rejected by the Arabs and has been followed by a series of wars would certainly have disappointed the president, who favored independence for the Arab states and the creation of a Jewish state in Palestine and hoped they would all be at peace with each other, even if not in the confederation he, like Churchill, would have preferred.

As a strong believer in low tariffs and the removal of barriers to international trade, Roosevelt entrusted the campaign for that to his secretary of state, Cordell Hull, and he would have been delighted to see the extension of the program of reciprocal trades agreements in the postwar years. Whatever the problems associated with and in some cases caused by the process of globalization, Roosevelt would probably have pointed to the trade wars, competitive currency devaluations, and preference schemes of the interwar years as far worse for all. The creation and subsequent evolution of the European Common Market and then the European Union certainly fit in with his preference for freer trade and a peaceful accommodation of European countries.

In conclusion, it might be said that the postwar vision of President Roosevelt came to be realized to a greater extent than that of any of the other World War II leaders. Not only were the expectations of the defeated terminated by their defeat, but Stalin, Chiang Kai-shek, Churchill, and de Gaulle would also see many of their hopes disappointed. Ironically, the countries of the defeated leaders emerged from the terrible experience of war and defeat in a way that came to seem on the whole quite acceptable to their inhabitants. The number of Germans, Italians, and Japanese who regret their inability to settle on farms in the Ukraine, hold office in a town in North Africa, or live in the shadow of an oil refinery in Borneo is certainly small. It is an open question whether there is a large or even small number of people in England and France who rue the fact that their governments no longer hold a condominium over the New Hebrides. It may, in fact, be doubted whether many of the English and French even know where on earth the country of Vanuatu, as it is now called, actually is located. Nostalgia for the great empires created in prior centuries is limited.

The world continues to change in many ways, and the process of change is certain to persist. The war in the middle of the twentieth century, the greatest of the wars we know of, certainly accelerated change. The leaders of the major powers involved each had his own vision of which direction those changes should take in the second half of the century. Those visions were not simply abstract musings but often influenced the military and diplomatic decisions that they made during the conflict. The final result made it possible for some and impossible for others of their hopes to be realized. Furthermore, unanticipated developments intervened to block or divert even the most determined of the victors. But the decisions made during the war in anticipation of the future certainly helped to shape the world that emerged from the ordeal of total war. If it resembles the vision of President Roosevelt more than those of the other seven leaders reviewed here, it may well be that he not only led one of the countries victorious in that war but also was more closely attuned to the currents of world history at a time when he saw and wished that colonial empire was a passing phenomenon. If what followed 1945 was in some ways an American half century, his vision surely played a part.

NOTES

INTRODUCTION

1. It should be noted that throughout the text the transliteration of Chinese names follows the old system in use at the time and that Japanese names are in the standard Japanese form, in which the family name comes first and the given name second.

2. The author has reviewed the evidence in "Zur Frage eines Sonderfriedens im Osten," in *Gezeitenwechsel im Zweiten Weltkrieg? Die Schlachten von Char'kov und Kursk im Frühjahr und Sommer 1943 in operativer Anlage, Verlauf, und politischer Wirkung*, ed. Roland G. Foerster (Hamburg: Mittler, 1996), 173–83. This is one field in which there is practically certain to be additional evidence still under lock and seal in the archives of the former Soviet Union. One can only hope that the records in these archives will be released before their chemical self-destruction makes them permanently inaccessible. Important new evidence on Stalin's interest in peace with Germany in the winter of 1941–42 and his willingness to go to war with the United States and Great Britain is being published as an appendix in Jochen von Lang, *Top Nazi: SS-General Karl Wolff: The Man Between Hitler and Himmler* (New York: Enigma Books, 2005).

CHAPTER 1. ADOLF HITLER

1. Rudolf Hess to Walter Hewel, 30 March 1927, National Archives, Nuremberg document 3753-PS; English translation in Gerhard L. Weinberg, *Germany, Hitler, and World War II* (New York: Cambridge University Press, 1995), chap. 2. Very important on this issue, Jochen Thies, *Architekt der Weltherrschaft: Die "Endziele" Hitlers* (Düsseldorf: Droste, 1976), 32–33, 152.

2. Constantin Goschler, ed., *Hitler: Reden, Schriften, Anordnungen Februar 1925 bis Januar 1933*, vol. 4, pt. 1 (Munich: Saur, 1994), no. 28, p. 95.

3. Gerhard L. Weinberg, ed., *Hitlers Zweites Buch: Ein Dokument aus dem Jahr 1928* (Stuttgart: Deutsche Verlags-Anstalt, 1961), 77. In the English language edition, Gerhard L. Weinberg, ed., *Hitler's Second Book: The Unpublished Sequel to Mein Kampf* (New York: Enigma Books, 2003), translated by Krista Smith, the passage is on p. 47.

4. Gerhard L. Weinberg, *The Foreign Policy of Hitler's Germany: Starting World War II, 1937–1939* (Atlantic Highlands, N.J.: Humanities Press, 1994), chaps. 10–11.

5. Ibid., chap. 14.

6. Weinberg, *Germany, Hitler, and World War II*, chaps. 12, 14–15.

7. Marianne Feuersenger, *Im Vorzimmer der Macht: Aufzeichnungen aus dem Whermachtführungsstab und Führerhauptquartier 1940–1945* (Munich: Herbig, 1999), 110.

8. Thies, *Architekt der Weltherrschaft*, 162–63, 174 ff.

9. An excellent introduction in Norman Rich, *Hitler's War Aims: The Establishment of the New Order* (New York: Norton, 1974), chaps. 7–8.

10. A satisfactory and thorough study of the German plans for the invasion and occupation of the United Kingdom remains to be written. There is a useful summary in Basil Collier, *History of the Second World War: The Defence of the United Kingdom* (London: Her Majesty's Stationery Office, 1957), chap. 11. A good early account is in Peter Fleming, *Operation Sealion* (New York: Simon & Schuster, 1957). A German survey of the purely military side is in Karl Klee, *Das Unternehmen "Seelöwe": Die geplante deutsche Landung in England 1940* (Göttingen: Musterschmidt, 1956). The Imperial War Museum in London has reprinted the arrest list and the administrative handbook for the planned German occupation.

11. See Norman J. W. Goda, *Tomorrow the World: Hitler, Northwest Africa, and the Path toward America* (College Station: Texas A & M Press, 1998).

12. A preliminary account is provided in Rich, *Hitler's War Aims*, 320–25. For a detailed, more recent study, see Lutz Klinkhammer, *Zwischen Bündnis und Besatzung: Das nationalsozialistische Deutschland und die Republik von Salo, 1943–1945* (Tübingen: Mohr, 1993).

13. Werner Jochmann, ed., *Adolf Hitler Monologe im Führerhauptquartier 1941–1944* (Hamburg: Knaus, 1980), no. 10.

14. Johanna M. Meskill, *Hitler and Japan: The Hollow Alliance* (New York: Atherton, 1966), chap. 3.

15. Gerhard L. Weinberg, "Deutsch-japanische Verhandlungen über das Südseemandat 1937–1938," *Vierteljahrshefte für Zeitgeschichte* 4 (1956): 390–98; Johanna M. Menzel, ed., "Der geheime deutsch-japanische Notenaustausch zum Dreimächtepakt," *Vierteljahrshefte für Zeitgeschichte* 5 (1957): 184–93.

16. Klaus Hildebrand, *Vom Reich zum Weltreich: Hitler: NSDAP und koloniale Frage 1919–1945* (Munich: Fink, 1969); Gerhard L. Weinberg, "German Colonial Plans and Policies, 1938–1942," in *World in the Balance: Behind the Scenes of World War II* (Hanover, N.H.: University Press of New England, 1981), 96–136; Dietrich Eichholtz, ed., "Die Kriegszieldenkschrift des Kolonialpolitischen Amtes der NSDAP von 1940," *Zeitschrift für Geschichtswissenschaft*, 22 (1974): 308–23.

17. Hitler's views of the United States before he became chancellor may be found in Weinberg, *Hitler's Second Book*, chap. 9. For a general survey, see Gerhard L. Weinberg, "Hitler's Image of the United States," in *World in the Balance*, 53–74.

18. Alton Frye, *Nazi Germany and the American Hemisphere, 1933–1941* (New Haven, Conn.: Yale University Press, 1967), 93–94, 122–23. The authenticity of the incident is confirmed by the document published as no. 137 in *Documents on German Foreign Policy 1918–1945*, ser. C, vol. 4 (Washington, D.C.: U.S. Government Printing Office, 1983).

19. Weinberg, *Hitler's Second Book*, chap. 9; Thies, *Architekt der Weltherrschaft*, 171.

20. Clemens Vollhans, ed., *Hitler Reden, Schriften, Anordnungen Februar 1925 bis Januar 1933*, vol. 1 (Munich: Saur, 1992), 127.

21. Henry Friedlander, *The Origins of Nazi Genocide: From Euthanasia to the Final Solution* (Chapel Hill: University of North Carolina Press, 1995).

22. *Documents on German Foreign Policy 1918–1945*, ser. D, vol. 8 (Washington, D.C.: U.S. Government Printing Office, 1954), no. 515. See also Zvi Elpeleg, *The Grand Mufti: Haj Amin Al-Husseini, Founder of the Palestinian National Movement* (London: Frank Cass, 1993).

23. Hitler's speech of 6 April 1920 in Eberhard Jäckel, ed., *Hitler: Sämtliche Aufzeichnungen 1905–1924* (Stuttgart: Deutsche Verlags-Anstalt, 1980), 120; cf. ibid., 28 June 1920, 152.

24. *Documents on German Foreign Policy 1918–1945*, ser. D, vol. 4 (Washington D.C.: U.S. Government Printing Office, 1951), 193. The original German reads: "Die Juden würden bei uns vernichtet."

25. On this deliberate misdating, see Gerhard L. Weinberg, "The Holocaust and World War II: A Dilemma in Teaching," in *Lessons and Legacies*, vol. 2, ed. Donald G. Schilling (Evanston, Ill.: Northwestern University Press, 1998), p. 27 and the detailed references for n. 3.

26. No complete text of the record of this meeting appears to have survived. The best text is in *Akten zur deutschen auswärtigen Politik 1918–1945*, ser. D, vol. 8, pt. 2, app. 3.

27. Excellent surveys include Raul Hilberg, *The Destruction of the European Jews*, 3d ed. (New Haven, Conn.: Yale University Press, 2003), and Christopher

Browning, *The Origins of the Final Solution: The Evolution of Nazi Jewish Policy, September 1939–March 1942* (Lincoln: University of Nebraska Press, 2004).

28. See n. 22.

29. Guenter Lewy, *The Nazi Persecution of the Gypsies* (New York: Oxford University Press, 2000); Michael Zimmermann, *Rassenutopie und Genozid: Die nationalsozialistische "Lösung der Zigeunerfrage"* (Hamburg: Christians, 1996).

30. Karl Dietrich Bracher et al., *Die nationalsozialistische Machtergreifung*, 2d ed. (Cologne: Westdeutscher Verlag, 1962), 214; Dorothee Klinksiek, *Die Frau im NS-Staat* (Stuttgart: Deutsche Verlags-Anstalt, 1982), 72–74.

31. See Michael Burleigh and Wolfgang Wippermann, *The Racial State: Germany 1933–1945* (Cambridge: Cambridge University Press, 1991).

32. Elke Fröhlich, ed., *Die Tagebücher von Joseph Goebbels* (hereafter cited as *Goebbels Tagebücher*), pt. 2, vol. 12 (Munich: Saur, 1995), 14 May 1944, 289–90.

33. For a summary of this operation in Poland, see Richard C. Lukas, *Forgotten Holocaust: The Poles under German Occupation 1939–1944* (Lexington: University Press of Kentucky, 1986), 25–27. See also the same author's *Did the Children Cry? Hitler's War against Jewish and Polish Children, 1939–1945* (New York: Hypocrene, 1994). There appears to be no study of the kidnapping operation as a whole. The "Lebensborn" organization of the SS was involved in it.

34. There are scattered references to the subject of "Totenehe," but there appears to be no systematic study. A summary is presented in Elizabeth D. Heineman, *What Difference Does a Husband Make? Women and Marital Status in Nazi and Postwar Germany* (Berkeley: University of California Press, 1999), 47–48.

35. For an excellent scholarly analysis, see Rüdiger Overmans, *Deutsche militärischen Verluste im Zweiten Weltkrieg* (Munich: Oldenbourg, 1999).

36. Oron J. Hale, ed., "Adolf Hitler and the Postwar German Birthrate," *Journal of Central European Affairs* 17 (1957): 166–73. This is a record by Martin Bormann of Hitler's comments on the subject.

37. Jochmann, *Adolf Hitler Monologe*, 49; see also ibid., 8–11 August 1941, 55; Ian Kershaw, *Hitler 1936–1945: Nemesis* (New York: Norton, 2000), 517; Bruno Wasser, *Himmlers Raumplanung im Osten: Der Generalplan Ost in Polen, 1940–1944* (Basel: Birkhäuser, 1993), 33–34.

38. Still useful is the pioneering work of Alexander Mitscherlich and Fred Mielke, *Das Diktat der Menschenverachtung* (Heidelberg: Lambert Schneider, 1947), 149 ff.

39. The best study is Jost Dülffer et al., *Hitlers Städte: Baupolitik im Dritten Reich* (Cologne: Böhlau, 1978).

40. An excellent survey of the subject is presented in Paul Jaskot, *The Architecture of Oppression: The SS, Forced Labor and the Nazi Monumental Building Economy* (New York: Routledge, 2000).

41. This ridiculous aspect of the project is summarized in Thies, *Architekt der Weltherrschaft*, 80. The plans for the world's biggest stadium, hall, street, airport, etc., are discussed in ibid., 80–81, 90–91.

42. On the planned museum for Linz, see the popular but useful account in Charles de Jaeger, *The Linz File: Hitler's Plunder of Europe's Art* (Exeter, England: Webb & Bower, 1981); for more details, see Günther Haase, *Kunstraub und Kunstschutz: Eine Dokumentation* (Hildesheim: Georg Olms, 1991), 30–31, 62–66, and relevant documents. See also Anja Heuss, *Kunst- und Kulturraub: Eine vergleichende Studie zur Besatzungspolitik der Nationalsozialisten in Frankreich und der Sowjetunion* (Heidelberg: C. Winter, 2000), 29–72.

43. Jochmann, *Adolf Hitler Monologe*, 19/20 February 1942, 285.

44. Thies, *Architekt der Weltherrschaft*, 131; Hans-Dietrich Loock, *Quisling, Rosenberg und Terboven: Zur Vorgeschichte und Geschichte der nationalsozialistischen Revolution in Norwegen* (Stuttgart: Deutsche Verlags-Anstalt, 1970), 457.

45. Jochmann, *Adolf Hitler Monologe*, 13 October 1941, 78; Thies, *Architekt der Weltherrschaft*, 77.

46. *Goebbels Tagebücher*, pt. 2, vol. 4, 31 May 1942, 406–07; ibid., 23 June 1942, 583–84. Hitler ordered that Vienna, including all its historic buildings, was to be totally demolished in 1945 to "spare" it occupation; see Susan Schwarz, "Operation Radetzky," *Austria Kultur*, 3, no. 4 (1993): 1–2.

47. Anton Joachimsthaler, *Die Breitspurbahn Hitlers: Eine Dokumentation über die geplante 3-Meter Breitspureisenbahn der Jahre 1942–1945* (Freiburg: Eisenbahn-Kurier Verlag, 1981), 42, 58–60, 80 ff., 250–51, and maps on 295, 306, 307.

48. Ibid., 380 n. 441.

49. Jochmann, *Adolf Hitler Monologe*, 29 August 1942, 375; Thies, *Architekt der Weltherrschaft*, 179–80; *Goebbels Tagebücher*, pt. 2, vol. 5, 24 August 1942, 308. It was for this very reason that he wanted Bavaria to be continued as a unit, because Munich, unlike Vienna, would not become a rival for Berlin; ibid., vol. 4, 22 June 1942, 583–84.

50. *Goebbels Tagebücher*, pt. 2, vol. 4, 26 April 1942, 177.

51. See Doris L. Bergen, *Twisted Cross: The German Christian Movement in the Third Reich* (Chapel Hill: University of North Carolina Press, 1996).

52. Jochmann, *Adolf Hitler Monologe*, 11/12 July 1941, 40–41; 14 October 1941, 82–85; 13 December 1941, 150–51; *Goebbels Tagebücher*, pt. 2, vol. 4, 24 May 1942, 360, and 30 May 1942, 410. The effort to refute the assessment of Hitler as intending to find a way to do away with Christianity in Richard Steigmann-Gall, *The Holy Reich: Nazi Conceptions of Christianity, 1919–1945* (Cambridge: Cambridge University Press, 2003), is entirely unconvincing.

53. *Goebbels Tagebücher*, pt. 2, vol. 5, 20 August 1942, 359–60. In March 1944 Hitler explained that after the war he would get rid of the generals and the

priests as Stalin had done and as he himself had done with the Jews. Ibid., vol. 11, 4 March 1944, 403–04.

54. Among the few, Rainer Zitelmann, *Hitler: Selbstverständnis eines Revolutionärs* (Hamburg: Berg, 1987); Ronald M. Smelser, *Robert Ley: Hitler's Labor Front Leader* (Oxford: Berg, 1988). Also helpful, David Schoenbaum, *Hitler's Social Revolution: Class and Status in Nazi Germany* (New York: Doubleday, 1966), and Shelley Baranowski, *Strength through Joy: Consumerism and Mass Tourism in the Third Reich* (Cambridge: Cambridge University Press, 2004).

55. Dieter Petzina, *Autarkiepolitik im Dritten Reich: Der nationalsozialistische Vierjahresplan* (Stuttgart: Deutsche Verlags-Anstalt, 1968).

56. *Goebbels Tagebücher*, pt. 1, vol. 4, 5 February 1941, 491–92.

57. Still very useful is Robert L. Koehl, *RKFDV: German Resettlement and Population Policy 1939–1945: A History of the Reich Commissioner for the Strengthening of Germandom* (Cambridge, Mass.: Harvard University Press, 1957). For a fine new survey, see Werner Röhr, ed., *Europa unterm Hakenkreuz: Analysen, Quellen, Register* (Berlin: Hüthig, 1996), 8:129–30; see also Norman Rich, *Hitler's War Aims: The Establishment of the New Order* (New York: Norton, 1974), 27–55.

58. See Peter Witte et al., eds., *Der Dienstkalender Heinrich Himmlers 1941/42* (Hamburg: Christians, 1999); Wasser, *Himmlers Raumplanung im Osten*, 47–52.

59. Lukas, *Forgotten Holocaust*; Gerhard Eisenblätter, "Grundlinien der Politik des Reiches gegenüber dem Generalgouvernement, 1939–1945" (Ph.D. diss., University of Frankfurt, 1969); Czeslaw Madajczyk, *Die Okkupationspolitik Nazideutschlands in Polen 1939–1945* (Berlin: Akademie Verlag, 1987).

60. See n. 16.

61. Thies, *Architekt der Weltherrschaft*, 126.

62. The proof coins are in Koblenz, Bundesarchiv, R 2/30737.

63. Rich, *Establishment of the New Order*, chaps. 6–8.

64. Eberhard Jäckel, *Frankreich in Hitlers Europa* (Stuttgart: Deutsche Verlags-Anstalt, 1966).

65. Robert O. Paxton, *Vichy France: Old Guard and New Order 1940–1944* (New York: Columbia University Press, 1972).

66. See n. 10.

67. Thies, *Architekt der Weltherrschaft*, 152.

68. *Goebbels Tagebücher*, pt. 2, vol. 10, 27 October 1943, 184–85.

69. Gerhard L. Weinberg, "Hitler and England, 1933–1945: Pretense and Reality," in *Germany, Hitler and World War II*, chap. 6.

70. See n. 17.

71. *Goebbels Tagebücher*, pt. 2, vol. 14, 2 December 1944, 324–27. On the systematic bribery of German military leaders by Hitler, see Gerd R. Ueberschär

and Winfried Vogel, *Dienen und Verdienen: Hitlers Geschenke an seine Eliten* (Frankfurt am Main: S. Fischer, 1999); Norman J. W. Goda, "Black Marks: Hitler's Bribery of His Senior Officers in World War II," *Journal of Modern History* 72 (2000): 413–52.

72. *Goebbels Tagebücher*, pt. 2, vol. 15, 485–86.

73. Gerhard L. Weinberg, "Der Überfall auf die Sowjetunion im Zusammmenhang mit Hitlers diplomatischen und militärischen Gesamtplanungen," in *"Unternehmen Barbarossa": Zum historischen Ort der deutsch-sowjetischen Beziehungen von 1933 bis Herbst 1941*, ed. Roland G. Foerster (Munich: Oldenbourg, 1993), 184; David Grier, "The Appointment of Admiral Karl Dönitz as Hitler's Successor," in *The Impact of Nazism: New Perspectives on the Third Reich and Its Legacy*, ed. Alan E. Steinweis and Daniel E. Rogers (Lincoln: University of Nebraska Press, 2003), 182–98.

74. Weinberg, *Foreign Policy of Hitler's Germany*, 462–63.

75. Albert Speer, *Spandauer Tagebücher* (Frankfurt am Main: Ullstein, 1975), 20 January 1953, 335.

CHAPTER 2. BENITO MUSSOLINI

1. Richard J. B. Bosworth, *Mussolini* (London: Arnold, 2002).

2. MacGregor Knox, *Mussolini Unleashed 1939–1941: Politics and Strategy in Fascist Italy's Last War* (Cambridge: Cambridge University Press, 1982); Robert Mallett, *The Italian Navy and Fascist Expansionism 1935–1940* (London: Frank Cass, 1998). The argument of G. Bruce Strang, *On the Fiery March: Mussolini Prepares for War* (Westport, Conn.: Praeger, 2003), that ideology influenced Mussolini's actions, is surely correct but in no way refutes the argument of Knox and Mallett.

3. All references to the diary of Count Galeazzo Ciano are to the new complete English language edition: *Diary 1937–1943* (New York: Enigma Books, 2002).

4. Mallett, *The Italian Navy*, 9–17; Denis Mack Smith, *Mussolini* (New York: Knopf, 1982), 195.

5. Smith, *Mussolini*, 225; Knox, *Mussolini Unleashed*, 38–39.

6. Knox, *Mussolini Unleashed*, 40; Mallett, *The Italian Navy*, 132.

7. Gerhard Schreiber, "Italiens Teilnahme am Krieg gegen die Sowjetunion: Motive, Fakten und Folgen," in *Stalingrad: Ereignis, Wirkung, Symbol*, ed. Jürgen Förster (Munich: Piper, 1992), 250–92; MacGregor Knox, *Hitler's Italian Allies: Royal Armed Forces, Fascist Regime, and the War of 1940–1943* (Cambridge: Cambridge University Press, 2000), chap. 2.

8. Mallet, *The Italian Navy*, 54–61, 110–11.

9. A naval base at Kisimayo (in Italian Somaliland) was to have been completed by 1943 but was not built; ibid., 108, 156.

10. Ciano, *Diary*, 13 August 1939, 258; 9 December 1939, 300.

11. Ibid., 25 February 1940, 323; 23 March 1940, 333.

12. Ibid., 2 April 1940, 338. On Hitler's views of a future Italian empire, see Chapter 1 of this book.

13. Bosworth, *Mussolini*, 366–70.

14. Knox, *Mussolini Unleashed*, 136; idem, *Hitler's Italian Allies*, 26 January 1940, 78.

15. Pompeo Aloisi, *Journal (25 juillet 1932–14 juin 1936)* (Paris: Plon, 1957), July 1936, 382; Smith, *Mussolini*, 190–92.

16. Zvi Epeleg, *The Grand Mufti: Haj Amin Al-Husseini, Founder of the Palestinian Nationalist Movement* (London: Frank Cass, 1993), 64–69.

17. Bosworth, *Mussolini*, chaps. 6–9.

18. Knox, *Mussolini Unleashed*, pp. 289–90 and n. 13.

19. Ibid., p. 10 and n. 38.

20. Ciano, *Diary*, 12 May 1940, 351; 2 December 1940, 400; 22 December 1941, 477.

21. A good summary of these schemes is in Peter Godman, *Hitler and the Vatican* (New York: The Free Press, 2004), 10–12.

22. Ciano, *Diary*, 10 April 1942, 510. Mussolini wanted to end sleeping cars, restaurant cars, and first-class on trains.

23. Ibid., 5 July 1940, 369.

24. Schreiber, "Italiens Teilnahme am Krieg gegen die Sowjetunion," 256 ff.

25. Ciano, *Diary*, 3–8 December 1941, 470–2; Smith, *Mussolini*, 273; Peter Herde, *Italien, Deutschland und der Weg in den Krieg im Pazifik* (Wiesbaden: Steiner, 1983).

26. Ciano, *Diary*, 5 July 1941, 441; Schreiber, "Italiens Teilnahme am Krieg gegen die Sowjetunion," 254 ff.

27. Max Domarus, *Mussolini und Hitler: Zwei Wege – Gleiches Ende* (Neustadt a.d. Aisch: Verlagsdruckerei Schmidt, 1977), 389–98. The story that Mussolini held on to some correspondence with Winston Churchill has no foundation in fact; see Richard Lamb, *Mussolini and the British* (London: John Murray, 1997), 322–23.

28. A full account is given in Gerhard Schreiber, *Die italienischen Militärinternierten im deutschen Machtbereich 1943–1945* (Munich: Oldenbourg, 1990).

29. Still very helpful is A. James Gregor, *The Ideology of Fascism: The Rationale of Totalitarianism* (New York: The Free Press, 1969).

30. References to the documents on this can be found in Gerhard L. Weinberg, *A World at Arms: A Global History of World War II* (Cambridge: Cambridge University Press, 1994).

CHAPTER 3. TOJO HIDEKI

1. Alvin D. Coox, *Tojo* (New York: Ballantine, 1975), 125 ff.; Kido Koichi, *The Diary of Marquis Kido: Selected Translations into English* (Frederick, Md.: University Publications of America, 1984), 18, 19 February 1944, 380–81.

2. F. C. Jones, *Japan's New Order in East Asia: Its Rise and Fall 1937–1945* (London: Oxford University Press, 1954), 332–36; Kido, 1 September 1942, 339–40; Ben-Ami Shillony, *Politics and Culture in Wartime Japan* (Oxford: Clarendon Press, 1991), 33–34.

3. Ugaki Matome, *Fading Victory: The Diary of Admiral Matome Ugaki 1941–1945* (Pittsburgh: University of Pittsburgh Press, 1991), 31 October 1942, 255. The article by Yukiko Koshiro, "Eurasian Eclipse: Japan's End Game in World War II," *American Historical Review* 109 (2004): 417–44, has many errors but no information on postwar plans during the period of Tojo's years as prime minister. Peter Duus, "Imperialism without Colonies: The Vision of a Greater East Asia Co-Prosperity Sphere," *Diplomacy & Statecraft* 7 (1996): 54–72, has a single reference to a speech of Tojo to the Japanese Diet (p. 64).

4. In addition to the points documented in notes 1 and 2, there is a 16 February 1942 entry showing that Tojo wanted an envoy sent to the Vatican and a 15 February 1943 entry repeating Tojo's view of Hitler's plan for winning the war.

5. See Shillony, *Politics and Culture in Wartime Japan*, passim; Edward J. Drea, *The 1942 Japanese General Election: Political Mobilization in Wartime Japan* (Lawrence: University Press of Kansas, 1979); Eugene Soviak, ed., *A Diary of Darkness: The Wartime Diary of Kiyosawa Kiyoshi* (Princeton, N.J.: Princeton University Press, 1999); Haruko Taya Cook and Theodore F. Cook, *Japan at War: An Oral History* (New York: New Press, 1992).

6. The full text of the document is printed as Appendix II in Richard Storry, *The Double Patriots: A Study of Japanese Nationalism* (London: Chatto & Windus, 1957), 317–19.

7. Gerhard L. Weinberg, "Deutsch-japanische Verhandlungen über das Südseemandat," *Vierteljahrshefte für Zeitgeschichte* 4 (1956): 390–98; Johanna M. Menzel, ed., "Der geheime deutsch-japanische Notenaustausch zum Dreimächtepakt," *Vierteljahrshefte für Zeitgeschichte* 5 (1957): 184–93.

8. Jones, *Japan's New Order in East Asia*, 349.

9. F. C. Jones et al., *Survey of International Affairs 1939–1946: The Far East 1942–1946* (London: Oxford University Press, 1955), 56–57.

10. Louis Allen, "Wartime Japanese Planning: A Note on Akira Iriye," in *Conflict and Amity in East Asia: Essays in Honor of Ian Nish*, ed. T. G. Fraser and Peter Lowe (London: MacMillan, 1992), 81–83.

11. Foreign Affairs Association of Japan, *The Japan Yearbook 1943–1944* (Tokyo: Japan Times, 1943), republished by the Interdepartmental Committee for the

Acquisition of Foreign Publications (Washington, D.C.: U.S. Government Printing Office, 1945), 1049–76.

12. John W. Dower, *Japan in War and Peace: Selected Essays* (New York: The Free Press, 1993), 82.

13. Gerhard Krebs, "Gibraltar oder Bosporus? Japans Empfehlungen für eine deutsche Mittelmeerstrategie im Jahre 1943, *"Militärgeschichtliche Mitteilungen* 58 (1999): 65–85; Gerhard L. Weinberg, "Zur Frage eines Sonderfriedens im Osten," in *Gezeitenwechsel im Zweiten Weltkrieg? Die Schlachten von Char'kov und Kursk im Frühjahr und Sommer 1943 in operativer Anlage, Verlauf und politischer Bedeutung*, ed. Roland G. Foerster (Hamburg: Mittler, 1996), 173–83.

14. Ray Flude, "The Axis Powers' lost opportunity: The failure to develop an air service between Europe and the Far East 1942–1945," (Ph.D. diss., De Montford University, 2000; courtesy of the author); Peter Herde, *Der Japanflug: Planungen und Verwicklichung einer Flugverbindung zwischen den Achsenmächten und Japan 1942–1945* (Stuttgart: Steiner, 2000).

15. John Hunter Boyle, *China and Japan at War 1937–1945: The Politics of Collaboration* (Stanford, Calif.: Stanford University Press, 1972), is helpful but needs to be brought up-to-date.

16. Jones, *Japan's New Order in East Asia*, 340–43.

17. Peter Wetzler, *Hirohito and War: Imperial Tradition and Military Decision Making in Prewar Japan* (Honolulu: University of Hawaii Press, 1998), 7–8. I owe reference to this book to Professor Miles Fletcher. Emperor Hirohito reciprocated Tojo's loyalty with a favorable view of Tojo in his evaluation after the war; see Herbert P. Bix, *Hirohito and the Making of Modern Japan* (New York: HarperCollins, 2000), 591.

18. There is a thoughtful comparison in L. H. Gann, "Reflections on the Japanese and German Empires of World War II," in *The Japanese Wartime Empire, 1931–1945*, ed. Peter Duus et al. (Princeton, N.J.: Princeton University Press, 1996), 335–62; cf. Wetzler, *Hirohito and War*, 8–9.

19. Drea, *The 1942 Japanese General Election*, 150–1; Courtney Browne, *Tojo: The Last Banzai* (New York: Da Capo Press, 1998), 175.

20. Oka Yoshitake, *Konoe Fumimaro: A Political Biography* (Tokyo: University of Tokyo Press, 1983), 106–10, 112–15.

21. Jones, *Japan's New Order in East Asia*, 421. I am not aware of any study of this organization.

22. Johanna M. Meskill, *Hitler & Japan: The Hollow Alliance* (New York: Atherton, 1966), chap. 4; Bernd Martin, *Deutschland und Japan im Zweiten Weltkrieg: Vom Angriff auf Pearl Harbor bis zur deutschen Kapitulation* (Göttingen: Musterschmidt, 1969), chap. 6.

23. Thus the detailed study by Sato Shigeru, *War, Nationalism and Peasants: Java under the Japanese Occupation 1942–1945* (Armonk, N.Y.: M. E. Sharpe, 1994),

provides no information on Tojo's role. The analysis of Paul H. Kratoska, *The Japanese Occupation of Malaya: A Social and Economic History* (Honolulu: University of Hawaii Press, 1997), merely refers to a speech of Tojo to the sultans when he visited Malaya in July 1943 (p. 70).

24. Joyce C. Lebra, *Japanese Trained Armies in Southeast Asia: Independence and Volunteer Forces in World War II* (New York: Columbia University Press, 1978).

25. Joyce C. Lebra, *Postwar Perspectives on Japan's Greater East Asia Co-Prosperity Sphere*, Harmon Memorial Lecture in Military History No. 34, U.S. Air Force Academy (Washington, D.C.: U.S. Government Printing Office, 1991). There is a useful discussion of categorization among Japanese settlers and local inhabitants in Marijo Asano Tamanoi, "Knowledge, Power, and Racial Classification: The 'Japanese' in 'Manchuria,'" *Journal of Asian Studies* 59 (2000): 248–76.

26. On Tojo's role in regard to prisoners of war, see Browne, *Tojo*, 145–46.

27. A preliminary survey is presented in George Hicks, *The Comfort Women: Japan's Brutal Regime of Enforced Prostitution in the Second World War* (New York: Norton, 1995).

CHAPTER 4. CHIANG KAI-SHEK

1. Marie-Louise Näth, *Chinas Weg in die Weltpolitik: Die nationalen und außenpolitischen Konzeptionen Sun Yat-sens, Chiang Kai-sheks und Mao Tse-tungs* (Berlin: Walter de Gruyter, 1976), 184–87; Conference on Chiang Kai-shek and Modern China (1986, Taipei, Taiwan), *Proceedings* (Taipei: China Cultural Service, 1987), 1:292–307. See also Jonathan Fenby, *Chiang Kai-shek: China's Generalissimo and the Nation He Lost* (New York: Carroll & Graf, 2004).

2. Näth, *Chinas Weg in die Weltpolitik*, 70, 89–92, 120–24.

3. Ibid., 137–9; You-li Sun, *China and the Origins of the Pacific War, 1931–1941* (New York: St. Martin's, 1999), chaps. 5–6.

4. Gerhard L. Weinberg, *The Foreign Policy of Hitler's Germany: Starting World War II, 1937–1939* (Atlantic City, N.J.: Humanities Press, 1995), 174–76.

5. On Germany's turn to Japan, see ibid., 177–84. On Sino–Soviet relations, see John W. Garver, "Chiang Kai-shek's Quest for Soviet Entry into the Sino-Japanese War," *Political Science Quarterly* 102 (1987): 295–316.

6. This is a major theme of Xiaoyuan Liu, *A Partnership for Disorder: China, the United States, and Their Policies for the Postwar Disposition of the Japanese Empire, 1941–1945* (Cambridge: Cambridge University Press, 1996).

7. See the excellent analysis by Stanley Hornbeck of 17 August 1942 in *Foreign Relations of the United States: 1942, China* (Washington, D.C.: U.S. Government Printing Office, 1956), 135–39.

8. John H. Boyle, *China and Japan at War 1937–1945: The Politics of Collaboration* (Stanford, Calif.: Stanford University Press, 1972).

9. Even a publication of the People's Republic of China recognizes this; see Cai Dejin, "Relations between Chiang Kai-shek and Wang Ching-wei during the War against Japan: An Examination of Some Problems," *Republican China* 14, no. 2 (1989): 3–20.

10. Wesley R. Fishel, *The End of Extraterritoriality in China* (Berkeley: University of California Press, 1952), chaps. 2, 11; Hollington K. Tong, *Chiang Kai-chek* (Taipei: China Publishing Company, 1953), 299.

11. Kit-cheng Chan, "The United States and the Question of Hong Kong, 1941–45," *Journal of the Hong Kong Branch of the Royal Asiatic Society* 19 (1979): 6, 8.

12. Liu, *A Partnership for Disorder*, 65, 77.

13. For a useful map, see Christopher Thorne, *The Limits of Foreign Policy: The West, the League and the Far Eastern Crisis of 1931–1933* (New York: Putnam's, 1972), 34.

14. Liu, *A Partnership for Disorder*, 108–11.

15. Sun, *China and the Origins of the Pacific War*, chap. 7; Liu, *A Partnership for Disorder*, passim.

16. Liu, *A Partnership for Disorder*, 226–8, 252–3; Conference on Chiang Kai-shek, *Proceedings*, 4:121–23.

17. Liu, *A Partnership for Disorder*, 239–40, 250–51.

18. Outer Mongolia had been under effective Soviet control for years.

19. See Dennis J. Doolin, *Territorial Claims in the Sino-Soviet Conflict: Documents and Analysis* (Stanford, Calif.: Hoover Institution, 1965).

20. Näth, *Chinas Weg in die Weltpolitik*, 104–07, 158–65.

21. Ibid.

22. Ibid., 239–43.

23. Liu, *A Partnership for Disorder*, 228–30.

24. Ibid., 110–11; William Roger Louis, *Imperialism at Bay: The United States and the Decolonization of the British Empire, 1941–1945* (Oxford: Clarendon Press, 1977), 279–80.

25. Liu, *A Partnership for Disorder*, 108–09.

26. Ibid., 44–45; see the summary of the memorandum of Dr. Sun Fo, President of the Legislative Yuan, included in the "Memorandum by the Foreign Office: Views of the Allied Governments on Reparations," 24 November 1942, PRO, FO 371/35305/U, published in *Dokumente zur Deutschlandpolitik*, series I, vol. 3, pt. 2, p. 1046.

27. Näth, *Chinas Weg in die Weltpolitik*, 218–19.

28. The best discussion of the sources and account is in Liu, *A Partnership for Disorder*, 128–47. There is useful information in Conference on Chiang Kai-shek, *Proceedings*, 4:163–68, 173; Tong, *Chiang Kai-shek*, 307–10; Louis, *Imperialism at Bay*, chap. 17; *Foreign Relations of the United States: The Conferences at Cairo*

and Teheran (Washington, D.C.: U.S. Government Printing Office, 1961), 323–25.

29. Liu, *A Partnership for Disorder*, 25–27.
30. Ibid., 119, 129–47.
31. Ibid., 181–82.
32. Ibid., 254–56.
33. Ibid., 26, 85, 176.
34. Ibid., 29, 176.
35. Ibid., 194.
36. A brief account with a helpful map is presented in Hsi-sheng Chi, *Nationalist China at War: Military Defeats and Political Collapse, 1937–1945* (Ann Arbor: University of Michigan Press, 1982), 74–79.
37. William Roger Louis, "Hong Kong, The Critical Phase, 1945–1949," *American Historical Review* 102 (1997): 1055.
38. Chiang Kai-shek, *China's Destiny* (New York: Roy, 1947).
39. The text is reprinted in ibid., 102–07.
40. For a devastating study of the sort of police force Chiang had supported – and that had supported him – see Frederic Wakeman, *Spymaster: Dai Li and the Chinese Secret Service* (Berkeley: University of California Press, 2003).

CHAPTER 5. JOSEF STALIN

1. Alvin D. Coox, *Nomonhan: Japan against Russia, 1939* (Stanford, Calif.: Stanford University Press, 1985).
2. Gerhard L. Weinberg, *The Foreign Policy of Hitler's Germany: Diplomatic Revolution in Europe 1933–1936* (Atlantic Highlands, N.J.: Humanities Press, 1994), chaps. 3, 8; idem, *The Foreign Policy of Hitler's Germany: Starting World War II 1937–1939* (Atlantic Highlands, N.J.: Humanities Press, 1994), chaps., 7, 13, 14.
3. See the piece by Jonathan Haslam in *The Rise and Fall of the Grand Alliance, 1941–1945*, ed. Ann Lane and Howard Temperley (London: MacMillan, 1995), 24–25.
4. Weinberg, *Foreign Policy 1937–1939*, chaps. 13, 14; Gerhard L. Weinberg, *Germany and the Soviet Union, 1939–1941* (Leyden: Brill, 1954); Sergej Slutsch, "Warum brauchte Hitler einen Nichtangriffspakt mit Stalin?" in *"Unternehmen Barbarossa": Zum historischen Ort der deutsch-sowjetischen Beziehungen von 1933 bis Herbst 1941*, ed. Roland G. Foerster (Munich: Oldenbourg, 1993), 69–88.
5. Sergej Slutsch, "Die deutsch-sowjetischen Beziehungen im Polenfeldzug und die Frage des Eintritts der UdSSR in den Zweiten Weltkrieg," in *Präventivkrieg? Der deutsche Angriff auf die Sowjetunion*, ed. Bianka Petrov-Ennker (Frankfurt am Main: Fischer, 2000), 95–112.

6. Boris J. Kaslas, "The Lithuanian Strip in Soviet-German Secret Diplomacy, 1939–1941," *Journal of Baltic Studies* 4, no. 3 (1973): 211–25; Gerhard L. Weinberg, *A World at Arms: A Global History of World War II* (Cambridge: Cambridge University Press, 1994), 987 nn. 50–51.

7. Ivo Banac, trans. and ed., *The Diary of Georgi Dimitrov 1933–1949* (New Haven, Conn.: Yale University Press, 2003), 115 (hereafter cited as *Dimitrov Diary*).

8. There is a useful map in the Official Blue-White Book of Finland, *Finland Reveals Her Secret Documents on Soviet Policy March 1940–June 1941* (New York: Wilfred Funk, 1941), x. For details, see H. Peter Krosby, *Finland, Germany, and the Soviet Union, 1940–1941: The Petsamo Dispute* (Madison: University of Wisconsin Press, 1968).

9. Weinberg, *A World at Arms*, 182–85.

10. The text of Stalin's instructions for Molotov may be found, translated into German, in Gerd R. Ueberschär and Lev A. Bezymenskij, eds., *Der deutsche Angriff auf die Sowjetunion 1941: Die Kontroverse um die Präventivkriegsthese* (Darmstadt: Primus, 1998), 174–76. See also Haslam in Lane and Temperley, *Rise and Fall of the Grand Alliance*, 30–2; MacGregor Knox, *Mussolini Unleashed: 1939–1941: Politics and Strategy in Fascist Italy's Last War* (Cambridge: Cambridge University Press, 1982), 64; Silvio Pons, *Stalin and the Inevitable War 1936–1941* (London: Frank Cass, 2002), 206–10.

11. *Documents on German Foreign Policy 1918–1945*, ser. D, vol. 8, no. 160.

12. Weinberg, *A World at Arms*, 107, 964 n. 232; Anna M. Cienciala, "Detective Work: Researching Soviet World War II Policy on Poland in Russian Archives (Moscow, 1994)," *Cahiers du Monde russe* 40 (1999): 257. In October and November 1940, the Soviets turned over 42,000 Polish prisoners of war from western Poland to the Germans, who killed the Jews among them, as they murdered most of the 60,000 Polish prisoners of war who were Jewish. Arno Lustiger, *Rotbuch: Stalin und die Juden* (Berlin: Aufbau-Verlag, 1998), 98.

13. See *Dimitrov Diary*, 25 November 1940, 134; James Barros and Richard Gregor, *Double Deception: Stalin, Hitler, and the Invasion of Russia* (De Kalb: Northern Illinois University Press, 1995).

14. Gerhard L. Weinberg, "Zur Frage eines Sonderfriedens im Osten," in *Gezeitenwechsel im Zweiten Weltkrieg? Die Schlachten von Char'kov und Kursk im Frühjahr und Sommer 1943 in operativer Anlage, Verlauf und politischer Bedeutung*, ed. Roland G. Foerster (Hamburg: Mittler, 1996), 173–83.

15. *Dimitrov Diary*, 12 June 1943, 279–80; Bodo Scheurig, *Verräter oder Patrioten: Das Nationalkomitee "Freies Deutschland" und der Bund Deutscher Offiziere in der Sowjetunion 1943–1945* (Berlin: Ullstein, 1993); Gerd R. Ueberschär, ed., *Das Nationalkomitee "Freies Deutschland" und der Bund Deutscher Offiziere* (Framkfurt am Main: Fischer, 1995).

16. The account is based on the extensive publication of relevant British and Soviet documents. The British documents may be found in Llewellyn Woodward, *History of the Second World War: British Foreign Policy in the Second World War* (London: H. M. Stationery Office, 1971), 2:221–36; Graham Ross, ed. *The Foreign Office and the Kremlin: British Documents on Anglo-Soviet Relations 1941–1945* (Cambridge: Cambridge University Press, 1984), 82–87; *Dokumente zur Deutschlandpolitik*, ser. 1, vol. 1, 592–97, and ser. 1, vol. 3, pt. 1, pp. 285–90; John Harvey, ed., *The War Diaries of Oliver Harvey* (London: Collins, 1978), 74–75; Albrecht Tyrell, *Grossbritannien und die Deutschlandplanung der Alliierten 1941–1946* (Frankfurt am Main: Metzner, 1987), 62–68. The Soviet documents are in Oleg Rzheshevsky, ed., *War and Diplomacy: The Making of the Grand Alliance, From Stalin's Archives* (Amsterdam: Harwood Academic Publishers, 1996), documents 4–14.

    It is worthy of note that after the Stalin-Eden meetings, on 28 January 1942, the Politburo established a nine-member commission to study possible postwar arrangements in Europe and Asia under Molotov's chairmanship. See A. Kem Welch, ed., *Stalinism in Poland 1944–1956* (London: MacMillan, 1999), 26.

17. Useful maps are contained in Romain Yakemtchouk, *La ligne Curson et la IIe guerre mondiale* (Louvain: Editions Nauwelaerts, 1957), 48, and Sarah Meiklejohn Terry, *Poland's Place in Europe: General Sikorski and the Origins of the Oder-Neisse Line, 1939–1943* (Princeton, N.J.: Princeton University Press, 1983), 121. Note that the Line B extension of the Curzon Line places Lvov on the Polish side. See also Cienciala, "Detective Work," 266–68.

18. A British Foreign Office memorandum tracing Stalin's shifting view from positive to negative is published in *Dokumente zur Deutschlandpolitik*, ser. 1, vol. 3, pt. 2, pp. 806–11.

19. PRO CAB 66/20 is published in ibid., 1:593.

20. The conflicting evidence is reviewed in Terry, *Poland's Place in Europe*, 245–56.

21. See Harvey, *War Diaries of Oliver Harvey*, 22 May 1942, 126; *Dokumente zur Deutschlandpolitik*, ser. 1, vol. 3, pt. 1, p. 44.

22. On Stalin's involvement in Soviet-Polish relations, see Cienciala, "Detective Work," 256–60; John Coutouvides and Jaime Reynolds, *Poland 1939–1945* (New York: Holmes & Meier, 1986), 83–85, 113, 156–57, 167–68; Alexander Contrast, *The Back Room: My Life with Krushchev and Stalin* (New York: Vantage Press, 1991), 128, 135, 150–51; Anita J. Prazmowska, *Britain and Poland, 1939–1943: The Betrayed Ally* (Cambridge: Cambridge University Press, 1995), 113, 120–21, 124–30, 147; *Foreign Relations of the United States, 1944*, 3:1305, 1372–96.

23. Detlef Brandes, "Eine verspätete tschechische Alternative zum Münchener 'Diktat': Edvard Beneš und die sudendeutsche Frage 1938–1945,"

Vierteljahrshefte für Zeitgeschichte 41 (1993): 221–41; Arnold Suppan and Elisabeth Vyslonzil, eds., *Eduard Beneš und die tschechoslovakische Aussenpolitik 1918–1948*, 2d. ed. (Vienna: Wiener Osteuropastudien, 2003).

24. *Dimitrov Diary*, 27 August 1941, 191; Geoffrey Swain, "Stalin's Wartime Vision of the Post War World," *Diplomacy and Statecraft* 7, no. 1 (1996): 83; Charles E. Bohlen, *Witness to History 1929–1969* (New York: Norton, 1973), 150–51; *Foreign Relations of the United States 1944*, 3:568, 587; *Foreign Relations of the United States: The Conferences at Cairo and Teheran*, 590–93.

25. *Dokumente zur Deutschlandpolitik*, ser. 1, vol. 3, pt. 1, pp. 259–61.

26. Weinberg, *A World at Arms*, 787–88; Paul Robert Magocsi, *The Shaping of a National Identity: Subcarpathian Rus', 1848–1949* (Cambridge, Mass.: Harvard University Press, 1978), 252–55.

27. Philip E. Moseley, "Across the Green Table from Stalin," *Current History* 15 (September 1948): 129–33, 164; Bruce R. Kuniholm. *The Origins of the Cold War in the Near East: Great Power Conflict and Diplomacy in Iran, Turkey, and Greece* (Princeton, N.J.: Princeton University Press, 1980), esp. maps 5, 7–9.

28. Ueberschär and Bezymenskij, *Der deutsche Angriff auf die Sowjetunion*, 183.

29. Xiauyuan Liu, *A Partnership for Disorder: China, the United States, and Their Policies for the Postwar Disposition of the Japanese Empire, 1941–1945* (Cambridge: Cambridge University Press, 1996), 250, 260 ff.; Contrast, *Backroom Boys*, 185–86, 195; Lane and Temperley, *Rise and Fall of the Grand Alliance*, 166–67; *Foreign Relations of the United States: The Conferences at Malta and Yalta*, 378–79.

30. See *Dimitrov Diary*, 16 June 1942, 337, and numerous other references there.

31. Bohlen, *Witness to History 1929–1969*, 139–40; *Foreign Relations of the United States: The Conferences at Cairo and Teheran*, 509, 514; but see *Dimitrov Diary*, 19 November 1944, 342–43.

32. Tyrell, *Grossbritannien und die Deutschlandplanung der Alliierten*, 117–18, 351 n. 20; *Foreign Relations of the United States: The Conferences at Cairo and Teheran*, pp. 513, 532–34.

33. Ibid., pp. 510–14; Tyrell, p. 475.

34. Gerhard L. Weinberg, "The Defeat of Germany in 1918 and the European Balance of Power," in *Germany, Hitler and World War II* (New York: Cambridge University Press, 1995), chap. 1.

35. Tyrell, *Grossbritannien und die Deutschlandplanung der Alliierten*, 469–73, 586.

36. Ibid., 260–63; Norman M. Naimark, *The Russians in Germany: A History of the Soviet Zone of Occupation, 1945–1949* (Cambridge, Mass.: Harvard University Press, 1995).

37. *Foreign Relations of the United States: The Conferences at Cairo and Teheran*, 530–32; Robert H. McNeal, "Roosevelt through Stalin's Spectacles," *International Journal* 18 (1963): 200–02.

38. McNeal, "Roosevelt through Stalin's Spectacles," 202–04; Robert C. Hilderbrand, *Dumbarton Oaks: The Origins of the United Nations and the Search for Postwar Security* (Chapel Hill: University of North Carolina Press, 1990), 44–46 and chap. 6.

39. Hilderbrand, *Dumbarton Oaks*, 63.

40. Ibid., 95–101.

41. Ibid., 215–17, 253, 255.

42. *Foreign Relations of the United States 1944*, 2:1017, 1019–21; Armand Van Dormael, *Bretton Woods: Birth of a Monetary System* (London: MacMillan, 1978); Harold James, *International Monetary Cooperation since Bretton Woods* (Washington, D.C.: International Monetary Fund and Oxford University Press, 1996).

43. William Roger Louis, *Imperialism at Bay 1941–1945: The United States and the Decolonization of the British Empire* (Oxford: Clarendon Press, 1977), 283–84; *Foreign Relations of the United States: The Conferences at Cairo and Teheran*, 532.

44. David Mayers, *The Ambassadors and America's Soviet Policy* (New York: Oxford University Press, 1995), 152–54.

45. *Foreign Relations of the United States 1944*, 4:973–75.

46. *Dimitrov Diary*, 28 June 1945, 358; see also Alexander Dallin, "Allied Leadership in the Second World War: Stalin," *Survey* 21 (1975): 11–19, esp. 16, 18. The dissolution of the Comintern is seen by one scholar more as a means for Stalin to give directives to individual communist parties in other countries directly rather than as a step toward better relations with the Western powers (Swain, "Stalin's Wartime Vision," 81–82).

47. Lane and Temperley, *Rise and Fall of the Grand Alliance*, 36–37.

48. Gerhard L. Weinberg, *World War II Leaders and Their Visions of the Future of Palestine* (Washington, D.C.: United States Holocaust Memorial Museum, 2002), 9–11, and the sources cited there; Constant, *Backroom Boys*, 131–32, 136–37, 140, 193. Arnold Krammer, *The Forgotten Friendship: Israel and the Soviet Bloc 1947–1953* (Urbana: University of Illinois Press, 1979), places the shift in Soviet policy at a much later date.

49. Albert Resis, "Spheres of Influence in Soviet Wartime Diplomacy," *Journal of Modern History* 53 (1981): 417–39; idem, "The Churchill-Stalin Secret 'Percentages' Agreement on the Balkans, Moscow, October, 1944," *American Historical Review* 83 (1978): 368–87; *Dimitrov Diary*, 8–9 December 1944, 345; 10 January 1945, 352–53.

50. Weinberg, *A World at Arms*, 201ff.

51. McNeal, "Roosevelt through Stalin's Spectacles," 197–200, 206.

52. James, *International Monetary Cooperation*, passim.

53. Lane and Temperley, *Rise and Fall of the Grand Alliance*, 207–10; David Holloway, *Stalin and the Bomb: The Soviet Union and Atomic Energy, 1939–1956* (New Haven: Yale University Press, 1094).

54. Timothy J. Colton, *Moscow: Governing the Socialist Metropolis* (Cambridge, Mass.: Belknap Press, 1995), 260, 332.

55. Vladimir V. Pozniakov, "Commoners, Commissars, and Spies: Soviet Policies and Society, 1945," in *Victory in Europe 1945: From World War to Cold War*, ed. Arnold A. Offner and Theodore A. Wilson (Lawrence: University Press of Kansas, 2000), 183–212.

56. The personal element in Stalin's decision to depart temporarily from prior and subsequent policy in regard to women flying combat planes is very well analyzed in Reina Pennington, *Wings, Women, and War: Soviet Airwomen in World War II Combat* (Lawrence: University Press of Kansas, 2001).

CHAPTER 6. WINSTON CHURCHILL

1. Cabinet minutes of 27 May 1940, PRO. CAB 65/13, quoted in David Dilks, "Allied Leadership in the Second World War: Churchill," *Survey* 21 (1975): 21.

2. The failure to recognize this critical point is a major defect of the valuable study by Klemens von Klemperer, *German Resistance to Hitler: The Search for Allies Abroad, 1938–1945* (Oxford: Clarendon, 1992).

3. Martin Gilbert, ed., *The Churchill War Papers*, vol. 2, *Never Surrender, May 1940–December 1940* (New York: Norton, 1995), 643, 708, 1230–31; John Colville, *The Fringes of Power: 10 Downing Street Diaries 1939–1955* (New York: Norton, 1985), 10 August 1940, 215; also 12 December 1940, 310 (hereafter cited as *Colville Diaries*); War Cabinet of 23 August 1940, PRO Cab 65/8, printed in *Dokumente zur Deutschlandpolitik*, ser. 1, vol. 1, pp. 198–99 (cf. ibid., 255).

4. Raymond A. Callahan, *Churchill: Retreat from Empire* (Wilmington, Del.: Scholarly Resources, 1984), 28, 112–16.

5. The full text of the speech is in Robert Rhodes James, ed., *Winston S. Churchill: His Complete Speeches 1897–1963*, vol. 4, *1935–1942* (New York: Bowker, 1974), 6691–95. On this question, see also William Roger Louis, *Imperialism at Bay: The United States and the Decolonization of the British Empire, 1941–1945* (Oxford: Clarendon Press, 1977), 181, 200–05; Richard J. Aldrich, *Intelligence and the War against Japan: Britain, America and the Politics of Secret Service* (Cambridge: Cambridge University Press, 2000), 117; *Foreign Relations of the United States: The Conferences at Cairo and Teheran* (Washington, DC: US Government Printing Office, 1961), 554.

6. Louis, *Imperialism at Bay*, 217–19; John Harvey, ed., *The War Diaries of Oliver Harvey* (London: Collins, 1978), 14 September 1942, 156; 18 October 1942, 168.

7. Louis, *Imperialism at Bay*, 124 ff.

8. Ibid., 40 n. 33; *Foreign Relations of the United States: The Conferences at Cairo and Teheran*, 485.

9. Louis, *Imperialism at Bay*, 433–35, 470.

10. The question of the Japanese mandated islands in the Pacific and their annexation or trusteeship status is reviewed in Chapter 8.

11. H. P. Willmott, *Grave of a Dozen Schemes: British Naval Planning and the War Against Japan, 1943–1945* (Annapolis, Md.: Naval Institute Press, 1996); Callahan, *Churchill*, 216–18.

12. Aldrich, *Intelligence and the War against Japan*, 4, 110–11; cf. 21, 196, 320–21. The project was dropped by Churchill's successor, Clement Attlee (ibid., 323).

13. See the excellent study by Ong Chit Chung, *Operation Matador: World War II – Britain's Attempt to Foil the Japanese Invasion of Malaya and Singapore* (Singapore: Times Academic Press, 1997).

14. Robert Rhodes James, *Churchill: A Study in Failure, 1900–1939* (New York: World Publishing Company, 1970), pt. 5.

15. Aldrich, *Intelligence and the War against Japan*, 158–59.

16. Callahan, *Churchill*, 185–88, 207–09.

17. John J. Sbrega, *Anglo-American Relations and Colonialism in East Asia, 1941–1945* (New York: Garland, 1983); idem, "Determination versus Drift: The Anglo-American Debate over the Trusteeship Issue, 1941–1945," *Pacific Historical Review* 55 (1986): 256–80.

18. Kit-chang Chan, "The United States and the Question of Hong Kong, 1941–1945," *Journal of the Hong Kong Branch of the Royal Asiatic Society* 19 (1979): 1–20.

19. Lord Moran, *Churchill, Taken from the Diaries of Lord Moran: The Struggle for Survival 1940–1965* (Boston: Houghton Mifflin, 1966), 24 November 1943, 140.

20. Ibid., 24 June 1954, 594; cf. Louis, *Imperialism at Bay*, 7.

21. Francis L. Loewenheim et al., eds., *Roosevelt and Churchill: Their Secret Wartime Correspondence* (New York: E. P. Dutton, 1975); Warren F. Kimball, ed., *Churchill and Roosevelt: The Complete Correspondence* (Princeton, N.J.: Princeton University Press, 1984); idem, *Forged in War: Roosevelt, Churchill and the Second World War* (New York: William Morrow, 1997).

22. There is good evidence on this in H. G. Nichols, ed., *Washington Despatches 1941–1945: Weekly Political Reports from the British Embassy* (Chicago: University of Chicago Press, 1981).

23. Gerhard L. Weinberg, "Roosevelt and Churchill – Conflicting Postwar Visions," in *World War II: Variants and Visions*, ed. Thomas O. Kelly II (Collingdale, Pa.: Diane Publishing Co., 1999), 181–93.

24. Joan Beaumont, *Comrades in Arms: British Aid to Russia 1941–1945* (London: Davis-Poynter, 1980); Martin H. Folly, *Churchill, Whitehall and the Soviet Union, 1940–1945* (New York: St. Martin's, 2000), 23–25.

25. See the maps in Earl F. Ziemke, *The U.S. Army in the Occupation of Germany 1944–1946* (Washington, D.C.: U.S. Government Printing Office, 1975), 120–21, and the discussion in Albrecht Tyrell, *Grossbritannien und die Deutschlandplanung der Alliierten 1941–1945* (Frankfurt am Main: Metzner, 1987), 230 ff.

26. Tyrell, *Grossbritannien und die Deutschlandplanung der Alliierten*, 404–08.

27. Callahan, *Churchill*, 226–28; Robert C. Hilderbrand, *Dumbarton Oaks: The Origins of the United Nations and the Search for Postwar Security* (Chapel Hill: University of North Carolina Press, 1990), 40. The British expected France to demand the Saar area and possibly more (Tyrell, *Grossbritannien und die Deutschlandplanung der Alliierten*, 354).

28. Tyrell, *Grossbritannien und die Deutschlandplanung der Alliierten*, 222–25, 349–50.

29. Ibid., 352–53.

30. Martin Gilbert, ed., *The Churchill War Papers*, vol. 3, *The Ever-Widening War 1941* (New York: Norton, 2000), 332; *Dokumente zur Deutschlandpolitik*, ser. 1, vol. 1, p. 266.

31. Gilbert, *Churchill War Papers*, 3:1112. The text reads, "In short, our aim is to make Germany 'fat but impotent.'"

32. Tyrell, *Grossbritannien und die Deutschlandplanung der Alliierten*, 506–15; John M. Blum, *From the Morgenthau Diaries*, vol. 3, *Years of War 1941–1945* (Boston: Houghton Mifflin, 1967), 369–72. Most writers on the subject have ignored Churchill's role in drafting the final version or the accompanying map, or both.

33. Tyrell, *Grossbritannien und die Deutschlandplanung der Alliierten*, 314, 390.

34. For Churchill on East Prussia, see *Dokumente zur Deutschlandpolitik*, ser. 1, vol. 1, p. 478.

35. Ironically, contiguity would come to several German states and provinces only after 1945.

36. Tyrell, *Grossbritannien und die Deutschlandplanung der Alliierten*, 384; Charles E. Bohlen, *Witness to History 1929–1969* (New York: Norton, 1973), 187; *Foreign Relations of the United States: The Conferences at Cairo and Teheran*, 510, 512; *Foreign Relations of the United States 1944*, 3:1325.

37. Tyrell, *Grossbritannien und die Deutschlandplanung der Alliierten*, 393–97, 467–68, 480; Gilbert, *Churchill War Papers*, 3:1657–58, 1660; *Dokumente zur Deutschlandpolitik*, ser. 1, vol. 2, pt. 1, pp. 125–52, 184–86; vol. 2, pt. 2, pp. 549–52, 555, 1144–46.

38. Tyrell, *Grossbritannien und die Deutschlandplanung der Alliierten*, 374–77; *Dokumente zur Deutschlandpolitik*, ser. 1, vol. 3, pt. 1, p. 57; vol. 2, pt. 2, pp. 549–52, 555, 576, 618–26, 663, 801–06, 844–45, 904.

39. Tyrell, *Grossbritannien und die Deutschlandplanung der Alliierten*, 543, 549.

40. Steven J. Lambakis, *Winston Churchill: Architect of Peace* (Westport, Conn.: Greenwood Press, 1993), 50–52; Folly, *Churchill, Whitehall, and the Soviet Union*, 77–80; Albert Resis, "The Churchill-Stalin Secret 'Percentages' Agreement on the Balkans, Moscow, October, 1944," *American Historical Review* 83 (1978): 368–87; *Foreign Relations of the United States 1944*, 2:112 ff.

41. Tyrell, *Grossbritannien und die Deutschlandplanung der Alliierten*, 402–03; Folly, *Churchill, Whitehall, and the Soviet Union*, 137; *Foreign Relations of the United States 1944*, 5:96–99; Sheila Lawlor, *Churchill and the Politics of War, 1940–1941* (New York: Cambridge University Press, 1994).

42. Lambakis, *Winston Churchill*, 44–46; Folly, *Churchill, Whitehall, and the Soviet Union*, 134–35, 143–46.

43. Folly, *Churchill, Whitehall, and the Soviet Union*, 162–3; Tyrell, *Grossbritannien und die Deutschlandplanung der Alliierten*, 395–96, 400–03, 457; Moran, *Churchill*, 301.

44. Folly, *Churchill, Whitehall, and the Soviet Union*, 166, 171.

45. Gilbert, *Churchill War Papers*, 3:137–39.

46. Tyrell, *Grossbritannien und die Deutschlandplanung der Alliierten*, 355–56; *Dokumente zur Deutschlandpolitik*, ser. 1, vol. 3, pt. 1, p. 470.

47. Gilbert, *Churchill War Papers*, 3:358–59; Moshe Gat, *Britain and Italy, 1843–1949: The Decline of British Influence* (Brighton, England: Sussex Academic Press, 1996); James E. Miller, "The Politics of Relief: The Roosevelt Administration and the Reconstruction of Italy, 1943–1944," *Prologue* 13 (1981): 205.

48. Richard Breitman, *Official Secrets: What the Nazis Planned, What the British and Americans Knew* (New York: Hill & Wang, 1998); *Dokumente zur Deutschlandpolitik*, ser. 1, vol. 3, pt. 2, pp. 742, 836–38.

49. *Dokumente zur Deutschlandpolitik*, ser. 1, vol. 3, pt. 2, pp. 555–56, 1129–32; Arieh J. Kochavi, *Prelude to Nuremberg: Allied War Crimes Policy and the Question of Punishment* (Chapel Hill: University of North Carolina Press, 1998); Robert H. Jackson, *Report of Robert H. Jackson, United States Representative to the Inter-national Conference on Military Trials, London 1945* (Washington, D.C.: U.S. Government Printing Office, 1949).

50. Gerhard L. Weinberg, *World War II Leaders and Their Visions for the Future of Palestine* (Washington, D.C.: United States Holocaust Memorial Museum, 2002), 13–16.

51. Gilbert, *Churchill War Papers*, 2:643, 708, 1230–31; *Colville Diaries*, 16 August 1940.

52. *Colville Diaries*, 13 December 1940, 312–13, 329, 326; *Dokumente zur Deutsch-landpolitik*, ser. 1, vol. 3, pt. 2, pp. 909, 915–16, 941.

53. Hilderbrand, *Dumbarton Oaks*, 38–40, 43–44, 51–54; Tyrell, *Grossbritannien und die Deutschlandplanung der Alliierten*, 98–108; Robert A. Divine, *Second Chance: The Triumph of Internationalism in America during World War II* (New York: Atheneum, 1971), 114; James, *Churchill: The Complete Speeches*, 3:6756–63; *Dokumente zur Deutschlandpolitik*, ser. 1, vol. 3, pt. 2, pp. 1196–202.

54. Hilderbrand, *Dumbarton Oaks*, 151–54.

55. Bohlen, *Witness to History, 1929–1969*, 168, 194.

56. Hilderbrand, *Dumbarton Oaks*, 51; Louis, *Imperialism at Bay*, 509, 530–31.

57. Callahan, *Churchill*, 182–83, 204–07.

58. Gilbert, *Churchill War Papers*, 2: 1256; *Foreign Relations of the United States 1944*, 3:10–14; James, *Churchill: The Complete Speeches*, 7:6755–63.

CHAPTER 7. CHARLES DE GAULLE

1. Marcel Vigneras, *United States Army in World War II: Rearming the French* (Washington, D.C.: U.S. Government Printing Office, 1957) This very important topic has been overlooked in the literature on Franco–American relations in World War II.

2. Martin Thomas, *The French Empire at War, 1940–1945* (Manchester: Manchester University Press, 1998), 134–29; R. T. Thomas, *Britain and Vichy: The Dilemma of Anglo-French Relations 1940–1942* (New York: St. Martin's, 1979), 124–26; Charles E. Bohlen, *Witness to History 1929–1969* (New York: Norton, 1973), 204–05.

3. See especially his speech at Oxford University on 25 November 1941, in Charles de Gaulle, *War Memoirs*, vol. 1, *The Call to Honor 1940–1942*, *Documents* (New York: Viking, 1955), 313–20.

4. Jean Lacouture, *De Gaulle: The Rebel 1890–1944* (New York: Norton, 1990), 321 ff.

5. Charles de Gaulle, *War Memoirs*, vol. 1, *The Call to Honor 1940–1942* (New York: Viking, 1955), 252. Note that when Molotov was in London in May 1942, de Gaulle took the occasion to complain to him about his British and American allies. See Molotov's report in Oleg Rzheshevsky, ed., *War and Diplomacy: The Making of the Grand Alliance, From Stalin's Archive* (Amsterdam: Harwood Academic Publishers, 1996), no. 45.

6. W. Averell Harriman and Elie Abel, *Special Envoy to Churchill and Stalin, 1941–1946* (New York: Random House, 1975), 231–32.

7. This is the information provided by de Gaulle's son to Erika S. Grams when she was working on the master's thesis cited in note 13.

8. See Douglas Johnson, "De Gaulle and France's Role in the World," in *De Gaulle and Twentieth Century France*, ed. Hugh Gough and John Horne (London: Arnold, 1994), 83–94; de Gaulle, *Memoirs, Documents*, 359–60; William Roger Louis, *Imperialism at Bay: The United States and the Decolonization of the British Empire, 1941–1945* (Oxford: Clarendon Press, 1977), 27.

9. John E. Dreifort, *Myopic Grandeur: The Ambivalence of French Foreign Policy toward the Far East, 1919–1945* (Kent, Ohio: Kent State University Press, 1991), chap. 9.

10. De Gaulle, *Memoirs, Documents*, 111; Thomas, *The French Empire at War, 1940–1945*, 109–10, 121–22, 236.

11. De Gaulle, *Memoirs, Documents*, 353–54.

12. Ibid., 99, 103, 222–23; Martin Gilbert, ed., *The Churchill War Papers*, vol. 3, *1941: The Ever Widening War* (New York: Norton, 2001), 1121; Lacouture, *De Gaulle*, 327. It should be noted that oil had not been discovered in Libya at that time.

13. Erika S. Grams, "Charles de Gaulle and Harry Truman: The Effects of Personality on Diplomacy during the Stuttgart and Val d'Aosta Incidents in Spring 1945" (master's thesis, University of North Carolina at Chapel Hill, 1994).

14. De Gaulle, *Memoirs, Documents*, 299; Albrecht Tyrell, *Grossbritannien und die Deutschlandplanung der Alliierten* (Frankfurt am Main: Metzner, 1987), 390.

15. John Colville, *The Fringes of Power: 10 Downing Street Diaries 1939–1955* (New York: Norton, 1985), 13 December 1940, 311.

16. John W. Wheeler-Bennett, ed., *Action This Day: Working with Churchill* (New York: St. Martin's, 1968), 82.

17. Lacouture, *De Gaulle*, 276 ff.

18. Tyrell, *Grossbritannien und die Deutschlandplanung der Alliierten*, 244, 522 nn. 10–11, 523–24, 525 n. 26; Jacques Bariéty, "Frankreich und das deutsche Problem nach dem Ersten und nach dem Zweiten Weltkrieg," in *Deutschland und der Westen im 19. und 20. Jahrhundert*, pt. 2, *Deutschland und Westeuropa*, ed. Klaus Schwabe and Francesca Schinzinger (Stuttgart: Steiner, 1994), 130–31; Cyril Buffet, "Zwischen Vorfeld und Hinterland: Frankreich, Deutschland und Europa, 1944–1962," in *Deutschland und der Westem: Internationale Beziehungen im 20. Jahrhundert, Festschrift für Klaus Schwabe*, ed. Guido Müller (Stuttgart: Steiner, 1998), 174–75; Dietrich Orlow, "Sozialistische Deutschlandpolitik: SFIO, SPD und die Zukunft Deutschlands 1945–1950," *Francia* 26, no. 3 (1999): 33, 48, and the sources cited there.

19. Tyrell, *Grossbritannien und die Deutschlandplanung der Alliierten*, 324–25.

20. This point is invariably ignored by those who have written on the Morgenthau Plan without looking at the map.

21. De Gaulle, *Memoirs, Documents*, 355–58.

22. Lacouture, *De Gaulle*, 504–07; Thomas, *The French Empire at War, 1940–1945*, 250–52.

23. Zvi Elpeleg, *The Grand Mufti: Haj Amin Al-Husseini, Founder of the Palestinian National Movement* (London: Frank Cass, 1993), 74–77.

24. De Gaulle, *Memoirs, Documents*, 227; Lacouture, *De Gaulle*, 325, 471–73.

CHAPTER 8. FRANKLIN D. ROOSEVELT

1. Raymond G. O'Connor, *Diplomacy for Victory: FDR and Unconditional Surrender* (New York: Norton, 1971), though rather dated, remains the best work on the subject.

2. The text is in *A Decade of American Foreign Policy: Basic Documents, 1941–1949* (Washington, D.C.: U.S. Government Printing Office, 1950), 2.

3. Albrecht Tyrell, *Grossbritannien und die Deutschlandplanung der Alliierten* (Frankfurst am Main: Metzner, 1987), 49.

4. Gerhard L. Weinberg, *A World at Arms: A Global History of World War II* (Cambridge: Cambridge University Press, 1994), 438–39. There is evidence that Churchill – and most likely Roosevelt – would have been willing to exempt Italy from the demand, but at the insistence of the British Cabinet Italy was included.

5. *Dokumente zur Deutschlandpolitik*, ser. 1, vol. 4, pp. 311–12.

6. Ibid., 499–500.

7. *Foreign Relations of the United States: The Conferences at Malta and Yalta 1945*, 158. Roosevelt did, however, want the subject studied carefully, as he told Hull in March 1943 (Cordell Hull, *The Memoirs of Cordell Hull* [New York: Macmillan, 1948], 1248).

8. *Dokumente zur Deutschlandpolitik*, ser. 1, vol. 3, pt. 1, pp. 201–02, vol. 3, pt. 2, pp. 1137–38, 1195–96; Anita J. Prazmovska, *Britain and Poland, 1939–1943: The Betrayed Ally* (Cambridge: Cambridge University Press, 1995), 178.

9. Roosevelt's map is in Maurice Matloff, *United States Army in World War II: Strategic Planning for Coalition Warfare, 1943–1944* (Washington D.C.: U.S. Government Printing Office, 1959), facing p. 341; cf. Earl F. Ziemke, *The U.S. Army in the Occupation of Germany 1944–1946* (Washington, D.C.: U.S. Government Printing Office, 1975), 115–22; Tyrell, *Grossbritannien und die Deutschlandplnung der Alliierten*, 239–41, 481; John Q. Barrett, ed., *Robert H. Jackson, That Man: An Insider's Portrait of Franklin D. Roosevelt* (New York: Oxford University Press, 2003), 107; Daniel J. Nelson, *Wartime Origins of the Berlin Dilemma* (University, Al.: University of Alabama Press, 1978): William M. Franklin, "Zonal Boundaries and Access to Berlin," *World Politics* 16 (1963): 1–31; John L. Harper, *American Visions of Europe: Franklin D. Roosevelt, George F. Kennan,*

and Dean G. Acheson (Cambridge: Cambridge University Press, 1994), 91–93; *Dokumente zur Deutschlandpolitik*, ser. 1, vol. 4, pp. 509–10.

10. Gretchen M. Skidmore, "The American Occupation of the Bremen Enclave, 1945–1947" (master's thesis, University of North Carolina at Chapel Hill, 1989).

11. The discussion of a French zone of occupation and seat on the Control Council for Germany can best be followed in *Foreign Relations of the United States: The Conferences at Malta and Yalta 1945* (Washington, D.C.: U.S. Government Printing Office, 1955).

12. John M. Blum, *From the Morgenthau Diaries: Years of War 1941–1945* (Boston: Houghton Mifflin, 1967), 352. For Roosevelt's earlier views, see Michaela Hoenicke, "Franklin D. Roosevelt's View of Germany: Formative Experiences for a Future President" (master's thesis, University of North Caroline at Chapel Hill, 1989).

13. The full text and map are printed in Henry Morgenthau Jr., *Germany Is Our Problem* (New York: Harper, 1945). The account in Tyrell (pp. 281–85) is helpful, but he ignores the differences between the maps there and on pp. 322–24. The main differences between Morgenthau's proposed map and the Oder-Neisse line were that Morgenthau's left all of Pomerania, much of Brandenburg, and a part of Silesia to Germany while placing additional territory in the West under French administration. See also Bernd Greiner, *Die Morgenthau-Legende: Die Geschichte eines umstrittenen Plans* (Hamburg: Hamburger Edition, 1995).

14. Blum, *Morgenthan Diaries*, 348–49, 412–14; Tyrell, *Grossbritannien und die Deutschlandplanung der Alliierten*, 286–91.

15. Robert A. Divine, *Second Chance: The Triumph of Internationalism in America during World War II* (New York: Atheneum, 1971), 49; Robert C. Hilderbrand, *Dumbarton Oaks: The Origins of the United Nations and the Search for Postwar Security* (Chapel Hill: University of North Carolina Press, 1990), 6–7, 12–13; Harley A. Notter, *Postwar Foreign Policy Preparations 1939–1945* (Washington, D.C.: U.S. Government Printing Office, 1949).

16. *Foreign Relations of the United States 1941*, 1:364–67; Theodore A. Wilson, *The First Summit: Roosevelt and Churchill at Placentia Bay 1941*, rev. ed. (Lawrence: University Press of Kansas, 1991).

17. Hilderbrand, *Dumbarton Oaks*, 15–16.

18. Edgar Snow, "Fragments from F.D.R.," *Monthly Review* 8 (1957): 317. The remark was made on 24 February 1942.

19. Averell W. Harriman and Elie Abel, *Special Envoy to Churchill and Stalin, 1941–1946* (New York: Random House, 1975), 236; Hilderbrand, *Dumbarton Oaks*, 58–60; T. G. Fraser, "Roosevelt and the Making of America's East Asia Policy, 1941–1945," in *Conflict and Amity in East Asia: Essays in Honor of Ian Nish*,

ed. T. G. Fraser and Peter Lowe (London: MacMillan, 1992), 98–107; *Foreign Relations of the United States 1942: China*, 185–87; Xiaoyuan Liu, *A Partnership for Disorder: China, the United States, and Their Policies for the Postwar Disposition of the Japanese Empire, 1941–1945* (Cambridge: Cambridge University Press, 1996), 21–23, 117. For Chinese records on this issue, see the references in Liu, p. 250.

20. Eggleston diary, entry for 14 November 1944, quoted in William Roger Louis, *Imperialism at Bay: The United States and the Decolonization of the British Empire, 1941–1945* (Oxford: Clarendon Press, 1977), 424. Roosevelt had made similar comments on 31 August 1943; see Liu, *A Partnership for Disorder*, 117.

21. Hilderbrand, *Dumbarton Oaks*, 60–61.

22. Divine, *Second Chance*, 48–49, 61–62; Ann Lane and Howard Temperley, eds., *The Rise and Fall of the Great Alliance, 1941–1945* (London: MacMillan, 1995), 4–5, 10–11. Note that originally Roosevelt had wanted a meeting of all four leaders – including Stalin and Chiang – in Khartoum in November 1942 rather than a meeting of just himself and Churchill at Casablanca in January 1943. See Geoffrey Ward, *Closest Companion* (Boston: Houghton Mifflin, 1995), 27 November 1942, 187; cf. ibid., 207.

23. Divine, *Second Chance*, 114; Ward, *Closest Companion*, 287; Harper, *American Visions of Europe*, 96–97, 107–08; *Dokumente zur Deutschlandpolitik*, ser. 1, vol. 4, pp. 189–90.

24. Divine, *Second Chance*, 136–137; Tyrell, *Grossbritannien und die Deutschlandplanung der Alliierten*, 120–22.

25. Charles E. Bohlen, *Witness to History 1929–1969* (New York: Norton, 1973), 144–45; Divine, *Second Chance*, 158.

26. Divine, *Second Chance*, 86, 93–97; Hilderbrand, *Dumbarton Oaks*, 27, 57–58, 64–65; See also Robert Dallek, "Allied Leadership in the Second World War: Roosevelt," *Survey* 21 (1975): 1–10. On Roosevelt's interest in the location of the UNO headquarters, see Hilderbrand, *Dumbarton Oaks*, 106.

27. Divine, *Second Chance*, 184–85, 206–08; Hilderbrand, *Dumbarton Oaks*, 34–37, 131, 180, 198–202. On Roosevelt's thinking about a permanent Council seat in the future for Brazil and for a Moslem state, see Hilderbrand, *Dumbarton Oaks*, 124–27.

28. Hilderbrand, *Dumbarton Oaks*, 226–28, 251–52.

29. Blum, *Morgenthau Diaries*, 16 February 1944, 373.

30. Divine, *Second Chance*, 117–18, 156–57; James Herbert George Jr., "United States Postwar Relief Planning: The First Phase, 1940–1943" (Ph.D. diss., University of Wisconsin, 1970).

31. Divine, *Second Chance*, 116–17.

32. Frances Perkins, *The Roosevelt I Knew* (New York: Viking, 1947), 339–41, 346; *Foreign Relations of the United States 1944*, 2:14 ff., 5:16–17.

33. Blum, *Morgenthan Diaries*, chap. 5; *Foreign Relations of the United States 1944*, 2:107 ff.; Alfred E. Eckes, *A Search for Solvency: Bretton Woods and the International Monetary System, 1941–1971* (Austin: University of Texas Press, 1975), 56–57, 81–82, 110–17. For the conference itself in July 1944, see Eckes, *A Search for Solvency*, chap. 6.

34. *Foreign Relations of the United States 1944*, 2:110–11.

35. Eckes, *A Search for Solvency*, 104–05, 113–14, 205–08. Earlier Roosevelt had been inclined to assist the Soviet Union with its reconstruction problems; see *Foreign Relations of the United States 1944*, 4:1046–48.

36. Alan P. Dobson, "The Other Air Battle: The American Pursuit of Post-War Civil Aviation Rights," *The Historical Journal* 28 (1985): 429–39; Louis, *Imperialism at Bay*, 268; *Foreign Relations of the United States: The Conferences at Cairo and Teheran*, 177–79; Beatrice Bishop Berle and Travis Beal Jacobs, eds., *Navigating the Rapids 1918–1971: From the Papers of Adolf A. Berle* (New York: Harcourt Brace Jovanovich, 1973), 483–84, 487, 496.

37. On Roosevelt and the development of the A-bomb, there is a forthcoming book by Lawrence Suid. For Roosevelt's critical decision of 9 October 1941 on moving forward, see Robin Edwards, *The Big Three: Churchill, Roosevelt and Stalin in Peace and War* (New York: Norton, 1991), 397; Harper, *American Visions of Europe*, 108–12.

38. Richard J. Aldrich, *Intelligence and the War against Japan: Britain, America and the Politics of Secret Service* (Cambridge: Cambridge University Press, 2000), chap. 8; *Foreign Relations of the United States 1942*, 1:599 ff.; Warren F. Kimball, ed., *Churchill and Roosevelt: The Complete Correspondence* (Princeton, N.J.: Princeton University Press, 1984), 1:400–04.

39. Wilson, *First Summit*, 108–10; Bohlen, *Witness to History*, 140; Aldrich, *Intelligence and the War against Japan*, 122 ff.; Douglas Brinkley and David R. Facey-Crowther, eds., *The Atlantic Charter* (New York: St. Martin's, 1994), chap. 4; Louis, *Imperialism at Bay*, 9, 29–30, chap. 5; Ward, *Closest Companion*, 187, 197–200; John J. Sbrega, "Determination versus Drift: The Anglo-American Debate over the Trusteeship Issue, 1941–1945," *Pacific Historical Review* 55 (1986): 266, 275–77; Snow, "Fragments from FDR," 318–21. The article by Robert B. Looper, "Roosevelt and the British Empire," *Occidente* 12, no. 4 (1956): 348–63; no. 5 (1956): 424–36, is still very helpful.

40. Elliott Roosevelt, ed., *F.D.R.: His Personal Letters 1928–1945* (New York: Duell, Sloan and Pearce, 1950), 2:1489; Bohlen, *Witness to History*, 140; Aldrich, *Intelligence and the War against Japan*, 205 ff.; Louis, *Imperialism at Bay*, 28, 41–42, 356–57, 436–38; *Foreign Relations of the United States 1944*, 5:1206; John A. L. Sullivan, "The United States, the East Indies and World War II: The American Efforts to Modify the Colonial Status Quo" (Ph.D. diss., University of Massachusetts, 1969). On the subject of the Portuguese portions

of Timor, Roosevelt held back in November 1944 because of the Allied need for bases in the Azores.

41. *Foreign Relations of the United States: The Conferences at Cairo and Teheran*, 307–08, 887–88; Kit-cheng Chan, "The United States and the Question of Hong Kong, 1941–1945," *Journal of the Hong Kong Branch of the Royal Asiatic Society* 19 (1979): 9–10, 16.

42. Berle and Jacobs, *Navigating the Rapids 1918–1971*, 476, 5 March 1945, quotes Roosevelt: "so far as he could see Churchill was running things on an 1890 set of ideas." See also Ward, *Closest Companion*, 207.

43. Louis, *Imperialism at Bay*, 95–96.

44. Ibid., chap. 22, pp. 44–45, 147–58, 484–87; Lane and Temperley, *Rise and Fall of the Great Alliance*, 10; *Foreign Relations of the United States 1942*, 3:378–81, *Foreign Relations of the United States 1942: China*, 185–87.

45. Sbrega, "Determination versus Drift," 275–77.

46. Hilderbrand, *Dumbarton Oaks*, 170–76; Louis, *Imperialism at Bay*, 262, 266–68, 211–12, 426; Jack Stokes Ballard, "Postwar American Plans for the Japanese Mandated Islands," *Rocky Mountain Social Science Journal* 3 (1966): 109–16.

47. Harper, *American Visions of Europe*, 108–12; *Dokumente zur Deutschlandpolitik*, ser. 1, vol. 4, p. 520.

48. Lane and Temperley, *Rise and Fall of the Great Alliance*, 56–57; *Foreign Relations of the United States 1942*, 1: 525–37.

49. David Reynolds, "Roosevelt, the British Left, and the Appointment of John G. Winant as United States Ambassador to Britain in 1941," *International History Review* 4 (1982): 393–413.

50. P. G. A. Orders, in his book, *Britain, Australia, New Zealand and the Challenge of the United States, 1939–1946: A Study in International History* (New York: Palgrave Macmillan, 2003), argues that there was no substantial turn of the two Dominions toward the United States; but whatever the frictions and distrust, the governments tended to turn toward Washington in crises during and after the war.

51. The incident occurred in February 1940; see Robert E. Sherwood, *Roosevelt and Hopkins: An Intimate History* (New York: Harper, 1948), 138.

52. *Dokumente zur Deutschlandpolitik*, ser. 1, vol. 3, pt. 1, pp. 201–02, 205–09.

53. Sherwood, *Roosevelt and Hopkins*, chap. 18. See also George C. Herring, Jr., *Aid to Russia: Strategy, Diplomacy, the Origins of the Cold War* (New York: Columbia University Press, 1973), 11–137 passim.

54. R. Michael Berry, *American Foreign Policy and the Finnish Exception* (Helsinki: Societas Historica Finlandiae, 1987).

55. Harriman and Abel, *Special Envoy to Churchill and Stalin*, 369–70, 373, chaps. 14–15; Bohlen, *Witness to History*, 187, 189–92; Alexander Contrast,

The Back Room: My Life with Khrushchev and Stalin (New York: Vantage Press, 1991), 139; *Foreign Relations of the United States 1944*, 3:1282.

56. The text is in *The Conferences at Malta and Yalta*, 977–78.

57. Geoffrey Warner, "From Teheran to Yalta: Reflections on F.D.R.'s Foreign Policy," *International Affairs* 48 (1967): 530–36; Harper, *American Visions of Europe*, 88–89, 121; Snow, "Fragments from F.D.R.," 398–402; *Foreign Relations of the United States 1944*, 2:112–15, 117 ff.; *Dokumente zur Deutschlandpolitik*, ser. 1, vol. 4, pp. 509–10.

58. Lane and Temperley, *Rise and Fall of the Great Alliance*, 12–14; Harper, *American Visions of Europe*, 90–91; *Dokumente zur Deutschlandpolitik*, ser. 1, vol. 4, pp. 189–90.

59. Lane and Temperley, *Rise and Fall of the Great Alliance*, 12–15.

60. *Dokumente zur Deutschlandpolitik*, ser. 1, vol. 2, p. 178.

61. Harriman and Abel, *Special Envoy to Churchill and Stalin*, 227–8; Olav Riste, "Free Ports in North Norway: A Contribution to the Study of F.D.R.'s Policy towards the USSR," *Journal of Contemporary History* 5, no. 4 (1970): 77–95.

62. Liu, *A Partnership for Disorder*, 74.

63. Ibid., 100–01, 240–45, 258–59; Snow, "Fragments from F.D.R.," 308; *Foreign Relations of the United States 1942: China*, 185–87.

64. Liu, *A Partnership for Disorder*, 203, 208–9, 233; Snow, "Fragments from F.D.R.," 395–98; Fraser, "Roosevelt and the Making of America's East Asia Policy," 98–107.

65. Liu, *A Partnership for Disorder*, 243.

66. Ibid., 212–13.

67. Marcel Vigneras, *United States Army in World War II: Rearming the French* (Washington, D.C.: U.S. Government Printing Office, 1957); *The Conferences at Cairo and Teheran*, 195; *Dokumente zur Deutschlandpolitik*, ser. 1, vol. 3, pt. 1, pp. 657–61.

68. Harper, *American Visions of Empire*, 113–16.

69. *The Conferences at Cairo and Teheran*, 195.

70. *Foreign Relations of the United States 1942*, 2:379–81.

71. *Foreign Relations of the United States 1944*, 1:98. Roosevelt wanted the announcement of this decision to be made on November 11.

72. Bohlen, *Witness to History*, 184–85.

73. See Roosevelt's comment on the "Iowa" on 15 November 1943, *The Conferences at Cairo and Teheran*, 196–97.

74. James E. Miller, "The Politics of Relief: The Roosevelt Administration and the Reconstruction of Italy, 1943–1944," *Prologue* 13 (1981): 193–208.

75. Rudolf V. A. Janssens, *"What Future for Japan?" U.S. Wartime Planning for the Postwar Era, 1942–1945* (Amsterdam: Rodopi, 1995), 4–60. There is a

generally unsatisfactory discussion of American planning and Roosevelt's role in it in Dale M. Hellegers, *We, the Japanese People: World War II and the Origins of the Japanese Constitution* (Stanford, Calif.: Stanford University Press, 2002), 1–7, 32–33; but see Roosevelt's approved but not issued statement to the Japanese of early December 1944 on pp. 86–87.

76. Fraser, "Roosevelt and the Making of America's East Asia Policy," 96–99.

77. There is a recent account in Hellegers, *We, the Japanese People*, chaps. 7–9.

78. See *Dokumente zur Deutschlandpolitik*, ser. 1, vol. 4, pp. 197–98 (22 February 1943).

79. Tyrell, *Grossbritannien und die Deutschlandplanung der Alliierten*, 49. There is a useful but not entirely satisfactory account in Arieh J. Kochavi, *Prelude to Nuremberg: Allied War Crimes Policy and the Question of Punishment* (Chapel Hill: University of North Carolina Press, 1998).

80. *Foreign Relations of the United States 1942*, 1:58–59; *Dokumente zur Deutschlandpolitik*, ser. 1, vol. 1, p. 483, vol. 4, pp. 301–04.

81. *Dokumente zur Deutschlandpolitik*, ser. 1, vol. 4, pp. 592–93.

82. Hull, *Memoirs of Cordell Hull*, 1289 ff.; Barrett, *Robert H. Jackson*, 109–10.

83. Gerhard L. Weinberg, *World War II Leaders and Their Visions for the Future of Palestine* (Washington, D.C.: U.S. Holocaust Memorial Museum, 2002), 13–14.

84. *Foreign Relations of the United States 1944*, 5:615–16.

85. Thomas Campbell and George C. Herring Jr., eds., *The Diaries of Edward R. Stettinius, Jr.* (New York: New Viewpoints, 1975), 10 November 1944, 170.

86. *Foreign Relations of the United States 1942*, 1:13, 25.

87. For a general survey placing relations with Latin America in context, see Robert Dallek, *Franklin D. Roosevelt and American Foreign Policy, 1932–1945* (New York: Oxford University Press, 1979).

88. John Morton Blum, *V Was for Victory: Politics and American Culture during World War II* (New York: Harcourt Brace Jovanovich, 1976), is still very useful. For a helpful recent survey, see John W. Jeffries, *Wartime America: The World War II Home Front* (Chicago: Ivan R. Dee, 1996).

89. D'Ann Campbell, *Women at War with America: Private Lives in a Patriotic Era* (Cambridge, Mass.: Harvard University Press, 1984); idem, "Women in Combat: The World War II Experience in the United States, Great Britain, Germany, and the Soviet Union," *Journal of Military History* 57 (1993): 301–23.

90. The book by Frances Perkins cited in note 32 provides some insight.

CHAPTER 9. THE REAL POSTWAR WORLD

1. Rüdiger Overmans, *Deutsche militärischen Verluste im Zweiten Weltkrieg* (Munich: Oldenbourg, 1999), contains an excellent analysis.

2. Georg Meyer, ed., *Generalfeldmarschall Ritter von Leeb: Tagebuchaufzeichnungen und Lagebeurteilungen aus zwei Weltkriegen* (Stuttgart: Deutsche Verlags-Anstalt, 1976), 10 December 1945, 80 n. 194.

3. Eduard Wagner to his wife, 31 August 1939, in Elizabeth Wagner, ed., *Der Generalquartiermeister: Briefe und Tagebuchaufzeichnungen des Generalquartiermeisters des Heeres General der Artillerie Eduard Wagner* (Munich: Olzog, 1963), 109.

4. There is a useful account in David G. Marr, *Vietnam 1945: The Quest for Power* (Berkeley: University of California Press, 1995).

5. Dennis J. Doolin, *Territorial Issues in the Sino-Soviet Conflict: Documents and Analysis* (Stanford, Calif.: Hoover Institution, 1965).

6. Robert A. Divine, *Second Chance: The Triumph of Internationalism in America During World War II* (New York: Atheneum, 1971), 313.

7. Roosevelt's map may be found in Maurice Matloff, *United States Army in World War II: Strategic Planning for Coalition Warfare, 1943–1944* (Washington, D.C.: U.S. Government Printing Office, 1959), facing p. 341.

8. Erika S. Grams, "Charles de Gaulle and Harry Truman: The Effects of Personality on Diplomacy during the Stuttgart and Val d'Aosta Incidents in Spring 1945" (master's thesis, University of North Carolina at Chapel Hill, 1994).

BIBLIOGRAPHY

Aldrich, Richard J. *Intelligence and the War against Japan: Britain, America and the Politics of Secret Service*. Cambridge: Cambridge University Press, 2000.

Aloisi, Pompeo. *Journal (25 juillet 1932–14 juin 1936)*. Paris: Plon, 1957.

Ballard, Jack Stokes. "Postwar American Plans for the Japanese Mandated Islands." *Rocky Mountain Social Science Journal* 3 (1966): 109–16.

Banac, Ivo, trans. and ed. *The Diary of Georgi Dimitrov 1933–1945*. New Haven, Conn.: Yale University Press, 2003.

Baranowski, Shelley. *Strength Through Joy: Consumerism and Mass Tourism in the Third Reich*. Cambridge: Cambridge University Press, 2004.

Bariéty, Jacques. "Frankreich und das deutsche Problem nach dem Ersten und nach dem Zweiten Weltkrieg." In *Deutschland und der Westen im 19. und 20. Jahrhundert*. Pt. 2. Edited by Klaus Schwabe and Francesca Schinziger, 121–36. Stuttgart: Steiner, 1994.

Barros, James, and Richard Gregor. *Double Deception: Stalin, Hitler, and the Invasion of Russia*. DeKalb: Northern Illinois University Press, 1995.

Beaumont, Joan. *Comrades in Arms: British Aid to Russia 1941–1945*. London: Davis Poynter, 1980.

Bergen, Doris L. *Twisted Cross: The German Christian Movement in the Third Reich*. Chapel Hill: University of North Carolina Press, 1996.

Berle, Beatrice Bishop, and Travis Beale Jacobs, eds. *Navigating the Rapids 1918–1971: From the Papers of Adolf A. Berle*. New York: Harcourt Brace Jovanovich, 1973.

Berry, R. Michael. *American Foreign Policy and the Finnish Exception*. Helsinki: Societas Historica Finlandiae, 1987.

Bix, Herbert P. *Hirohito and the Making of Modern Japan*. New York: Harper-Collins, 2000.

Blum, John M. *V Was for Victory: Politics and American Culture during World War II*. New York: Harcourt Brace Jovanovich, 1976.

———, ed. *From the Morgenthau Diaries: Years of War 1941–1945*. Boston: Houghton Mifflin, 1967.

Bohlen, Charles E. *Witness to History 1929–1969*. New York: Norton, 1973.

Bohn, Robert. *Reichskommisariat Norwegen: "Nationalsozialistische Raumordnung" und Kriegswirtschaft*. Munich: Oldenbourg, 2000.

Borton, Hugh. *American Presurrender Planning for Japan*. New York: East Asia Institute, 1967.

Bosworth, Richard J. B. *Mussolini*. London: Arnold, 2002.

Boyle, John Hunter. *China and Japan at War 1937–1945: The Politics of Collaboration*. Stanford, Calif.: Stanford University Press, 1972.

Bracher, Karl Dietrich, et al. *Die nationalsozialistische Machtergreifung*. 2d ed. Cologne: Westdeutscher Verlag, 1982.

Brandes, Detlef. "Eine verspätete tschechische Alternative zum Münchener 'Diktat': Edvard Beneš und die sudetendeutsche Frage." *Vierteljahrshefte für Zeitgeschichte* 41 (1993): 221–41.

Breitman, Richard. *Official Secrets: What the Nazis Planned, What the British and Americans Knew*. New York: Hill & Wang, 1998.

Brinkley, Douglas, and David R. Facey-Crawther, eds. *The Atlantic Charter*. New York: St. Martin's, 1996.

Browne, Courtney. *Tojo: The Last Banzai*. New York: Da Capo Press, 1998.

Browning, Christopher. *The Origins of the Final Solution: The Evolution of Nazi Jewish Policy, September 1939–March 1942*. Lincoln: University of Nebraska Press, 2004.

Buffet, Cyril. "Zwischen Vorfeld und Hinterland: Frankreich, Deutschland und Europa, 1944–1962." In *Deutschland und der Westen: Internationale Beziehungen im 20. Jahrhundert: Festschrift für Klaus Schwabe*, edited by Guido Müller, 174–85. Stuttgart: Steiner, 1998.

Burleigh, Michael, and Wolfgang Wippermann. *The Racial State: Germany 1933–1945*. Cambridge: Cambridge University Press, 1991.

Caj Dejin. "Relations between Chiang Kai-shek and Wang Ching-wei during the War against Japan: An Examination of Some Problems." *Republican China* 14, no. 2 (1989): 2–20.

Callahan, Raymond. *Churchill: Retreat from Empire*. Wilmington, Del.: Scholarly Resources, 1984.

Campbell, D'Ann. *Women at War with America: Private Lives in a Patriotic Era.* Cambridge, Mass.: Harvard University Press, 1984.

———. "Women in Combat: The World War II Experience in the United States, Great Britain, Germany and the Soviet Union." *Journal of Military History* 57 (1993): 301–23.

Campbell, Thomas, and George C. Herring, Jr., eds. *The Diaries of Edward R. Stettinius, Jr.* New York: New Viewpoints, 1975.

Carlton, David. *Churchill and the Soviet Union.* Manchester: Manchester University Press, 2000.

Chan, Kit-cheng. "The United States and the Question of Hong Kong." *Journal of the Hong Kong Branch of the Royal Asiatic Society* 19 (1979): 1–20.

Chi, His-sheng. *Nationalist China at War: Military Defeat and Political Collapse, 1937–1945.* Ann Arbor: University of Michigan Press, 1982.

Chiang Kai-shek. *China's Destiny.* With notes and commentary by Philip Jaffe. New York: Roy Publishers, 1947.

Chung, Ong Chit. *Operation Matador.* Singapore: Times Academic Press, 1997.

Ciano, Galeazzo. *Diary 1937–1943.* Translated by Robert L. Miller. New York: Enigma Books, 2002.

Cienciala, Anna M. "Detective Work: Researching Soviet World War II Policy on Poland in Russian Archives (Moscow, 1994)." *Cahiers du Monde Russe* 40 (1999): 251–70.

Cohen, Michael J. *Churchill and the Jews.* London: Frank Cass, 1985.

Collier, Basil. *History of the Second World War: The Defence of the United Kingdom.* London: H. M. Stationery Office, 1957.

Colton, Timothy J. *Moscow: Governing the Socialist Metropolis.* Cambridge, Mass.: Belknap Press, 1995.

Colville, John. *The Fringes of Power: 10 Downing Street Diaries 1939–1955.* New York: Norton, 1985.

Conference on Chiang Kai-shek and Modern China (Taipei, Taiwan, 1986). *Proceedings of the Conference on Chiang Kai-shek and Modern China.* 5 vols. Taipei: China Cultural Service, 1987.

Contrast, Alexander. *The Back Room: My Life with Khrushchev and Stalin.* New York: Vantage Press, 1991.

Cook, Haruko Raya, and Theodore F. Cook, eds. *Japan at War: An Oral History.* New York: New Press, 1992.

Coox, Alvin D. *Nomonham: Japan against Russia 1939.* 2 vols. Stanford, Calif.: Stanford University Press, 1985.

———. *Tojo.* New York: Ballantine, 1975.

Coutouvides, John, and Jaime Reynolds. *Poland 1939–1945.* New York: Holmes & Meier, 1986.

Dallek, Robert. "Allied Leadership in the Second World War: Roosevelt." *Survey* 21 (1975): 1–10.

———. *Franklin D. Roosevelt and American Foreign Policy, 1932–1945.* New York: Oxford University Press, 1979.

Dallin, Alexander. "Allied Leadership in the Second World War: Stalin." *Survey* 21 (1975): 11–19.

Deakin, F. W. *The Brutal Friendship: Mussolini, Hitler and the Fall of Italian Fascism.* New York: Harper & Row, 1962.

A Decade of American Foreign Policy, 1941–1949. Washington, D.C.: U.S. Government Printing Office, 1950.

De Gaulle, Charles. *War Memoirs.* Vol. I. *The Call to Honor 1940–1942.* Translated by Jonathan Griffin. 2 pts. New York: Viking, 1955.

De Jaeger, Charles. *The Linz File: Hitler's Plunder of Europe's Art.* Exeter, England: Webb & Bower, 1981.

Dilks, David. "Allied Leadership in the Second World War: Churchill." *Survey* 21 (1975): 20–29.

Dirks, Carl, and Karl-Heinz Janßen. *Der Krieg der Generäle: Hitler als Werkzeug der Wehrmacht.* Berlin: Propyläen, 1999.

Divine, Robert A. *Second Chance: The Triumph of Internationalism in America during World War II.* New York: Atheneum, 1971.

Dobson, Alan P. "The Other Air Battle: The American Pursuit of Post-War Civil Aviation Rights." *The Historical Journal* 28 (1985): 429–39.

Documents on German Foreign Policy 1918–1945. Washington, D.C.: U.S. Government Printing Office, 1948–76. Documents from this set are cited by series and volume number in the notes.

Dokumente zur Deutschlandpolitik. Ser. 1, vols. 1–4. *Vom 1. September 1939 bis 8. Mai 1945.* Frankfurt am Main: Metzner, 1984–.

Domarus, Max. *Mussolini und Hitler: Zwei Wege – Gleiches Ende.* Neustadt an der Aisch: Verlagsdruckerei Schmidt, 1977.

Doolin, Dennis J. *Territorial Claims in the Sino-Soviet Conflict: Documents and Analyses.* Stanford, Calif.: Hoover Institution, 1965.

Dower, John W. *Japan in War and Peace.* New York: The Free Press, 1983.

Drea, Edward J. *The 1942 Japanese General Election: Political Mobilization in Wartime Japan.* Lawrence: University Press of Kansas, 1979.

Dreifort, John E. *Myopic Grandeur: The Ambivalence of French Foreign Policy toward the Far East, 1919–1945.* Kent, Ohio: Kent State University Press, 1991.

Dülffer, Jost, et al. *Hitler's Städte: Baupolitik im Dritten Reich.* Cologne: Böhlau, 1978.

Dunn, F. S. *Peace-Making and the Settlement with Japan.* Princeton, N.J.: Princeton University Press, 1963.

Duus, Peter. "Imperialism without Colonies: The Vision of the Greater East Asia Co-Prosperity Sphere." *Diplomacy and Statecraft* 7 (1996): 54–72.

———. *The Japanese Wartime Empire, 1931–1945.* Princeton, N.J.: Princeton University Press, 1996.

Eckes, Alfred E. *A Search for Solvency: Bretton Woods and the International Monetary System, 1941–1971.* Austin: University of Texas Press, 1975.

Edmonds, Robin. *The Big Three: Churchill, Roosevelt and Stalin in Peace and War.* New York: Norton, 1991.

Eichholz, Dietrich, ed. "Die Kriegszieldenkschift des Kolonialpolitischen Amtes der NSDAP von 1940." *Zeitschrift für Geschichtswissenschaft* 22 (1974): 308–23.

Eisenblätter, Gerhard. "Grundlinien der Politik des Reiches gegenüber dem Generalgouvernment, 1919–1945." Ph.D. diss., University of Frankfurt, 1969.

Elpeleg, Zvi. *The Grand Mufti: Haj Amin Al-Husseini: Founder of the Palestinian National Movement.* Translated by David Harvey, edited by Shmuel Himelstein. London: Frank Cass, 1993.

Fenley, Jonathan. *Chiang Kai-shek: China's Generalissimo and the Nation He Lost.* New York: Carroll & Graf, 2004.

Feuersenger, Marianne. *Im Vorzimmer der Macht: Aufzeichungen aus dem Wehmachtführungsstab und Führerhauptquartier 1940–1945.* Munich: Herbig, 1999.

Fishel, Wesley R. *The End of Extraterritoriality in China.* Berkeley: University of California Press, 1952.

Fleming, Peter. *Operation Sealion.* New York: Simon & Schuster, 1957.

Flude, Roy. "The Axis Powers' Lost Opportunity: The Failure to Develop an Air Service between Europe and the Far East 1942–1945." Ph.D. diss., DeMontford University, 2000.

Foerster, Roland G., ed. *Gezeitenwechsel im Zweiten Weltkrieg? Die Schlachten bei Char'kov und Kursk im Frühjahr und Summer 1943 in operativer Anlage, Verlauf und politischer Wirkung.* Hamburg: Mittler, 1996.

———. *"Unternehmen Barbarossa": Zum historischen Ort der deutsch-russischen Beziehungen von 1933 bis Herbst 1941.* Munich: Oldenbourg, 1993.

Folly, Martin H. *Churchill, Whitehall and the Soviet Union, 1940–1945.* New York: St. Martin's, 2000.

Foreign Policy Association of Japan. *The Japan Yearbook 1943–1944.* Tokyo: The Japan Times, 1943.

Foreign Relations of the United States. Volumes from this series are cited by year and volume number or title in the notes.

Förster, Jürgen, ed. *Stalingrad: Ereignis. Wirkung, Symbol.* Munich: Piper, 1992.

Franklin, T. G., and Peter Lowe, eds. *Conflict and Amity in East Asia: Essays in Honor of Ian Nish.* London: MacMillan, 1992.

Franklin, William M. "Zonal Boundaries and Access to Berlin." *World Politics* 16 (1963): 1–31.

Friedlander, Henry. *The Origins of Nazi Genocide: From Euthanasia to the Final Solution.* Chapel Hill: University of North Carolina Press, 1995.

Fröhlich, Elke, ed. *Die Tagebücher von Joseph Goebbels.* Pt. 2. 15 vols. Munich: Saur, 1995.

Frye, Alton. *Nazi Germany and the Western Hemisphere, 1933–1941.* New Haven, Conn.: Yale University Press, 1967.

Garrett, John Q., ed. *Robert H. Jackson, That Man: An Insider's Portrait of Franklin D. Roosevelt.* New York: Oxford University Press, 2003.

Garver, John. W. "Chiang Kai-shek's Quest for Soviet Entry into the Sino-Japanese War." *Political Science Quarterly* 102 (1987): 295–316.

Gat, Moshe. *Britain and Italy, 1943–1949: The Decline of British Influence.* Brighton, England: Sussex Academic Press, 1991.

George, James Herbert, Jr. "United States Postwar Relief Planning: The First Phase, 1941–1943." Ph.D. diss., University of Wisconsin, 1970.

Gietz, Axel. *Die Neue Alte Welt: Roosevelt, Churchill und die europäische Nachkriegsordnung.* Munich: W. Fink, 1986.

Gilbert, Martin, ed. *The Churchill War Papers.* Vol. 2. *Never Surrender May 1940–December 1940.* New York: Norton, 1995.

———. *The Churchill War Papers.* Vol. 3. *The Ever Widening War 1941.* New York: Norton, 2000.

Goda, Norman J. W. "Black Marks: Hitler's Bribery of His Senior Officers in World War II." *Journal of Modern History* 72 (2000): 413–52.

———. *Tomorrow the World: Hitler, Northwest Africa, and the Path toward America.* College Station: Texas A & M University Press, 1998.

Godman, Peter. *Hitler and the Vatican.* New York: The Free Press, 2004.

Gorodetsky, Gabriel. *Grand Delusion: Stalin and the German Invasion of Russia.* New Haven, Conn.: Yale University Press, 1999.

Goschler, Constantin, ed. *Hitler: Reden, Schriften, Anordnungen Februar 1925 bis Januar 1933.* Vol. 4, pt. 1. Munich: Saur, 1994.

Gough, Hugh, and John Horne, eds. *De Gaulle and Twentieth Century France.* London: Arnold, 1994.

Grams. Erika S. "Charles de Gaulle and Harry Truman: The Effects of Personality on Diplomacy during the Stuttgart and Val d'Aosta Incidents in Spring 1945." Master's thesis, University of North Carolina at Chapel Hill, 1994.

Gregor, A. James. *The Ideology of Fascism.* New York: The Free Press, 1969.

Greiner, Bernd. *Die Morgethau-Legende: Die Geschichte eines umstrittenen Plans.* Hamburg: Hamburger Edition, 1995.

Haase, Günther. *Kunstraub und Kunstschutz: Eine Dokumentation.* Heidelberg: Georg Olms, 1991.

Hale, Oron J., ed. "Adolf Hitler and the Postwar German Birthrate." *Journal of Central European Affairs* 17 (1957): 166–73.

Harper, John L. *American Visions of Europe: Franklin D. Roosevelt, George F. Kennan and Dean G. Acheson.* Cambridge: Cambridge University Press, 1994.

Harriman, W. Averell, and Elie Abel. *Special Envoy to Churchill and Stalin 1941–1946.* New York: Random House, 1975.

Harvey, John, ed. *The War Diary of Oliver Harvey.* London: Collins, 1978.

Hattori Takushiro. *The Complete History of the Greater East Asia War.* Tokyo: Hara Shoto, 1965.

Heineman, Elizabeth D. *What Difference Does a Husband Make?: Women and Marital Status in Nazi and Postwar Germany.* Berkeley: University of California Press, 1999.

Hellegers, Dale M. *We, the Japanese People: World War II and the Origins of the Japanese Constitution.* 2 vols. Stanford, Calif.: Stanford University Press, 2002.

Herde, Peter. *Italien, Deutschland und der Weg in den Krieg im Pazifik.* Wiesbaden: Steiner, 1983.

———. *Der Japanflug: Planungen und Verwirklichung einer Flugverbindung zwischen den Achsenmächten und Japan 1942–1945.* Stuttgart: Steiner, 2000.

Herring, George C., Jr. *Aid to Russia: Strategy, Diplomacy, the Origins of the Cold War*. New York: Columbia University Press, 1973.

Herzstein, Robert. *When Nazi Dreams Come True*. London: Abacus, 1982.

Heuss, Anja. *Kunst- und Kulturraub: Eine vergleichende Studie zur Besatzungspolitik der Nationalsozialisten in Frankreich und der Sowjetunion*. Heidelberg: C. Winter, 2000.

Hicks, George. *The Comfort Women: Japan's Brutal Regime of Enforced Prostitution in the Second World War*. New York: Norton, 1995.

Hilberg, Raul. *The Destruction of the European Jews*. 3d ed. 3 vols. New Haven, Conn.: Yale University Press, 2003.

Hildebrand, Klaus. *Vom Reich zum Weltreich: Hitler, NSDAP und koloniale Frage 1919–1945*. Munich: Fink, 1969.

Hilderbrand, Robert C. *Dumbarton Oaks: The Origins of the United Nations and the Search for Postwar Security*. Chapel Hill: University of North Carolina Press, 1990.

Hoenicke, Michaela. "Franklin D. Roosevelt's View of Germany: Formative Experiences for a Future President." Master's thesis, University of North Carolina at Chapel Hill, 1989.

Holloway, David. *Stalin and the Bomb: The Soviet Union and Atomic Energy, 1939–1956*. New Haven, Conn.: Yale University Press, 1994.

Hoopes, Townsend, and Douglas Brinkley. *FDR and the Creation of the United Nations*. New Haven, Conn.: Yale University Press, 1997.

Housden, Martyn. *Hans Frank: Lebensraum and the Holocaust*. New York: Palgrave Macmillan, 2003.

Hull, Cordell. *Memoirs*. 2 vols. New York: Macmillan, 1948.

Hunt, Michael H. *The Genesis of Chinese Communist Foreign Policy*. New York: Columbia University Press, 1996.

Israel, Ministry of Foreign Affairs, and Ministry of Foreign Affairs of the Russian Federation. *Documents on Israeli-Soviet Relations, 1941–1953*. 2 vols. London: Frank Cass, 2000.

Jäckel, Eberhard. *Frankreich in Hitlers Europa*. Stuttgart: Deutsche Verlags-Anstalt, 1966.

———, ed. *Hitler: Sämtliche Aufzeichnungen 1905–1934*. Stuttgart: Deutsche Verlags-Anstalt, 1980.

Jackson, Robert H. *Report of Robert H. Jackson, United States Representative to the International Conference on Military Trials*. Washington, D.C.: U.S. Government Printing Office, 1949.

James, Harold. *International Monetary Cooperation since Bretton Woods.* Washington, D.C.: International Monetary Fund and Oxford University Press, 1996.

James, Robert Rhodes. *Churchill: A Study in Failure 1900–1939.* New York: World Publishing Co., 1970.

———, ed. *Winston S. Churchill: His Complete Speeches 1897–1963.* 8 vols. New York: Bowker, 1974.

Janssens, Rudolf V. A. *"What Future for Japan?" U.S. Wartime Planning for the Postwar Era, 1942–1945.* Amsterdam: Rodopi, 1995.

Jaskot, Paul. *The Architecture of Oppression: The SS, Forced Labor and the Nazi Monumental Building Economy.* New York: Routledge, 2000.

Jeffries, John W. *Wartime America: The World War II Home Front.* Chicago: Ivan R. Dee, 1996.

Joachimsthaler, Anton. *Die Breitspurbahn Hitlers: Eine Dokumentation über die geplante 3-Meter Breitspureisenbahn der Jahre 1942–1945.* Freiburg: Eisenbahn-Kurier Verlag, 1981.

Jochmann, Werner, ed. *Adolf Hitler: Monologe im Führerhauptqurtier 1941–1944, Die Aufzeichnungen Heinrich Heims.* Hamburg: Kraus, 1980.

Jones, F. C. *Japan's New Order in East Asia: Its Rise and Fall 1937–1945.* London: Oxford University Press, 1954.

Jones, F. C., et al. *Survey of International Affairs 1939–1946: The Far East 1942–1946.* London: Oxford University Press, 1955.

Kaslas, Boris J. "The Lithuanian Strip in Soviet-German Secret Diplomacy, 1939–1941." *Journal of Baltic Studies* 4, no. 3 (1971): 211–25.

Kido Koichi. *The Diary of Marquis Kido: Selected Translations into English.* Frederick, Md.: University Publications of America, 1981.

Kimball, Warren E. *Forged in War: Roosevelt, Churchill and the Second World War.* New York: William Morrow, 1997.

———, ed. *Churchill and Roosevelt: The Complete Correspondence.* 3 vols. Princeton, N.J.: Princeton University Press, 1984.

Klee, Karl. *Das Unternehmen "Seelöwe": Die geplante deutsche Landung in England 1940.* Göttingen: Musterschmidt, 1956.

Klemperer, Klemens von. *German Resistance to Hitler: The Search for Allies Abroad, 1938–1945.* Oxford: Clarendon Press, 1992.

Klinkhammer, Lutz. *Zwischen Bündnis und Besatzung: Das nationalsozialistische Deutschland und die Republik von Salo, 1943–1945.* Tübingen: Mohr, 1993.

Klinksiek, Dorothee. *Die Frau im NS-Staat.* Stuttgart: Deutsche Verlags-Anstalt, 1982.

Knox, MacGregor. *Hitler's Italian Allies: Royal Armed Forces, Fascist Regime, and the War of 1940–1943.* Cambridge: Cambridge University Press, 2001.

———. *Mussolini Unleashed 1939–1941: Politics and Strategy in Fascist Italy's Last War.* Cambridge: Cambridge University Press, 1982.

Kochavi, Arieh J. *Prelude to Nuremberg: Allied War Crimes Policy and the Question of Punishment.* Chapel Hill: University of North Carolina Press, 1998.

Koehl, Robert L. *RKFDV: German Resettlement and Population Policy 1939–1945, A History of the Reich Commissioner for the Strengthening of Germandom.* Cambridge, Mass.: Harvard University Press, 1957.

Krammer, Arnold. *The Forgotten Friendship: Israel and the Soviet Bloc. 1947–1953.* Urbana, Il.: University of Illinois Press, 1974.

Kratoska, Paul H. *The Japanese Occupation of Malaya: A Social and Economic History.* Honolulu: University of Hawaii Press, 1997.

Krebs, Gerhard. "Gibraltar oder Bosporus? Japans Empfehlungen für eine deutsche Mittelmeerstrategie im Jahre 1943." *Militärgeschichtliche Mitteilungen* 58 (1999): 65–85.

Krosby, H. Peter. *Finland, Germany, and the Soviet Union 1940–1941: The Petsamo Dispute.* Madison: University of Wisconsin Press, 1968.

Kuniholm, Bruce R. *The Origins of the Cold War in the Near East: Great Power Conflict and Diplomacy in Iran, Turkey, and Greece.* Princeton, N.J.: Princeton University Press, 1980.

Lacouture, Jean. *De Gaulle: The Rebel, 1890–1944.* Translated by Patrick O'Brian. New York: Norton, 1990.

Lamb, Richard. *Mussolini and the British.* London: John Murray, 1997.

Lambakis, Steven J. *Winston Churchill: Architect of Peace.* Westport, Conn.: Greenwood Press, 1993.

Lane, Ann, and Howard Temperley, eds. *The Rise and Fall of the Grand Alliance 1941–1945.* New York: St. Martin's, 1991.

Lawlor, Sheila. *Churchill and the Politics of War, 1940–1941.* New York: Cambridge University Press, 1994.

Lebra, Joyce C. *Japanese Trained Armies in Southeast Asia: Independence and Volunteer Forces in World War II.* New York: Columbia University Press, 1978.

———. *Postwar Perspectives on the Greater East Asia Co-Prosperity Sphere.* Harmon Memorial Lecture no. 34. Washington, D.C.: U.S. Government Printing Office, 1991.

——, ed. *Japan's Greater East Asia Co-Prosperity Sphere in World War II: Selected Readings and Documents*. Kuala Lumpur: Oxford University Press, 1975.

Lewy, Guenter. *The Nazi Persecution of the Gypsies*. New York: Oxford University Press, 2000.

Liu, Xiaoyua. *A Partnership for Disorder: China, the United States, and Their Policies for the Postwar Disposition of the Japanese Empire, 1941–1945*. Cambridge: Cambridge University Press, 1996.

——. "Sino-American Diplomacy over Korea during World War II." *Journal of American-East Asia Relations* 1, no. 2 (1992): 223–64.

Loewenheim, Francis, et al., eds. *Roosevelt and Churchill: Their Secret Correspondence*. New York: E. P. Dutton, 1975.

Longerich, Peter. *The Unwritten Order: Hitler's Role in the Final Solution*. Charleston, S.C.: Tempus, 2001.

Look, Hans-Dietrich. *Quisling, Rosenberg und Terboven: Zur Vorgeschichte und Geschichte der nationalsozialistischen Revolution in Norwegen*. Stuttgart: Deutsche Verlags-Anstalt, 1970.

Looper, Robert B. "Roosevelt and the British Empire." *Occidente* 12, no. 4 (1956): 348–63, no. 5 (1956): 424–36.

Louis, William Roger. "Hong Kong, The Critical Phase, 1945–1949." *American Historical Review* 102 (1997): 1045–84.

——. *Imperialism at Bay: The United States and the Decolonization of the British Empire, 1941–1945*. Oxford: Clarendon Press, 1977.

Lukas, Richard C. *Did the Childen Cry? Hitler's War against Jewish and Polish Children, 1939–1945*. New York: Hypocrene, 1991.

——. *Forgotten Holocaust: The Poles under German Occupation 1939–1944*. Lexington: University Press of Kentucky, 1986.

Lustiger, Arno. *Rotbuch: Stalin und die Juden*. Berlin: Aufbau-Verlag, 1998.

Madajczyk, Czeslaw, *Die Okkupationspolitik Nazideutschlands in Polen 1939–1945*. Berlin: Akademie-Verlag, 1987.

Magocsi, Paul R. *The Shaping of a National Identity: Subcarpathian Rus', 1848–1949*. Cambridge, Mass.: Harvard University Press, 1978.

Maguire, G. E. *Anglo-American Policy towards the Free French*. New York: St. Martin's, 1995.

Mallett, Robert. *The Italian Navy and Fascist Expansionism 1935–1940*. London: Frank Cass, 1998.

Marr, David G. *Vietnam 1945: The Quest for Power*. Berkeley: University of California Press, 1995.

Martin, Bernd. *Deutschland und Japan im Zweiten Weltkrieg: Vom Angriff auf Pearl Harbor bis zur deutschen Kapitulation.* Göttingen: Musterschmidt, 1969.

Matloff, Maurice. *United States Army in World War II: Strategic Planning for Coalition Warfare 1943–1944.* Washington, D.C.: U.S. Government Printing Office, 1959.

Mayers, David. *The Ambassadors and America's Soviet Policy.* New York: Oxford University Press, 1995.

Mazower, Mark. "Hitler's New Order, 1939–45." *Diplomacy and Statecraft* 7 (1996): 29–53.

McNeal, Robert H. "Roosevelt through Stalin's Eyes." *International Journal* 18 (1963): 194–201.

Meskill, Johanna M. *Hitler and Japan: The Hollow Alliance.* New York: Atheneum, 1966.

———, ed. "Der geheime deutsch-japanische Notenaustausch zum Dreimächtepakt." *Vierteljahrshefte für Zeitgeschichte* 5 (1957): 182–95.

Meyer, Georg, ed. *Generalfeldmarschall Ritter von Leeb: Tagebuchaufzeichnungen und Lagebeurteilungen aus zwei Weltkriegen.* Stuttgart: Deutsche Verlags-Anstalt, 1976.

Miller, James E. "The Politics of Relief: The Roosevelt Administration and the Reconstruction of Italy, 1943–44." *Prologue* 13 (1981): 193–208.

Mitscherlich, Alexander, and Fred Mielke. *Das Diktat der Menschenverachtung.* Heidelberg: Lambert Schneider, 1947.

Moran, Lord. *Churchill: Taken from the Diaries of Lord Moran: The Struggle for Survival 1940–1965.* Boston: Houghton Mifflin, 1966.

Morgenthau, Henry, Jr. *Germany Is Our Problem.* New York: Harper, 1945.

Mortimer, Edward. *The World That FDR Built.* New York: Scribner's, 1989.

Moseley, Philip E. "Across the Green Table from Stalin." *Current History* 15 (September 1948): 129–33, 164.

Näth, Marie-Luise. *Chinas Weg in die Weltpolitik: Die nationalen und außenpolitischen Konzeptionen Sun Yat-sens, Chiang Kai-sheks und Mao Tse-tungs.* Berlin: Walter de Gruyter, 1976.

Naimark, Norman M. *The Russians in Germany: A History of the Soviet Zone of Occupation 1945–1949.* Cambridge, Mass.: Harvard University Press, 1995.

Nelson, Daniel J. *Wartime Origins of the Berlin Dilemma.* Tuscaloosa: University of Alabama Press, 1978.

Nichols, H. G., ed. *Washington Despatches 1941–1945: Weekly Political Reports from the British Embassy.* Chicago: University of Chicago Press, 1981.

Notter, Harley A. *Postwar Foreign Policy Preparation*. Washington, D.C.: U.S. Government Printing Office, 1949.

O'Connor, Raymond G. *Diplomacy for Victory: FDR and Unconditional Surrender*. New York: Norton, 1971.

Offner, Arnold A., and Theodore A. Wilson, eds. *Victory in Europe 1945: From World War to Cold War*. Lawrence: University Press of Kansas, 2000.

Oka Yoshitake, *Konoe Fumimaro: A Political Biography*. Tokyo: University of Tokyo Press, 1983.

Orders, P. G. A. *Britain, Australia, New Zealand and the Challenge of the United States, 1939–1946: A Study in International History*. New York: Palgrave Macmillan, 2003.

Orlow, Dietrich. "Between Nationalism and Internationalism: French and German Socialists and the Question of Boundary Changes after World Wars I and II." In *The Establishment of European Borders after the Two World Wars*, edited by Christian Baechler and Carole Fink, 99–114. New York: Peter Lang, 1996.

———. "Sozialistische Deutschlandpolitik: SFIO, SPD und die Zukunft Deutschlands 1945–1950." *Francia* 26, no. 3 (1999): 19–48.

Overmans, Rüdiger. *Deutsche militärischen Verluste im Zweiten Weltkrieg*. Munich: Oldenbourg, 1999.

Overy, Richard. *Why the Allies Won*. London: Jonathan Cape, 1995.

Paxton, Robert O. *Vichy France: Old Guard and New Order 1940–1944*. New York: Columbia University Press, 1972.

Pennington, Reina. *Wings, Women, and War: Soviet Airwomen in Combat in World War II*. Lawrence: University Press of Kansas, 2001.

Perkins, Francis. *The Roosevelt I Knew*. New York: Viking, 1947.

Petzina, Dieter. *Autarkiepolitik im Dritten Reich: Der nationalsozialistische Vierjahresplan*. Stuttgart: Deutsche Verlags-Anstalt, 1968.

Pietrow-Ennker, Bianka, ed. *Präventivkrieg? Der deutsche Angriff auf die Sowjetunion*. Frankfurt am Main: Fischer, 2000.

Pons, Silvio. *Stalin and the Inevitable War 1936–1941*. London: Frank Cass, 2002.

Prazmowska, Anita J. *Britain and Poland, 1939–1943: The Betrayed Ally*. Cambridge: Cambridge University Press, 1995.

Range, Willard. *Franklin D. Roosevelt and World Order*. Athens: University of Georgia Press, 1959.

Resis, Albert. "The Churchill-Stalin 'Percentages' Agreement on the Balkans, Moscow, October 1944." *American Historical Review* 83 (1978): 368–87.

————. "Spheres of Influence in Soviet Wartime Diplomacy." *Journal of Modern History* 53 (1981): 417–39.

Reynolds, David. "Roosevelt, the British Left, and the Appointment of John G. Winant as United States Ambassador to Britain in 1941." *International History Review* 4 (1982): 393–413.

Rich, Norman. *Hitler's War Aims: The Establishment of the New Order.* New York: Norton, 1974.

Riste, Olav. "Free Ports in North Norway: A Contribution to the Study of F.D.R.'s Policy towards the Soviet Union." *Journal of Contemporary History* 5, no. 4 (1970): 77–95.

Röhr, Werner, ed. *Europa unterm Hakenkreuz: Analysen, Quellen, Register.* Berlin: Hüthig, 1996.

Rohwer, Jürgen, and Mikhael S. Monakov. *Stalin's Ocean-going Fleet: Soviet Naval Strategy and Shipbuilding Programmes, 1935–1953.* Portland, Ore.: Frank Cass, 2001.

Roosevelt, Elliott, ed. *F.D.R.: His Personal Letters 1928–1945.* 2 vols. New York: Duell, Sloan & Pearce, 1950.

Ross, Graham. *The Foreign Office and the Kremlin: British Documents on Anglo-Soviet Relations 1941–45.* Cambridge: Cambridge University Press, 1984.

Rzheshevszy, Oleg A., ed. *War and Diplomacy: The Making of the Grand Alliance: From Stalin's Archives.* Amsterdam: Harwood Academic Publishers, 1996.

Sato, Shigeru. *War, Nationalism and Peasants: Java under Japanese Occupation 1942–1945.* Armonk, N.Y.: M. E. Sharpe, 1994.

Sbrega, John J. *Anglo-American Relations and Colonialism in East Asia, 1941–1945.* New York: Garland, 1983.

————. "Determination versus Drift: The Anglo-American Debate over the Trusteeship Issue, 1941–1945." *Pacific Historical Review* 55 (1986): 256–80.

Scheurig, Bodo. *Verräter oder Patrioten: Das Nationalkomitee "Freies Deutschland" und der Bund Deutscher Offiziere in der Sowjetunion 1943–1945.* Berlin: Ullstein, 1993.

Schild, Georg. *Bretton Woods and Dumbarton Oaks: American Economic and Political Planning in the Summer of 1944.* New York: St. Martin's, 1995.

Schilling, Donald G., ed. *Lessons and Legacies.* Vol. 2. Evanston, Ill.: Northwestern University Press, 1998.

Schoenbaum, David. *Hitler's Social Revolution: Class and Status in Nazi Germany 1933–1939.* New York: Doubleday, 1966.

Schreiber, Gerhard. *Die italienischen Militärinterniierten im deutschen Machtbereich 1943–1945*. Munich: Oldenbourg, 1990.

Sherwood, Robert E. *Roosevelt and Hopkins: An Intimate History*. New York: Harper, 1948.

Shillony, Ben-Ami. *Politics and Culture in Wartime Japan*. Oxford: Clarendon Press, 1991.

Sichel-Achenbach, Sebastian. *Lower Silesia from Nazi Germany to Communist Poland, 1942–1949*. London: MacMillan, 1994.

Skidmore, Gretchen M. "The American Occupation of the Bremen Enclave, 1945–1947." Master's thesis, University of North Carolina at Chapel Hill, 1989.

Smelser, Ronald M. *Robert Ley: Hitler's Labor Front Leader*. Oxford: Berg, 1988.

Smith, Dennis Mack. *Mussolini*. New York: Knopf, 1982.

Snow, Edgar. "Fragments from F.D.R." *Monthly Review* 8, pt. 1 (1957): 316–21, pt. 2 (1957): 394–404.

Soviak, Eugene, ed. *A Diary of Darkness: The Wartime Diary of Kiyosawa Kiyoshi*. Translated by Eugene Soviak and Kamiyama Tamie. Princeton, N.J.: Princeton University Press, 1999.

Speer, Albert. *Spandauer Tagebücher*. Frankfurt am Main: Ullstein, 1975.

Steinweis, Alan E., and Daniel E. Rogers, eds. *The Impact of Nazism: New Perspectives on the Third Reich and Its Legacy*. Lincoln: University of Nebraska Press, 2003.

Storry, Richard. *The Double Patriots: A Study of Japanese Nationalism*. London: Chatto & Windus, 1957.

Strang, G. Bruce. *On the Fiery March: Mussolini Prepares for War*. Westport, Conn.: Praeger, 2003.

Sullivan, John A. L. "The United States. The East Indies and World War II: The American Efforts to Modify the Colonial Status Quo." Ph.D. diss., University of Massachusetts, 1969.

Sun, You-li. *China and the Origins of the Pacific War, 1931–1941*. New York: St. Martin's, 1999.

Suppan, Arnold, and Elisabeth Vyslonzil, eds. *Eduard Beneš und die tschechoslowakische Aussenpolitik 1918–1948*. Vienna: Wiener Osteuropastudien, 2003.

Swain, Geoffrey. "Stalin's Wartime Vision of the Post-War World." *Diplomacy and Statecraft* 7, no. 1 (1986): 73–96.

Tamanoi, Marijo Asano. "Knowledge, Power, and Racial Classification: The 'Japanese' in Manchuria." *Journal of Asian Studies* 59 (2000): 248–76.

Terry, Sarah Meiklejohn. *Poland's Place in Europe: General Sikorski and the Origins of the Oder-Neisse Line, 1939–1943*. Princeton, N.J.: Princeton University Press, 1983.

Thies, Jochen. *Architekt der Weltherrschaft: Die "Endziele" Hitlers*. Düsseldorf: Droste, 1976. English translation forthcoming from Enigma Books, New York.

Thomas, Martin. *The French Empire at War, 1940–45*. Manchester: Manchester University Press, 1998.

Thomas, R. T. *Britain and Vichy: The Dilemma of Anglo-French Relations 1940–1942*. New York: St. Martin's, 1979.

Thompson, Kenneth W. *Winston Churchill's World View: Statesmanship and Power*. Baton Rouge: Louisiana State University Press, 1983.

Tong, Hollington K. *Chiang Kai-shek*. Taipei: China Publishing Co., 1953.

Tyrell, Albrecht. *Grossbritannien und die Deutschlandplanung der Alliierten 1941–1945*. Frankfurt am Main: Metzner, 1987.

Ueberschär, Gerd R. *Das Nationalkomitee "Freies Deutschland" und der Bund Deutscher Offiziere*. Frankfurt am Main: Fischer Taschenbuch Verlag, 1995.

Ueberschär, Gerd R., and Winfried Vogel. *Dienen und Verdienen: Hitlers Geschenke an seine Eliten*. Frankfurt am Main: S. Fischer, 1999.

Ueberschär, Gerd R., and Lev A. Bezymenskij, eds. *Der deutsche Angriff auf die Sowjetunion 1941: Die Kontroverse um die Präventivkriegsthese*. Darmstadt: Primus, 1998.

Ugaki Matome. *Fading Victory: The Diary of Admiral Matome Ugaki 1941–1945*. Translated by Masataka Chihaya with Donald M. Goldstein and Katherine V. Dillon. Pittsburgh: University of Pittsburgh Press, 1991.

Van Dormal, Armand. *Bretton Woods: Birth of a Monetary System*. London: MacMillan, 1978.

Vigneras, Marcel. *United States Army in World War II: Rearming the French*. Washington, D.C.: U.S. Government Printing Office, 1957.

Wagner, Elisabeth, ed. *Der Generalquartiermeister: Briefe und Tagebuchaufzeichnungen des Generalquartiermeisters des Heers General der Artillerie Eduard Wagner*. Munich: Olzog, 1963.

Wakeman, Frederic, Jr. *Spymaster: Dai Li and the Chinese Secret Service*. Berkeley: University of California Press, 2003.

Ward, Geoffrey C., ed. *Closest Companion: The Unknown Story of the Intimate Friendship between Franklin Roosevelt and Margaret Suckley*. Boston: Houghton Mifflin, 1995.

Warner, Geoffrey. "From Teheran to Yalta: Reflections on F.D.R.'s Foreign Policy." *International Affairs* 43 (1967): 530–36.

Wasser, Bruno. *Himmlers Raumplanung im Osten: Der Generalplan Ost in Polen 1940–1944*. Basel: Birkhäuser Verlag, 1993.

Weinberg, Gerhard L. "Deutsch-japanische Verhandlungen über das Südseemandat." *Vierteljahrshefte für Zeitgeschichte* 4 (1956): 390–98.

———. "Economic Planning for the Postwar World: Roosevelt and Hitler Compared." In *Germany and America: Essays in Honor of Gerald R. Kleinfeld*, edited by Wolfgang Uwe-Friedrich, 1–11. New York: Berghahn Books, 2001.

———. *The Foreign Policy of Hitler's Germany: A Diplomatic Revolution in Europe 1933–1936*. Atlantic Highland, N.J.: Humanities Press, 1994.

———. *The Foreign Policy of Hitler's Germany: Starting World War II 1937–1939*. Atlantic Highlands, N.J.: Humanities Press, 1994.

———. *Germany, Hitler and World War II*. New York: Cambridge University Press, 1995.

———. *Germany and the Soviet Union, 1939–1941*. Leyden: Brill, 1954, 1971.

———. "Roosevelt and Churchill: Conflicting Postwar Visions." In *World War II: Variants and Visions*, edited by Thomas O. Kelly II, 181–93. Collindale, Pa.: Diane Publishing Co., 1999.

———. *A World at Arms: A Global History of World War II*. Cambridge: Cambridge University Press, 1994.

———. *World in the Balance: Behind the Scenes of World War II*. Hanover, N.H.: University Press of New England, 1981.

———. *World War II Leaders and Their Visions for the Future of Palestine*. Washington, D.C.: United States Holocaust Memorial Museum, 2002.

———, ed. *Hitler's Second Book: The Unpublished Sequel to Mein Kampf*. Translated by Krista Smith. New York: Enigma Books, 2003.

Welch, A. Kem, ed. *Stalinism in Poland*. London: MacMillan, 1994.

West, Nigel [Rupert Allason], and Oleg Tsarev. *The Crown Jewels: The British Secrets at the Heart of the K.G.B. Archives*. New Haven, Conn.: Yale University Press, 1999.

Wetzler, Peter. *Hirohito and War: Imperial Tradition and Military Decision Making in Prewar Japan*. Honolulu: University of Hawaii Press, 1998.

Wheeler-Bennett, John W., ed. *Action This Day: Working with Churchill*. New York: St. Martin's, 1969.

Willmott, H. P. *Grave of a Dozen Schemes: British Naval Planning and the War against Japan, 1943–1945*. Annapolis, Md.: Naval Institute Press, 1996.

Wilson, Theodore A. *The First Summit: Roosevelt and Churchill at Placentia Bay 1941*. Rev. ed. Lawrence: University Press of Kansas, 1991.

Witte, Peter, et al., eds. *Der Dienstkalender Heinrich Himmlers 1941/42*. Hamburg: Christians, 1999.

Woodward, Llewellyn. *History of the Second World War: British Foreign Policy in the Second World War*. 5 vols. London: Her Majesty's Stationery Office, 1971.

Yakemtchouk, Romain. *La ligne Curzon et la IIe guerre mondiale*. Louvain: Editions Nauwalaerts, 1957.

Ziemke, Earl F. *The U.S. Army in the Occupation of Germany 1944–1946*. Washington, D.C.: U.S. Government Printing Office, 1975.

Zimmermann, Michael. *Rassenutopie und Genozid: Die nationalsozialistische "Lösung der Zigeunerfrage"*. Hamburg: Christians, 1996.

Zitelman, Rainer. *Hitler: Selbstverständnis eines Revolutionärs*. Hamburg: Berg, 1987.

INDEX

For the names of leaders who have chapters of their own, the number of the chapter is followed by page references for information on them in other chapters. Provinces or other portions of countries are listed under the country to which they belonged in 1939 (except for Austria and Manchuria), while cities are listed separately. The names used at the time are employed here even if the name of the city or territory changed after World War II. The occasional mention of subsequent names is to assist the reader and has no political connotation.